Community Theatre

Global perspectives

Eugene van Erven

London and New York

First published 2001
by Routledge
2 Park Square, Milton Park, Abingdon, Oxon, OX14 4RN

Simultaneously published in the USA and Canada
by Routledge
270 Madison Ave, New York NY 10016

Routledge is an imprint of the Taylor & Francis Group

Transferred to Digital Printing 2005

© 2001 Eugene van Erven

Typeset in Goudy by
M Rules

British Library Cataloguing in Publication Data
A catalogue record for this book is available from the British
Library

Library of Congress Cataloging in Publication Data
Van Erven, Eugene
    Community theatre: global perspectives/Eugene van Erven.
        p. cm.
    Includes bibliographical references and index.
    1. Community theater. 2. Drama in education. 3. Theater and
    society. 4. Community development. I. Title.

PN3305.E94 2001   00-041506
792–dc21

ISBN 0-415-19034-7 (hbk)
ISBN 0-415-19031-2 (pbk)

To Orn, Lennin and Harry

Contents

Preface

In August 1995, when I was in Los Angeles to complete a manuscript I
had been writing together with Professor Susan Mason, Sally Gordon
invited me to a performance of one of her community plays and thereby
inadvertently planted the first seed for this project. Sally, who has been
creating community theatre plays for over twenty years without much
recognition, wondered out loud how community theatre artists elsewhere in the world were coping with such frustrations, what methods
they used, how they financed themselves, and what it is that keeps them
going. In the same breath she suggested I write a book about it.

After seeing Sally's work in Northeast Los Angeles, I realized people
should know about it, not only to give her the recognition she deserves,
but also because the art she and others elsewhere in the world practise is
of immense significance. The stories that form the basis for its scripts
come straight out of life and are presented unapologetically, sometimes
literally on a street corner, by the very people who live them.
Community theatre is moving, pertinent, powerful, and effective in
strengthening the groups of people it caters to. Yet, because it mostly
manifests itself in out-of-the-way places, this art form is often ignored by
inner city elites, by policy-makers, and by cultural commentators. These
dedicated artists who assist unsung heroes to sing their songs in the shadows will never be nominated for national theatre awards, let alone Nobel
Prizes. I wanted to find out who they are, what drives them, and how
they work. What kind of theatre do they create and how do participants
and audiences respond to it? And although community theatre enjoys a
growing interest, few if any fully fledged courses on the topic are offered
at universities or theatre academies, mainly because so few scholars and
theatre educators have taken the trouble to document it properly. With
'properly' I mean 'observing creative processes from beginning to end'
and generally spending sufficient time with artists and community

participants to determine what techniques and strategies they use to create and produce their original community theatre performances. As a result, I underwent my own tailor-made year-long intercultural course on community theatre, an experience that I wanted to somehow share with others. I hope that all those who shared their experiences with me find themselves 'properly' represented here, but I alone, of course, must claim full responsibility for all the stupidities still left in this book and video.

Acknowledgements

I could not have completed this task without a certain degree of western privilege that provided me access to advanced education and then a tenured position at a Dutch university, which helped me open necessary doors to funding and technical facilities. I also want to acknowledge the support I received from a great many individuals and institutions. After Sally, New Zealand film maker Rod Prosser got on board. Then Maria van Bakelen of IDEA, Wiljan van den Akker of Utrecht University's Research Institute for History and Culture (OGC) and the staff of Ocean Film Productions recognized the project's potential and subsequently provided the institutional back-up necessary for fundraising, field work and film production. A lot of hard grant writing and production work was done by Esther Pardijs and Marinde Hurenkamp, who also gave invaluable research support and assistance in the tedious transcription and translation process. All other funding and video production credits are appended at the end of the film, although I should single out the contributions of actress Jetty Mathurin, audiovisual technicians Hans Schuurman and Fokke Walstijn and OMI-video, who through their volunteer efforts basically financed a Dutch version of the film that was screened at Stut's Theatre's twentieth anniversary symposium on 30 October 1998. I am also indebted to Kees Epskamp for introducing me to Maria van Bakelen, and to Ton van Vlijmen, Rien Sprenger, Jet Vos, Tera Jonker, Masja Knops, Fons Eikholt, Hans Klein Schiphorst and Bodine de Walle of the Theatre and Education Programme within the Utrecht School of the Arts for their ongoing support. Phillip Mann provided me with a welcome opportunity to do a trial run by allowing me to videotape one of his playmaking workshops. He also introduced me to the Remould Theatre Company in Hull and its artistic director, Rupert Creed, who continued to be a source of inspiration throughout this project.

I thank my American Studies colleagues and Hans Bertens, Head of Utrecht University's Department of Modern Foreign Languages, for facilitating my leave in 1997, and OGC's Frans Ruiter and Henrieke Crielaard and Hetty Winkel and Job Mulder of Utrecht University's International Relations Office for helping me find sponsors for most of my foreign trips. The greatest sacrifices, I am sure, were made by my wife Ria Green, my son Carlos, my step-children Peggy and Roy, and by Rod Prosser's family.

In the Philippines I am grateful for the friendship and trust I received from Jack and Hiroko Yabut, the fabulous Q sisters Dessa and Mae Quesada, Beng Santos, Maribel Legarda, Bong and Gail Billones, Mel Bernardo, Ernie Cloma, Nanding Josef, Nonoy Regalado, Eli Obligacion, Trini Malaga, Joey Ayala, and the members of Teatro Balangaw. In Utrecht, I owe thanks to Jos Bours, Marlies Hautvast, Elsbeth Reijmers, Jamal Hamid, Frans de Vette and the *Tears in the Rain* cast for always making me feel welcome. Were it not for Majella Perry I might never have found Aguamarina and hence would never have befriended Gerardo Arias Elizondo, Marvin Lara, and Eduardo Martinez. Thanks also to Danilo Montoya, Vicky Montero, Joaquin Salazar, Rafael Cuevas Molina, Alfredo Catania, and Vladimir de la Cruz for allowing me to interview them and, of course, to all the other members of Aguamarina and Liliane, *La Mona Azul* from Quepos. In Kenya, I deeply appreciated the hospitality of the entire Sigoti community, but I am particularly grateful to Susan Adhiambo Odongo, Emma Mumma, and Helida Molo Odongo of the Kawuonda Women's group, to Carolyn Odero, to Augustino Mumma, to George Ochieng Anang'a and his family, and to Kanang'a, George Otula, Opiyo Swa, and Elija Kogamedada. Julius Obala of the Entertainment Masters in Nairobi provided us with indispensable technical support, while Jones Munene Mputhia and the Kairithu Youth Group warmly received us in Meru. I am also thankful to Dr Opiyo Mumma of the University of Nairobi for introducing us to the Free Travelling Theatre and the KDEA network, for personally taking us to Sigoti, and for providing invaluable background information about community theatre in his country. Back in the Netherlands, Odak Isaiah helped me with additional translations from Doluo to English.

In Los Angeles, Alpha Sorensen gave us a home away from home, Eriberto Reyes loaned indispensable wheels, Michael Archuleta and Lorenzo Martinez shared their contagious *ritmo de la gente*, the 'Saquen la sopa ya!' cast contributed their vitality and creativity, Pat Bowie and the staff of the Hathaway Family Resource Center provided office facilities and a supportive working environment, Hector Aristizabel, José Cruz

Gonzalez, Jay McAdams, Susan Mason, Susan Suntree, Lillian Lehman, Robert and Kelly Alexander, Betty Bernhard and Kailash Pandya provided relaxation and food for stomach, soul, and thought. Susan Suntree also came over to Holland twice to give me a break from teaching and to offer the English narration for the video as her personal gift. In Australia, in addition to our crew members Ronnie Morelos and Peter Clark, I owe thanks to Harley Stumm, Fiona Winning, John Baylis, Janine Peacock, Mona Zaylaa, Anthony Babicci, Richard Vella, Boris Kelly, Monica Barone, Bonnie, Richard Murphet, Jenny Kemp, Venetia Gillot, Madeleine Blackwell, Mingus Formentor, PACT Youth Theatre, City Moon Youth Theatre, Powerhouse Youth Theatre, the University of Western Sydney's audiovisual department, Gordon Beattie, Anne Marshall, Hey You, You Too, David Watt, and the 'Trackwork' cast.

Finally, I am grateful to Lenie van der Heiden and Jander van Dijk van 't Velde for lending me their quiet little house in Old Zealand, where I was able to virtually complete this book. I will not say it has not been a difficult job at times, but it was a breeze compared to the many odds community theatre artists themselves continuously have to overcome over a much, much longer period of time than this project has taken me. I humbly take my hat off to them and particularly thank Sally, Ernie, Dessa, Jos, Marlies, Susan, Emma, Carolyne, George, Gerardo, and Harley for their faith and wisdom.

I dedicate this entire enterprise to the memory of my Uncle Harry – the playful undertaker – and to Lennin Kenyanito and Orn-Anong Vong-Asavathepchai, two energetic community theatre artists, from Kenya and Thailand respectively, who died right at the time they should have blossomed.

Eugene van Erven, Kloetinge
14 January 2000

Introduction

This is a book about an inter-continental community theatre project. It is an attempt to gain a better understanding of this increasingly popular cultural practice that operates on the cutting edge between performing arts and sociocultural intervention. The main emphasis in this book, and in the accompanying video, has been placed on the diverse mechanics and inspirations of community theatre as an artistic process that always evolves under very particular local sociocultural conditions. Through written word and moving image, this package thus documents, contextualizes, and theorizes the methods that were used to create six community performances in distinct locations around the world in the course of 1997. Both in the video and in the book I have opted to tell these six tales as relatively independent narratives. I recommend watching the appropriate video segments before reading each book chapter, which provides the background about (community) theatre in each particular region, the facilitators, the organizations they work in, the evolution of their method, and a more technically oriented case study of the distinctive approach they used to create one specific community theatre performance in 1997.

Roots of community theatre

Although the usual anthropological arguments could be dusted off to place the origins of community theatre, as indeed of all theatrical expression, back in pre-colonial and pre-Graeco-Roman times, its more immediate antecedents lie buried in the various forms of counter-cultural, radical, anti- and post-colonial, educational, and liberational theatres of the 1960s and 1970s. Etymologically, the term 'community theatre' has been around since at least the 1920s, when in upstate New York Cornell University Professor Alexander Drummond used it to refer to his stimulation programme for developing 'fine original plays authored by the people of the area' (Gard 1993: 28). Drummond's and Gard's idea of community theatre was, however, to organize what in essence were historical playwriting courses for rural folk with the academic facilitators subsequently artistically fashioning the material to make it fit for performance in their university auditorium (ibid.: 37). This was not quite the improvisation-based collectively oriented community theatre that first started to evolve in South America in the early 1960s and not long thereafter independently sprung up in Africa, Asia, Australia, Europe, and the United States, where, to avoid confusion with the umpteenth amateur production of, say, *Death of a Salesman*, North-American academic commentators now generally prefer to call it 'community-based' or 'grassroots theatre' (Kuftinec 1996: 91).

Community theatre is a worldwide phenomenon that manifests itself in many different guises, yielding a broad range of performance styles. It is united, I think, by its emphasis on local and/or personal stories (rather than pre-written scripts) that are first processed through improvisation and then collectively shaped into theatre under the guidance either of outside professional artists – who may or may not be active in other kinds of professional theatre – or of local amateur artists residing among groups of people that, for lack of a better term, could perhaps best be called 'peripheral'. Community theatre yields grass roots performances in which the participating community residents themselves perform and during the creative process of which they have substantial input. Not only the participants are considered 'peripheral', community theatre as an art form is as well. While there exist generic connections with drama and theatre in education, radical people's theatre, theatre of liberation, theatre for development, youth theatre, reminiscence theatre, and adult and informal education, it is generally distinguished from high art, mass culture, and mainstream as well as avant garde theatre, although recently there have been some cases of well-known avant garde theatre artists entering the field either temporarily (Peter Sellars in Los Angeles) or semi-permanently (John Baylis in Sydney). The surprising lack of attention to community theatre in post-colonial and inter-cultural performance studies is a function, I suspect, of this marginal position within international and national art hierarchies. Community theatre performances are seldom reviewed by national media and, because they frequently occur outside 'legitimate' arts milieux, they have consequently tended to escape the attention of cultural theorists and theatre scholars. The related question of how much artistic satisfaction professionals can derive from community theatre yields widely divergent answers and depends largely on personalities and sociocultural circumstances. I will address this issue more elaborately in the conclusion, where, with the help of the project partners and an eclectic selection of theoretical writings, I shall speculate further on common concerns in community theatre. At the outset, however, it should be clear that in the first place it privileges the artistic pleasure and sociocultural empowerment of its community participants. Its material and aesthetic forms always emerge directly (if not exclusively) from 'the' community, whose interests it tries to express. Community theatre thus is a potent art form that allows once largely silent (or silenced) groups of people to add their voices to increasingly diverse and intricately inter-related local, regional, national and international cultures, whether these are evolving in insular Southeast Asia, provincial Europe, on the metropolitan southern Californian coast, coastal Central America, rural East Africa, or suburban Australia.

I estimate that, worldwide, at the very least a few hundred other projects fitting the loose definition above were unfolding during 1997. Why then these six and why in this order? Why not Boal, why not South Africa, why not Papua New Guinea? Quite simply because I personally knew them, they quickly agreed to participate, and all had interesting activities going on in the period I was able to set aside for the project. Identifying others and establishing relations with them would have taken too long and might well have resulted in missing this unique opportunity to bring together community theatre experiences from around the world.

The order of the trips, which to avoid bias or confusion, I have duplicated in the book and the video, was dictated by the production schedules of the theatre partners, who luckily but not altogether unexpectedly had lined up projects with a broad range of themes, urban as well as rural settings, and a balanced representation of women – both as facilitators and as participants. The other important variable affecting the order and length of our journeys were film director Rod Prosser's and my own young family, as well as the limited time I was given off from my teaching duties.

Hi tech gazing

Rod Prosser and I spent a maximum of five weeks with each of the projects and, in order to mimimize our unavoidable outsider gazing, worked with local camera operators and sound recordists in most of the places we visited. While we would have liked to have greater gender equity in these crews, the sad reality is that there still are very few women professionals in the film and video field. Moreover, the very presence of sophisticated technical equipment and the crew, who, although recruited by our theatre partners and proficient in the local languages, may well have affected the very community theatre processes we were trying to document with as little disturbance as possible. As Sally Gordon pointed out, people in Los Angeles are probably more media conscious than any-where else in the world and the presence of a foreign film crew also gave prestige to her project, thus perhaps motivating her participants to work harder than they normally would have and providing her community play with more publicity than it might otherwise have generated. In Sigoti, Kenya, a place with hardly any media to speak of, the very fact that a western film crew was interested in the local women's group con-vinced the men to give the women more space to maneouvre, at least temporarily. I am also quite sure that our physical presence gave the two young female performers in the Sydney train project a slightly greater sense of security at the moment that they were being verbally harrassed by an elderly couple not at all in the mood for their wacky performance. And while the *Legends and Traditions* performance had already been fixed as part of an annual community theatre festival in Costa Rica before we even came into the picture, the subsequent reconstructions of Aguamarina's collective creation method quite likely would not have happened at all if we had not come. In the Philippines, where we had the smallest crew, and in the Netherlands (home turf, I guess), I felt our pres-ence least affected the dynamics of the theatre process, but even there one can never be completely sure.

Method

In Marinduque we worked with Nonoy Regalado, a nationally respected self-directing camera man from Manila with links to PETA. In Los Angeles we worked with two young second-generation Chicano camera operators specializing in music videos, Art Santamaria and Jack Gonzalez, whom we recruited through Cal State-LA's broadcasting department. In Puntarenas we worked with camera operator Joaquin Salazar and sound recordist Francisco Esquivel Rodriguez, both from public broadcasting corporation SINART/Canal 13. In Kenya we worked with cameraman Julius Obala, who used to work for the Kenyan Broadcasting System (KBS) as a cameraman-reporter, and George Anang'a, a young university-educated storyteller who assisted as an inter-preter, sound recordist, and location manager. In Sydney, we worked with an old friend, videographer and theatre maker Ronaldo Morelos, and freelance sound recordist Peter Clark, whom we had found through another friend, Madeleine Blackwell, who was then studying at the National Film School. And in Utrecht we worked with award-winning camera man Albert van der Wildt and sound recordists Fokke Walstijn and Hans Schuurman, both experienced audiovisual technicians working for Utrecht University. In all the localities we visited, we recorded every workshop and rehearsal session we possibly could on either audio or video, we interviewed facilitators and participants at key moments of the process, documented the final performances, and invited reactions from spectators. In each place, I conducted additional library and archival research to collect scripts, reviews, and local cultural studies texts to inform my contextual pieces without which, I believed, the case studies could not be fully appreciated.

From January through to March 1998, I selected what I thought were the most relevant materials from 70 hours of video and 100 hours of audio transcriptions and fed these to Rod Prosser, who, in turn, used it and his own judgement to compose a provisional editing script, which, after another round of consultations and revisions, finally became the guideline for the offline and online editing process that, in July 1998, resulted in the video documentary that accompanies this book. In that same month, Sally Gordon of Teatro de la Realidad in Los Angeles, Jos Bours and Marlies Hautvast of Stut Theatre in Utrecht, Beng Santos Cabangon, Maribel Legarda, and Bong Billones of PETA in Manila, Harley Stumm of Urban Theatre Projects formerly known as Death Defying Theatre in Sydney, Gerardo Arias Elizondo of Aguamarina in Puntarenas, and Susan Adhiambo Odongo, Emma Mumma and several other members of the Kawuonda Women's Group in Sigoti came together in four consecutive seminar sessions at the Third World Congress of IDEA, in Kisumu, Kenya, to view and comment on the video documentary and on each other's ways of making community theatre. Since then, all of the partners have taken the opportunity to correct draft versions of the separate chapters I subsequently wrote on each of the participating community theatre groups. These chapters, following the chronological order of the video, form the heart of this book. With the obvious exception of the conclusion, all the chapters are similarly structured. I first provide a sociocultural impression of the country followed by a brief history of community theatre there, the country's overall arts scene, and a background of the featured artists and the particular organization they work with. Then, in the case study, I zoom in on a specific locality and comment in detail on the community theatre process that took place there, highlighting its distinguishing features.

The Philippines

The book (Chapter 1) and the video open with the Philippines, because chronologically that is where the journeys began, but also because I somehow wanted to continue where I had left off in my previous book, *The Playful Revolution: Theatre and Liberation in Asia* (1992). The main focus of this chapter is on PETA, the Philippines Educational Theater Association, a multifunctional theatre organization that includes a semi-professional performance ensemble, women's, children's and youth theatre units, a film and broadcasting department, and a so-called School for People's Theatre, which conducts community theatre training. PETA, too, has roots in the university and union-based anti-imperial struggle of the late 1960s, but also has affinity with American and European ideas about radical people's, epic, and educational theatre, as well as with Boal. Internationalist in spirit, PETA has always looked to connect with like-minded artists, drama teachers, and solidarity activists overseas. For many years now, the company has been collaborating with Black Tent Theatre of Tokyo. It has also been actively involved in international organizations that promote educational and community theatre, which have brought to light substantial ongoing community theatre activities in other Asian and Polynesian countries as well.[1] Most importantly for the purposes of this book and video, however, after the fall of Ferdinand Marcos in 1986, PETA has been consciously shifting its grass roots outreach work from explicitly issue-driven liberation theatre to community theatre. I have maintained good working relations with PETA since 1986. Moreover, PETA's Basic Integrated Theatre Arts (BITAW) approach is arguable one of the clearest methods of community theatre to come out of Asia and Ernie Cloma and Dessa Quesada among the most experienced facilitators (van Erven 1998). When the opportunity presented itself to observe these two at work on the environmentally devastated island of Marinduque, the choice was easily made. In April and May 1997, we spent two weeks on the island living with Teatro Balangaw, and two weeks in Manila for further research. The main focus in this chapter's case study is on the BITAW as an educational instrument for rapidly generating quality community theatre with young people on burning issues.

The Netherlands

Utrecht, which follows the Philippines in the book (Chapter 2) and video, was another obvious choice. I could literally go to Stut's Monday night rehearsals on my bicycle. I also knew the city well. I had migrated there from the southern countryside at age nine in 1964 and had lived there for most of my teenage years, growing up in what was then still a working-class neighbourhood but has since become middle class, as I have. From 1977 to 1988, partly to avoid the draft but mostly to satisfy an urge to find out everything I could about political theatre, I lived abroad (van Erven 1988). First on scholarship in Nashville, then on savings and a New Zealand research grant in the Asia-Pacific region. I returned home in 1988 to take a job at Utrecht University, where I have since been teaching American Studies and drama, producing inter-cultural theatre projects on the side. Although I was born in the rural south and have lived for extended periods of time in other cultures, I consider myself culturally and socially a Utrechter. Hence Utrecht, where in Jos Bours and Marlies Hautvast of Stut Theatre, themselves transplanted southerners (from rural Limburg), I found loyal research partners with artistic roots going back to the 1970s.

In the Netherlands, as in most of western Europe, community theatre developed either out of professional radical people's theatre companies or out of theatre-in-education and cultural action initiatives that started becoming more participatory and community-based after 1965 (Jackson 1993: 18–21). Stut Theatre quite coincidentally discovered the value of letting people perform in their own plays during an outreach project in a working-class neighbourhood, the product of which the artists had originally intended to be performed by trained actors. For a long time, the few community theatre companies that did manage to survive in Europe operated in isolation from each other and in the margins between the arts and social welfare worlds in their own countries. It is only now, after working for more than twenty years in some cases, that they are beginning to gain recognition for the powerful theatre they create and for the positive impact they have on European working-class neighbour-hoods, where inter-cultural tension and youth unemployment are becoming a real concern.[2] Consequently, since the early 1990s, Stut has been tackling themes related to cultural diversity as formerly monocul-tural parts of town have witnessed a steady increase of migrant and refugee residents. Stut has high production standards, which it tries to meet by working with a professional playwright, a professional director, professional technicians and designers, and by a creative process that typ-ically lasts a year, considerably longer than any of the other groups in this book and video. From February through to October 1997, whenever I was home from a foreign trip I went to Stut rehearsals and intermittently interviewed Jos and Marlies and Carla and Feryal, a Dutch and a Turkish participant, respectively. As with all the other groups, I also collected earlier scripts, video documentation and all the secondary literature I could lay my hands on. The focus of Chapter 2 is on the role of the professional playwright and director in inter-cultural working-class community theatre.

Los Angeles

In May–June 1997, we visited Sally Gordon's Teatro de la Realidad in Los Angeles, the subject of Chapter 3. Gordon started her career in Off-Off Broadway theatre collectives in New York in the 1960s and came to the West Coast by way of children's theatre tours through rural eastern states in the early 1970s. She cites theatre educator Robert Alexander of Washington's Living Stage as the main influence on her way of working, and to a lesser degree Nicaragua's Alan Bolt and Brazil's Augusto Boal. Gordon works in relative isolation from other professional community theatre artists, like Colombian Hector Aristizabel or higher profile community theatre companies as Cornerstone in Santa Monica, the Roadside Theatre in Whitesburg, Kentucky, Junebug Productions in New Orleans, and the Puerto Rican *Pregones* Theatre in New York's South Bronx.[3] These enterprises make use of professional performers with or without amateurs (Cocke *et al.* 1993: 56), frequently work with existing scripts (Kuftinec 1996: 93–96), or professionally develop their own from local materials. In terms of their organizational structure and the foregrounding of their own artistry, they seem more akin to regionally implanted Radical People's Theatre companies. In some ways, their professional organizational, artistic, and community celebratory approach is represented here by Urban Theatre Projects of western Sydney. Gordon's work, in contrast, has obvious links to art therapy, but although many of her participants have suffered traumatic experiences from migration and domestic abuse, in her community theatre projects she insists on treating them as artists. Sally Gordon's work, in addition to the sensitivity required for dealing with delicate personal issues, tells the tale of the frustrations associated with making community theatre within the organizational structure of a not-for-profit social welfare agency.

Costa Rica

Majella Perry, an Irish student in the theatre and education department of the Utrecht School of the Arts, introduced me to Costa Rica, where she had gone for an internship with 'Aguamarina' in 1994. Through her, in 1996 I began corresponding with that group's administrator, Gerardo Arias Elizondo, after attempts to link up with the 'Taller Nacional de Teatro' had fallen through. I gathered from Majella's report and Gerardo's letters that 'Aguamarina' practised a type of *creación colectiva* similar to other South and Central American community theatre collectives and, moreover, had been around since the early 1970s, which was the height of the *Nuevo Teatro Popular* ('New Popular Theatre') movement that was then spreading throughout Latin America and the Caribbean and to which Augusto Boal has also been linked. I consciously opted not to concentrate on Boal, however, because community theatre, despite his undeniable influences, cannot be equated with theatre of the oppressed. Besides, Filipino-Australian multimedia artist Ronaldo Morelos, our first camera operator in Sydney, had just completed a video documentary on Boal's legislative theatre in Brazil and written reflections on Boal's theory and practical applications all over the world were already abounding at the time this project went underway (Cohen-Cruz and Schutzman 1994; Boal 1995). Our work in Costa Rica was different from anywhere else, because when we arrived 'Aguamarina' did not have a new project on the drawing board but, unbeknownst to us, was in the middle of training a group of new young recruits. To suit us and them, the three Aguamarina leaders reconstructed the way they worked on four earlier projects: one for and with local fisherfolk, another one about AIDS, a third about local legends and traditions, and a fourth about prisoners. Although perforce less spontaneously than in the other countries, we nevertheless managed to document the technical intricacies of Latin American community-based collective creation, focusing particularly on the fishermen's project. Through additional interviews with cultural historians and library research I subsequently put together a cultural-historical context for collective creation in Costa Rican community theatre.

Kenya

The community theatre work of Ngũgĩ wa Thiong'o first attracted me to Kenya. I wanted to find out what legacy his initiatives had left and therefore accepted an invitation from Opiyo Mumma, then president of the Kenyan Drama/Theatre and Education Association (KDEA). Dr Mumma, whom I had first met at a community theatre conference in Utrecht in 1994, proposed that we work with a women's theatre collective in his native village Sigoti in western Kenya, the report of which appears in the case study of Chapter 5. It is preceded by a post-colonial

history of Kenyan community theatre in which the quintessential contributions of Ngũgĩ and the University of Nairobi's Free Travelling
Theatre are highlighted.

Community theatre in Africa has clear roots in the anti-colonial struggle (Pickering 1957) and, today, through local cultural festivals, has
become intricately intertwined with drama in schools and theatre in
public awareness campaigns, in which guise it is commonly called
'Theatre for Development' (Abah 1996a and 1996b; Boeren and
Epskamp 1992; Byram 1985; Kamlongera 1989; Mda 1993; wa Mirii
1989; Malamah-Thomas 1987; Mlama 1991; Ndumbe 1991; Prentki
1996). Kenyan novelist and playwright Ngũgĩ wa Thiongo explicitly
mentions the propaganda theatre created by the anti-imperial Mau-Mau
guerrillas in the 1950s and the pre-colonial theatricalized expressions of
his ancestors as inspirations for his own community theatre activities
(Ngũgĩ 1981: 69; 1986: 37). Although he had written plays before, Ngũgĩ
began to develop a more explicit interest in participatory community
theatre after 1974, when John Ruganda brought the Free Travelling
Theatre concept to Kenya from Uganda, where it had existed since 1966
(Cook 1966; Kayanja 1967). This interest was further fed at the Second
World Festival of African Arts and Culture (FESTAC) held in January
and February 1977 in Lagos, Nigeria, almost immediately after which he
and others began to work on the now legendary *I Will Marry When I
Want* project in the Kamiriithu community. After President Moi's clam-
pdown and Ngũgĩ's consequent exile in 1982, Kenyan community
theatre was absorbed for almost a decade in school-based theatre activities and women's groups, from which it has reluctantly emerged as a
distinct art form once again after 1991, when governmental control
began to ease up. The case study emphasizes the seamless integration of
community theatre activities in Sigoti's daily life, highlighting particularly the beneficial effects it has on local gender relations.

Australia

Australia, the last in line, is represented here less for geocultural parity
reasons than for the useful lessons it offers in terms of governmental
community arts policy, the scope and the sophistication of the theoretical reflections it has produced, and the fascinating flirtations of some of
its longest-surviving community theatre companies with the avant-garde
and vice versa. Australian community theatre has direct, but in terms of
post-colonial theory, complicated links with western radical people's
theatre and the theatre-in-education movement of Britain in the 1960s

and 1970s (Fotheringham 1992: 18). A fundamental change in government arts funding under Prime Minister Whitlam in 1973 led to a prolific and widespread community arts movement, whose priorities and definitions of 'community' and 'art' have clearly shifted over the past twenty years (Hawkins 1993). Death Defying Theatre, now called Urban Theatre Projects (UTP), is arguably one of the most innovative companies to have come out of this Australian Community Arts scene. Monica Barone and Boris Kelly, two Australian theatre artists I had known since 1993 and with whom I had collaborated on a five-week student theatre project in Utrecht in 1996, first introduced me to UTP. In 1996, Monica was serving on UTP's Artistic Board and was working on the original proposal that would lead to *Trackwork*, a large-scale moveable community theatre event whose logistical and curatorial aspects I particularly emphasize in the case study.

Notes

1 Since its foundation in 1967, PETA has been associated with several attempts to set up international organizations for people's theatre, first through UNESCO's International Theatre Institute channels and later through such networks as the International People's Theatre Alliance (IPTA), the Asian Theatre Forum, and, indirectly, through the Asian Council For People's Culture (ACPC). It has been an active member of the International Drama/Theatre and Education Association (IDEA) since that organization's foundation in 1991 and is also actively involved in international children's and youth theatre networks.

2 To celebrate its twentieth anniversary, Stut Theatre organized a three-day symposium that drew representatives from community theatre groups in Nijmegen, Leeuwarden, Eindhoven, and Rotterdam (all in the Netherlands), Ghent and Antwerp (Belgium), Berlin (Germany), Hull (England), and Taiwan. In the preparations for the event, solidly established groups were also discovered in Louvain and Liege (Belgium), Hamburg and Cologne (Germany), and in Paris and Lyon (France). I suspect, community theatre also exists in Scandinavian countries, where, just as in the UK and Ireland, it may well be practised in combination with theatre-in-education (Jackson 1993: 22). Sally Gordon from Los Angeles, George Anang'a from Kenya, Phillip Mann from New Zealand, and Ernie Cloma and Dessa Quesada (along with eight other actors from PETA) also participated in the Stut symposium, which drew a lot of interest from local politicians and social welfare policy-makers, but was largely ignored by the mainstream theatre.

3 *Pregones* ('town criers') runs a performance ensemble and a cultural centre in a remodelled gym in the South Bronx, where it performs collectively created shows to popular audiences from the Spanish-speaking Caribbean. The artistic director of Pregones, Rosalba Rolón, studied theatre at the University of Puerto Rico and migrated to New York in 1963. Pregones thus has direct roots in the Latin American *creación colectiva* or 'New Popular

Theatre' movement. Three of its actors joined the company after having worked for years with Puerto Rico's well-known theatre collective *Animo*. The company also collaborates with such leading Latin American *creación colectiva* groups as La Candalaria from Colombia and Yuyachkani from Peru (Ralli) and further coordinates its activities with other Latino theatre companies on the East Coast and with the TENAZ Chicano theatre network in the Southwest.

4 The history of community theatre in the Caribbean also has roots in colonial times. In Jamaica, for example, it has been connected to the School Drama Festivals and the Little Theatre Movement that began in the 1940s, which in turn engendered the Jamaica School of Drama and a number of grass roots community theatre companies, including Sistren (Epskamp 1994: 21–22). Epskamp also reports community theatre activities on other Anglo-Caribbean islands as well as in the French and Dutch Antilles.

Bibliography

Abah, Ogah Steve (1996a) 'Theatre for Development as an Informal Method of Education in Nigeria', *Research in Drama Education* 1, 2: 245–260.

—— (1996b) *Performing Life: Case Studies in Theatre for Development*, Zaria: Shekut Books.

Boal, Augusto (1995) *The Rainbow of Desire*, London: Routledge.

Boeren, Ad (1983) 'Theatre in Swaziland', *Third World Popular Theatre Newsletter* 3: 10–11.

Boeren, Ad and Epskamp, Kees (eds) (1992) *The Empowerment of Culture: Development Communication and Popular Media*, The Hague: CESO.

Byram, M.L. (1985) *Theatre for Development: A Guide to Training*, Amherst, MA: University of Masachussetts Center for International Education.

Cocke, Dudley, Newman, Harry and Salmons-Rue, Janet (eds) (1993) *From the ground Up: Grassroots Theater in Historical and Contemporary Perspective*, Ithaca, NY: Community Based Arts Project at Cornell University.

Cohen-Cruz, Jan and Schutzman, Mady (eds) (1994) *Playing Boal: Theatre, Therapy, Activism*, London: Routledge.

Cook, D. (1966) 'Theatre Goes to the People!', *Transition* 25: 23–33.

Epskamp, Kees (1994) 'Gemeenschapstheater: tussen lokale en nationale identiteitsopbouw', *Theater & Educatie* 2 (Fall): 8–29.

Erven, Eugene van (1988) *Radical People's Theatre*, Bloomington: Indiana University Press.

—— (1992) *The Playful Revolution: Theatre and Liberation in Asia*, Bloomington: Indiana University Press.

—— (1998) 'Some Thoughts on Uprooting Asian Grassroots Theatre', in Jeanne Colleran and Jenny S. Spencer (eds) *Staging Resistance: Essays on Political Theatre*, Ann Arbor, MI: The University of Michigan Press: 98–120.

Fotheringham, Richard (ed.) (1992) *Community Theatre in Australia*, Sydney: Currency Press.

Gard, Robert (1959) *Community Theatre: Idea and Achievement*, New York: Duell, Sloan and Pearce.

—— (1993) 'Robert Gard,' in Dudley Locke *et al.* (eds) *From the Ground Up: Grassroots Theater in Historical and Contemporary Perspective*, Ithaca, NY: Community Based Arts Project at Cornell University.

Gaudibert, Pierre (1977) *Action Culturelle: intégration et/ou subversion*, Paris: Casterman.

Gecau, K. (1991) *Community-Based Theatre in Zimbabwe*, Harare: Zimbabwe Foundation for Education with Production.

Gunner, L.(ed.) (1991) special issue on Theatre and the Performing Arts in Southern Africa, *Journal of Southern African Studies* 16, 2.

Hawkins, Gay (1993) *From Nimbin to Mardigrass: Constructing Community Arts*, St Leonards, NSW: Allen & Unwin.

Jackson, Tony (ed.) (1993) *Learning Through Theatre: New Perspectives on Theatre in Education*, London: Routledge.

Kamlongera, C. (1989) *Theatre for Development in Africa with Case Studies from Malawi and Zambia*, Bonn: German Foundation for International Development.

Kayanja, L. (1967) 'The Makerere Travelling Theatre in East Africa', *Journal of Modern African Studies* 5: 141–142.

Kuftinec, Sonja (1996) 'A Cornerstone for Rethinking Community Theatre', *Theatre Topics* 6, 1: 91–102.

Malamah-Thomas, D.H. (1987) 'Community Theatre with and by the People: The Sierra Leone Experience,' *Convergence* 20, 1: 59–69.

—— (1989) 'Bibliography of Documentation on the Participatory Research of Community Theatre for Education and Development in Sierra Leone', *Journal of the African Association for Literacy and Adult Education* 4, 1: 36–37.

Mda, Z. (1993) *When People Play People: Development Communication Through Theatre*, London: Zed Books.

Mirii, Ngũgĩ wa (1989) 'Using Theatre to Communicate', *Group Media Journal* (June): 15–16.

Mlama, P.M. (1991) *Culture and Development: The Popular Theatre Approach in Africa*, Uppsala, Sweden: The Scandinavian Institute of African Studies.

Ndumbe Eyoh, H. (1991) *Beyond the Theatre*, Bonn: DSE.

Pickering, A.K. (1957) 'Village Drama in Ghana', *Fundamental and Adult Education* 9, 4: 178–183.

Prentki, Tim (1996) 'The Empire Strikes Back: The Relevance of Theatre for Development in Africa and South-East Asia to Community Drama in the UK', *Research in Drama Education* 1, 1: 33–50.

Ralli, T. (1989) 'Teatro Peruano: Una Pedagogica Alternativa', *Autoeducacción* 9, 26: 55–59.

Thiongo, Ngũgĩ wa (1981) *Writers In Politics*, Nairobi: East African Educational Publishers.

—— (1986) *Decolonizing the Mind: The Politics of Language in African Literature*, Nairobi: East African Educational Publishers.

Chapter 1

Philippine community theatre in the 1990s

We arrived at Ninoy Aquino International Airport on 17 April 1997. PETA staff member Gail Billones took us in a hired jeepney through rush-hour traffic across town to the PETA office in Lantana street, Cubao, where we could safely store our equipment. The next day, we had a briefing with PETA executive director Beng Santos Cabangon, treasurer Mel Bernardo and Ernie Cloma, the energetic veteran artist-teacher who would lead the Marinduque expedition. They gave us our schedule and connected me by phone to Eli Obligacion, the coordinator there. My friend Jack Yabut, head of PETA's marketing and promotions, then took me book shopping at the Ateneo University Press store and later his wife Hiroko, a Japanese anthropologist, showed me the ins and outs of the university library.

I spent the entire Saturday in the library before swallowing a full hit of black Manila rush-hour exhaust gas on my way to Fort Santiago, where I wanted to see PETA's production of two Orlando Nadres plays. Nadres, a gifted writer and director who had worked with PETA in the 1970s, had died in 1991. To celebrate its thirtieth anniversary, PETA had taken two of his best-known shorter plays out of the drawer and cast several popular television and movie actors, all former PETA members, in the leading roles. Due to congested traffic and missed jeepney connections, I arrived half an hour late, catching only a glimpse of the first. The second play, *Hanggang Dito na Lamang at Maraming Salamat* ('Until Here and No Further, Thank You Very Much') I got to see in full. It featured Joel Lamangan, now a famous film director, and an outrageous Khryss Adalia, who, I understood, had become quite a star in a local soap. Joel played an aging, repressed gay pawnshop owner. The play is set in his tastefully decorated, comfortably furnished backyard adjacent to the railroad tracks, for which the catwalk in the middle of PETA's outdoor theatre (with the audience sitting on either side on more comfortable plastic chairs than the stiff wooden ones I remembered from 1988) was put to good use.

The play opens with Joel reading a letter from a protégé whose education he had been financing for a number of years. The student turns out to be an attractive young man, with whom Joel's character is secretly in love. Khryss plays a transsexual houseguest, who has entered the Gay Miss Philippines contest. He displays an awesome register of mood changes and clearly is the favourite of the countless male and female gay couples in the audience. Enter the kid, who has no clue what he is walking into. Joel tries to charm him with uncle-nephew-type horseplay and beer drinking, but when he elicits no response he corners the boy for a forced kiss on the mouth, which causes the latter to escape in disgust. Equally disgusted with himself, the uncle then falls into a depression lasting several days. In the meantime, Khryss returns as the newly crowned Gay Miss Philippines, but Joel takes his frustrations out on his transsexual friend, tearing the dress and wig to pieces and humiliatingly exposing Khryss/Julie's underwear. Having thus chased his best friend away, Joel is left to face himself in all his naked solitude. The protégé re-enters and is almost tempted to comfort his mentor, but a quick conciliatory hug is all he can muster. With lots of unresolved conflictual feelings, Joel finally symbolically releases the white balloon that Julie/Khryss had brought back for him from the contest. An obvious symbol of liberation, I could follow it for minutes as it drifted away into the night time sky over Manila Bay, while the audience around me broke into a standing ovation, reminding me what an important play this must have been for gay emancipation back in the mid-1970s in Asia's latin, dictatorial, macho archipelago.

The Philippines and its theatre in the late 1990s

Community theatre in the Philippines has a rich history going back to pre-colonial times (Fernandez 1996). As I recorded in *The Playful Revolution*, it assumed explicit political overtones in the 1970s and 1980s, culminating in a nationwide network of theatre workers fighting against the Marcos dictatorship. Since then, under the successive regimes of upper-class ex-housewife Corazon Aquino, of ex-general Fidel Ramos, and now of ex-moviestar Joseph Estrada, the Philippines has undergone substantial political and cultural changes, which have affected its theatre as well.

Renato Constantino (1996: 99), the ageing cultural commentator of the democratic left, sounds a useful warning to 'overrated foreign "Filipinologists"', urging us not to ignore the unheralded efforts by Filipino intellectuals in our attempts to find local endorsement from sell-out intellectuals for our self-aggrandizing orientalist projects. Since the fall of Marcos, Constantino has continued to express concern over the fragmentation of the left as a result of the evil enemy's disappearance while old hierarchically institutionalized inequities remain intact. By 1997, military encounters between government forces and private armies, on one side, and combat units of the communist New People's Army or various armed bands of Muslim separatists on the other, had subsided, creating, on the surface at least, an illusion of peace. But the Philippine Alliance of Human Rights Advocates concludes otherwise:

> The downtrend in politically inspired human rights abuses has been offset by human rights violations coming from other sources. While the areas of armed conflict have narrowed, the intensity of the government's military response to the renewed armed activities of Moro rebel groups in Mindanao has led to an alarming rise in displacements. The human rights violators of the past – the police, military and paramilitary forces who were never made to account for their crimes against human rights during the Marcos and Aquino years – have not learned to respect human rights more. They have merely shifted targets: the main victims are no longer political dissenters but ordinary people in the streets; no longer suspected communist insurgents but suspected criminals and terrorists.
>
> (PAHRA 1996: 61)

And although the Philippine economy recorded spectacular annual growth rates before the 1998 Asian stock market crisis, this had not trickled down to reduce poverty or bring about a more just distribution of wealth (Buenconsejo Garcia 1994; Broad and Cavanagh 1991). Meanwhile, graft, corruption and abuse of power remain rampant throughout the archipelago at all levels of governance and business (Constantino 1996: 124–132).

The Philippines of the late 1990s is a complex place, ranging from indigenous tribes trying to preserve age-old traditional ways in the Cordillera highlands in the north and Mindanao forests in the south, to rapping youngsters in the smoggy, overcrowded streets of metropolitan Manila. North American culture remains an influential yardstick for Filipinos from all walks of life, because of American-style printed and electronic media, because of air-conditioned mega malls with mirror-glass façades encroaching on the big cities, and, most importantly, because of family contacts with between 1.5 (Pertierra 1995: 62) and 2.5 million Filipino immigrants in the United States and Canada (Chant and McIlwaine 1995: 34, n18).

The Philippine economy relies heavily on the earnings of temporary migrants to the Middle East, Europe, and Asian countries such as Hong Kong, Singapore, Malaysia and Japan, almost half of whom are women (Chant and McIlwaine 1995: 34). The position of many Filipinas at home and abroad is not enviable as they are frequently at the receiving end of abuse and exploitation of all kinds. To compound this, the official position of the Catholic Church, the most popular institutionalized religion in the country, remains conservative on such issues as abortion and divorce. And the fact that a woman became the first President after Marcos did little to change the predicament of the majority of women (ibid.: 40–41). Non-government-supported grass roots activities on behalf of women seem to have been more effective, although there, too, urban middle-class domination and ideological fragmentation are reported to have caused stagnation (ibid.: 42).

By 1997, the Philippine population was estimated at 70 million with almost half living in urban areas. The country's foreign debt remained among the highest in the world and its GNP among the lowest in Asia-Pacific. Health, housing, and welfare conditions are dismal, particularly for the urban poor, at least 8 million of whom live in slums around Metro Manila but who continue to maintain cultural and kinship ties with their rural roots (Chant and McIlwaine 1995: 67). Conversely, most Filipino rural residents are now connected, through migrated relatives, to life in the big city and the world beyond. For this reason, Raul Pertierra argues, contemporary Philippine cultural identity, which is simultaneously composed of 'premodern, late modern and even postmodern elements' (1995: 14) has become 'increasingly polymorphic and no longer confined to the accidents of its colonial past' (ibid.: 11).

Pertierra points out that in terms of literacy levels and women's participation in education the Philippines ranks very high internationally, but that nevertheless many schools are 'not properly integrated with the country's cultural, institutional, and economic requirements' (ibid.: 75). PETA's Ernie Cloma agrees:

> There are schools in the remote areas where in one classroom there are four different grades and the teacher is teaching them all at the same time. While one is gardening, another is doing mathematical exercises, and a third is being taught how to read. What will the fourth do? Maybe drawing. All the materials come from Manila and are not adapted to regional particulars and most teachers train their students to prepare for exams, because high scores enhance the school's reputation.[1]

Ernie Cloma

Cloma, who heads PETA's School for People's Theatre, has been working for over two and a half decades now to change what he calls 'the olympic mentality' of schools and teachers, who usually do not consider creativity important:

> Schooling should be about teaching you about who you are as a person and the society and culture you live in. What is the point of teaching white-collar values to people who are going to work on the land or in a factory, thereby training them, in effect, to be better and cheaper labor for the first world by not teaching them to think and decide for themselves and be critical?

PETA has been expanding its operations in the Philippines educational system since the fall of Marcos, which, ironically, coincided with the removal of drama as an elective subject from the curricula. It has therefore become an important task of PETA's School for People's Theatre to nurture teachers' enthusiasm for drama through its 'Creative Pedagogy' programme, a special after-hours initiative designed to increase their creativity.

Ernie Cloma's own involvement in community theatre goes back to his days as a primary school teacher in his hometown Pasig, a heavily industrialized area in Southeast Metro Manila. As a university student he had orginally been trained as a dancer, but after Martial Law was declared in September 1972 he gradually became more active in the anti-dictatorial protest movement. He remembers how several of his former pupils went on to become radical theatre organizers and some, like the legendary guerrilla poet Eman Lacaba, even went underground. He finally joined PETA in 1977 at the age of 37.

Cloma continued to teach in Pasig, acting in his spare time in PETA's Kalinangan Ensemble productions, most of Lino Brocka's internationally successful feature films (David, 1995), and conducting theatre workshops for children. He was politicized, he believes, through his art activism and through the radicalization in his own community:

> When I was young, Pasig was still very rural; it didn't become industrialized until the late 1960s. Back then there was still a strong sense of community, which is why the labourers were so easily organized, also because the unions came in right away with the first factories. Exploitation was rampant then. When I was already with PETA, the unions were putting up theatre groups in each *barrio*; these were at the vanguard of the demonstrations.

Back in the period when Ernie Cloma joined the company, PETA's most radical members were coming up through the Metro Teen Theatre League (MTTL), a network of youth theatre groups based in different highschools around Manila. Dessa Quesada, who can be seen working alongside Ernie Cloma in the video, and Beng Santos Cabangon, PETA's current executive director, were part of this first MTTL generation in the late 1970s.

Changes in the BITAW

From 1975 to 1985 community-based political theatre groups were spontaneously sprouting up all over the Philippines as a result of the widespread implementation of so-called 'Basic Integrated Theater Arts Workshops' (BITAW) in schools, progressive church parishes, universities, and grass-roots organizations (van Erven 1992: 64–94). The BITAW method, a phased, modular approach to grass-roots theatre training, had been concocted from exercises adapted from Viola Spolin and Dorothy Heathcote and a philosophy inspired by the Philippine reality in combination with Liberation Theology and Freire's Pedagogy of the Oppressed. But although it eventually led to a numerically strong national network of people's theatre groups that played a significant role in the mass mobilizations against Marcos, according to Ernie Cloma BITAWs were conducted without much sense of strategy, subtlety, or self-criticism:

> I first realized this in the early 1980s, when we were in Basilan helping a local group choreograph a dance for a Holy Mass. All they did were western jazz movements, Alvin Ailey and all that. So I told myself, 'This island is so rich in authentic movements of its own; aren't we committing cultural imperialism here?' After that, we began to reflect more seriously on this issue and started studying local traditional theatre forms.

In the early 1980s, after several PETA artists had attended a Boal workshop in Paris, they made the same mistake once again, this time uncritically blending Theatre of the Oppressed techniques with the existing PETA workshop approach. Eventually, a hard-fought self-reflection process led to an internal split between two schools of thought. While both camps agreed that the social, political, economic and cultural conditions should always be the starting point for PETA's theatre processes and that participants should be empowered by writing their own scripts and directing themselves, they differed on the question whether facilitators should be allowed to present their own aesthetics and perspectives. Those who disagreed were afraid they might be imposing their own ideology and artistic standards, preferring instead to only stimulate the participants' creativity. The other camp, to which Cloma belonged, believed that it would do no harm to raise the aesthetics of the participants. 'I give participants always an idea of my own aesthetics,' he comments. 'We were invited because they feel we can give them something. Growing one's own aesthetics is also okay, but to nurture it they have to see other forms.'

PETA's executive director Beng Santos Cabangon has a slightly different analysis of the internal conflict. She believes that in the late 1980s PETA was not really effective at integrating artist-teachers working at the regional grass roots with the more performance-oriented artists who continued to play in Manila for urban middle-class audiences:

> The question arose: when you go to the regions, do you really just provide artistic consultancy and further leave it up to them, or are you intervening at the expense of imposing professional Manila-based

standards on these organizations? During this period we would always invite one community organization to come perform at Fort Santiago. Some of them worked; some didn't. But the purpose was also to show our Manila audiences what we had been doing in the regions.[2]

One of the most successful examples of showcasing work from the grass roots was *Lin Awa* ('Wellspring of Life'), a performance by a tribal group from Lúbuagan in Mountain Province led by charismatic school teacher, elder, and performer Cirilio Bawer. To help them prepare for the Manila gig, PETA staff member Jack Yabut travelled to the tribal community, but all he did was suggest certain scenes to be shortened and adjust the blocking for the Manila stage. 'It was beautiful and we hardly touched it,' PETA's artistic director Maribel Legarda recalls:

> It came straight out of the community. They did their dances, which – and this is perhaps where PETA's input could be detected – they strung together with a story. It worked, even for sophisticated Manila audiences. But later we also had a production from Laguna; a German play transposed into *Komedya* style, which was so forced. So, there really is no set answer to this question.[3]

PETA's community theatre workshops
The aesthetics debate, in combination with a subsequent clash of personalities and funding problems, led to the departure of several veteran PETA members and an organizational overhaul in the late 1980s. It cleared the way for more efficient decision-making and a more flexible community theatre methodology that could be adapted to any cultural or social circumstances. As a result, most PETA workshops are now more narrowly issue-based than the general anti-imperialist stance that characterized their work before 1990.

PETA facilitators design their syllabi according to a specific social theme provided by their hosts. After (1) building trust and releasing inhibitions through theatre games, the essential ingredient in PETA's community theatre method is (2) the so-called 'exposure,' a field trip to an area where life is strongly affected by the issue at hand. The stories gathered in the exposure then become the basis for (3) a collectively created performance.

Community theatre training at different levels

PETA offers its workshops to a variety of target groups, ranging from church and community theatre groups to teachers
and NGO staffs.

• Level 1: these introductory workshops go through all three
  phases: from basic theatre skills training and exposure, to an
  in-house showcase.
• Level 2: contains the same three phases but includes
  advanced actor training and basic playwriting and concludes with a theatrically more challenging public
  performance. The case study is an example of a LEVEL 2
  workshop. Portions of it are included in the accompanying
  video.
• Level 3: is designed for people who have already gone
  through Levels 1 and 2 and are interested in conducting
  workshops of their own. After going through the basic
  exercises, they learn to design workshop syllabi themselves,
  trying them out under supervision.
• Level 4: teaches trainees to tailor-make workshops for all
  kinds of different needs and circumstances.

Respecting local cultural traditions

Catholicism is still widely practised all over the Philippines and the
effective community theatre artist therefore has no option but to respect
it, cooperating even with conservative priests, and, if need be, building
on local liturgical theatrical traditions. During Holy Week, many rural
communities still mount religious dramas, like the *Sinakulo* dramatizations of Christ's crucifixion, for example (van Erven 1992: 31–32).
Town *fiestas* on the occasion of local patron saints and Christmas are
other attractive occasions for community theatre activities. When they
are invited to work with parish-based groups, PETA artists usually try to
insert a historical or social dimension in liturgical plays. Ernie Cloma
has been involved in many such religiously packaged community
theatre projects: 'For example, I did a community production of the
Kalvaryo with young people. Everything starts traditional, but when
Judas makes his statement, I had other Judases appear from behind

him – the Judases of today. In this way, the people could see that the play is still relevant and that Judases are still with us now.' And as Raul Pertierra (1995: 42–53) illustrates with an example from Zamora (Ilocos Sur), traditional *Komedya* productions by local community members for the annual *fiesta* can easily turn into hard-fought secular political battles.

Community theatre networking in the 1990s

Cloma estimates that, if one includes church-based, children's theatre, youth theatre and cause-oriented groups, there are some 300 community theatre companies active in his country. But he no longer believes there is a need for a national coordinating body in the vein of BUGKOS (van Erven 1992: 92–94). Around 1990, when former PETA stalwart Nanding Josef joined the staff of the Cultural Center of the Philippines (CCP), this government institution took over most of the coordinating work from BUGKOS, which by then was slowly dying. BUGKOS had derived its main inspiration from clear-cut political objectives, such as getting rid of the dictator and the US military bases, but when there were no longer any big targets left it vanished. 'It was a very difficult period in terms of finding out what the new essence of our cultural work and art had become,' Nanding Josef recalls:

> Many artists stopped because they got married and had to support a family. Some got government jobs, became coopted by the system, and stopped being critical. There are also some who misused funds. That's what happened to KAFI in Mindanao and BANAAG in the Visayas. It was a major factor in the decline of the cultural movement in those places. Kaliwat, a community theatre group that came out of the Mindano Community Theatre Network [MCTN], is one of the few groups succeeding to keep its integrity intact. The likes of Nestor Horfilla are hanging on, consciously developing second-liners.[4]

Government-sponsored arts training

In the Philippines, government funding for the arts is in the hands of a National Commission for Culture and the Arts (NCCA) that comes under the Cultural Center of the Philippines (CCP). The NCCA coordinates twenty-four national arts committees, including the Committee on Dramatic Arts (CDA). Nanding Josef was CDA chair from 1989 until 1996, when he fell out with then newly appointed arts commissioner Alayla, a former Minister of Education under Marcos. Nestor Horfilla (van Erven 1992: 82–90), representing the Mindanao region, is the current chair, while PETA executive director Beng Santos Cabangon continues as vice chair for the National Capital Region. Other former people's theatre activists stayed on as vice chairs for Luzon and the Visayas, respectively. Josef, who during his CDA tenure had organized three national drama festivals to celebrate the regional, aesthetic and orientational diversity of Philippine theatre, now dedicates himself fully to training young artists at the Philippine Highschool for the Arts (PHA) in Laguna, where he has been director since 1995.

Josef envisions his school turning out community-minded artists through a new curriculum with a strong emphasis on cultural identity and social awareness. His school offers training in seven main disciplines: visual arts, film, broadcasting, architecture, theatre, music, and dance, which are all taught from a post-colonial perspective. Community exposure and the study of indigenous cultural expressions under the guidance of tribal artists are also important elements in his curriculum. For this reason, he has made it a point to recruit young students from indigenous areas, although he encourages them to return home after graduating: 'One of my "correctives" is to invite elders from their communities to come over here and stay with us for a while. Our tribal students thus understand better that their task is to develop their art here but to bring it back to their homes because it should be kept alive there.' Even so, particularly artists from Mindanao resist Josef's plans for cultural synthesis. Some even regard it as a potentially dangerous dilution of regional heritages that are already seriously threatened with extinction to begin with. Yet, the days of factionalizations, so prevalent in the 1970s and 1980s, have passed. The dialogue between Manila-based artists and those in the region now continues through the Committee on Dramatic Arts while critical 'anti-synthesis' artists like Nestor Horfilla are regularly invited as guest lecturers to the Highschool for the Arts.

Government versus non-government

Josef is careful not to let his school get in the way of PETA's activities and emphasizes that while the PHA is active in seven different art disciplines, PETA only works in theatre and film. Moreover, he knows that as a government institution his school has to adopt a neutral profile. The NGO-sponsored PETA can afford to choose its own partners independently.

Until 1990, PETA used to have outreach projects all over the Philippines. Now, through its School for People's Theatre, it works in only five designated partner areas, where it has established long-term programmes and cooperates with other NGOs to explore how cultural work can be integrated in community development processes. Beng Santos Cabangon sees the grass-roots activities in these five regional partnerships – in Cordillera, Mindoro, southern Luzon, and the greater metropolitan area of Manila – as PETA's essential task:

> It provides people with a non-threatening space to tell what happened to them, so they feel a bit better about themselves. In addition, I would say theatre is still one of the better alternatives, especially for our children and youth. There is something fundamentally wrong with our educational system, because it blocks communication with peers and lowers self-esteem. A lot of young people would like to talk to others and to learn to like themselves a little better, find out who they are and what they can do in life. Theatre is an effective way to positively redirect their energies, so they can contribute something good to their community and their families.

Funding

Some 60 per cent of PETA's annual budget of approximately US$ 200,000 (1997) comes from five external funding agencies, one of which is Philippine based. Some 40 per cent is raised through local counterparts, including some support from the National Commission for Culture and the Arts (NCCA) and an audience development subsidy through 'Philstage', another government agency. Dutch funding agent ICCO provides institutional funding for PETA's general operations; not for any specific programme. The Canadian Catholic Organization for Development and Peace funds PETA's work in schools and another grant is specifically for its work with children. The MTTL programme is funded by the Children and Youth Foundation of the Philippines, which, in turn, raises its funds locally and through connections with North America. The German Evangelisches Missions Werk (Evangelical Missionary Work) and Terre des Hommes fund PETA's women's programmes.

In 1989, at the end of a regular three-year funding cycle, PETA's sponsors concluded that it was suffering from unmanaged growth and insisted that the company reorganize. As a result, by 1990 the extensive outreach programmes all over the Philippines were replaced by the five geographically closer partnerships listed above. Encouraged by its financial backers, PETA also decided to make its professional productions self-supporting through sponsorship, ticket sales, and extended provincial tours. According to PETA's marketing coordinator Jack Yabut, the potential theatre audience in Manila does not exceed 10 per cent of the population. His strategy to attract new audiences with quality productions was particularly successful with PETA's political musicals: 'But we're still new at this game,' he admits: 'we have to compete with 75 cable stations and popular spectator sports like basketball. Yet, we will always defend our freedom of form and content even if we enter into a sponsorship deal with a respectable commercial enterprise.'[5] A related problem he faces is casting. Some of the older PETA members are growing increasingly concerned over the star-struck attitudes of young newcomers, who all too easily drop out of a PETA production to tape a much more lucrative commercial or a soap episode. 'At PETA we pay less than minimum wage,' acknowledges Yabut: '200 Pesos per day. So if you count three weeks rehearsals and a run of twelve shows our actors make 8,000 Pesos (US$ 200) max. Compare that to the 5,000 Pesos (US$ 125) they can earn for a small part in a one-day shoot for a television soap.'[6]

PETA's calendar of activities

PETA's outdoor performance season at the Fort Santiago theatre in downtown Manila starts at the end of November, closing briefly for Christmas and New Year and picking up again in early January through to mid-April. Summer workshops are held in April and May. June is assessment time. In July, rehearsals start for the annual provincial tour that takes place from August to December. Each year, PETA creates four new productions, two for the open-air theatre in Manila and two for regional tours. Some of these new works emerge from PETA's playwright development programme; other original plays or foreign adaptations are commissioned from senior playwrights Rody Vera, Chris Millado, and until his death in 1995 from Charley de la Paz. Each Fort Santiago production runs for twelve to fifteen shows on weekends only, attracting between 300 to 400 spectators per night. The touring productions have thirty to fifty stops and tend to cater to children and high-school-age youth. Tour gigs, which are sponsored by schools, local governments, churches, and private foundations, easily draw between 800 and 2,000 people in town plazas. PETA asks a flat fee of 30,000 pesos (US$ 750) for each show, for which it brings its own lights and sound equipment. If it is outside Manila, the host also has to provide transportation, board and lodging. From the flat fee, PETA pays the actors; any profits flow back to the programme that initiated the play. For example, in the case of a children's play to the children's theatre programme.

Recent PETA productions

The 1992–1993 PETA season featured *Domestic Helper* (1992–1993), a play about how migrant Filipina maids keep their bodies and souls intact while supporting their families back home. That same season PETA also produced a Filipino music theatre version of the Indian *Ramayana* epic, written by Rody Vera and directed by Gardy Labad. Other noteworthy PETA productions of the early 1990s included *Kahapon, Ngayon, at Bukas* ('Yesterday, Today and Tomorrow'), a revolutionary allegorical *sarswela* originally written by Aurelio Tolentino in 1903, which Chris Millado adapted and directed. It contained images of revolt, from all the way back to the Spanish time to contemporary manifestations of cultural imperialism. *Miisna'y Isang Gamu-Gamo*, a stage adaptation of a famous Nora Aunor film with the movie star in the lead, drew crowds that had never attended theatre before. The stage version addressed the effects of American military bases in the Philippines on a nurse, who is in the middle of packing her bags to emigrate to the States. *Miserere Nobis*, which Chris Millado adapted from a Pete Lacaba film script, deals with activists and the detrimental psychological effects their political obsessions have on them and on their families. In 1995, PETA also collaborated with the San Francisco Mime Troupe on a musical election satire entitled *Sebiong Engkanto*. That same year, Charley De la Paz also wrote the libretto for the musical *1896*, a large-scale production that featured famous pop singer Ariel Rivera and which PETA put on to commemorate the centennial of the Filipino revolution against the Spanish. Unlike their productions during martial law and the People Power Revolt, then, PETA's productions of the 1990s reflect the company's shift from national sovereignty issues to the effects of macro political issues on a more personal level.

PETA's School for People's Theatre

In addition to its more than 100 annual performances, PETA teams engage in outreach work with community theatre groups or create small productions upon special request. Throughout the year, PETA also conducts in-house teacher training to prepare its own artists for the summer workshops. In addition, it trains young writers, assists schools with productions for the Youth Theatre Festival it organizes each February, and helps children prepare a small production for its annual Children's Theatre Festival in December. Training sessions for schools run the whole year, as do the Metro Teen Theatre League and the Women's Theatre programmmes. To do this work, PETA permanently employs thirty people, half of whom are artist-teachers and the other half office staff. Furthermore, between twenty and thirty PETA members are on call for *ad hoc* productions and workshops.

The PETA School for People's Theatre works according to its own separate calendar and draws on a specially trained pool of twenty-four artist-teachers, who are paid a small honorarium and a transport and food allowance. Between July and December, the School for People's Theatre conducts twenty to thirty outreach workshops, which can vary in length from one day to two weeks. Although PETA expects workshop hosts to pay for expenses, lack of resources are never allowed to be an obstacle. Workshops are always meticulously documented and evaluated in an annual report that forms the basis for the next year's cycle of activities. From December to May, Ernie Cloma and his colleague Bong Billones prepare for the summer workshops, but even in this period they give occasional workshops. In January and February they conduct in-house teacher's training for the four-to-six-week summer workshops, which take place between the end of March and the middle of May. Open to the general public, these usually contain courses on children's theatre, youth theatre, general theatre arts, and, if there is enough interest, trainor's training and creative pedagogy for school teachers. The summer school courses follow PETA's familiar structure of a release and trust-building phase followed by an exposure and awareness phase, but also allow for considerably more time to polish theatre techniques than the more intensive shorter workshops. Usually they have midway showcases as well as a more elaborate final performance. Even the specialized acting courses, although they cater to people who want to find employment in show business, always include an exposure trip. Yet, Ernie Cloma is well aware of the difficulty to inspire a new generation of a-political middle-class artists:

> After martial law, a bunch of PETA artists went into the movies or were eaten up by commercials and we were left with martial law babies. We couldn't really make them feel the significance of what we were trying to do. When we do a conflict exercise, they ask us what for? We give them orientational training but without first-hand experiences it is almost impossible. So now we send them out to the grass roots; to the provinces. What helps a lot is our constant education. Every three months we organize sociopolitical seminars. All our workshops, even in the MTTL, are thematic and we always put in a module on the social, economic and cultural situation. We take them on exposure to urban poor areas. But it remains difficult: so many of them join PETA because they want to have an acting career in film and TV. Commitment is the key; if you don't have that, then you'll be pulled out by other forces. So we cannot be too ambitious. If one or two catch the bug, that's enough.

Ernie Cloma regards the electronic media, which are rapidly expanding their influence all over the Philippines, as a detrimental force that affects people at all levels of society: 'When we go to an urban poor area, during improvisations participants sometimes regurgitate complete dialogues of what they saw on TV the night before, including the violence.' He also knows that it will not be easy to train young, culturally sensitive artist-trainers with a passion for community theatre. Yet, he remains optimistic. Changes no longer come as quickly as they once did in the mid-1980s, he knows, but gradually, through its workshops, PETA has been able to affect fundamental improvements in all kinds of governmental and non-governmental organizations. He particularly singles out PETA's work with children as crucial:

> We work with all kinds of people now and sometimes we are criticized for that by underground activists, who think we are being coopted. True, when government agencies request us to help them we no longer refuse. We even work with children of cops. They also

have rights. We need to learn to work with everybody. One of our big concerns now is working with sexually abused children, which is a tremendous problem that cuts right through the classes and sectors. And if we can make teachers aware that they help the child more by making it more creative and critical, rather than cramming dates and facts into their memories only to be spit out without thinking, then I think we're getting somewhere.

PETA still has a lot to offer to the deceptively less repressive Philippines of the late 1990s. It has undisputedly some of the country's best theatre artists, who each year create original, relevant shows for both city dwellers and rural folk. It tries to develop quality television and film productions through its revamped Film and Broadcasting Unit and has effective children's, youth, and women's theatre units. Most importantly, PETA tries to combat continuing social problems by transferring its creativity and its theatre skills to a broad range of communities in and around the country's main island, Luzon. As it did in the week-long workshop in Marinduque that we documented.

CASE STUDY: TEATRO BALANGAW, BOAC, MARINDUQUE

April to June is summer holiday in the Philippines and hence a good time to hold community and youth theatre workshops: kids are free from school and empty classrooms abound. So, also in Marinduque, a mere fifty airborne minutes from Manila Domestic Airport.

At 7 a.m. on Sunday morning 20 April, we circle in a Fokker 50 over Mount Malindig, a dormant volcano that rises 1,157 metres above dense coconut groves. We are welcomed by local cultural worker Eli Obligacion, who takes us in a hired jeepney to a pension, a few minutes walk from his wooden home and from the primary school where the PETA workshop will be held. Although it is hot and muggy, the sea breeze makes the island much more bearable than the noisy and dirty national capital.

In the afternoon, Eli takes us to a fishing community at the mouth of the Boac River, from which all life has disappeared after thousands upon thousands of gallons of toxic waste water from a giant open-pit copper mine poured into it in March 1996. After this sobering excursion, which also offers us a quick glimpse of the pompous seaside mansion of local Congresswoman Carmencita Reyes, members of Eli's immediate community offer us a traditional *putong* welcoming ritual. It reminds me of Pacific Islander ceremonies in which visitors are honoured with songs, dances, and flower garlands. Over the next few days we also meet Provincial Governor José Antonio Carrion, community politicians, mine officials, local musicians, and environmental activists. Early one morning we go fishing with Melo Miciano and his three sons, two of whom, Harald and Hajun, are members of Eli's community youth theatre group, Teatro Balangaw. We catch nothing at all, something which, Melo informs us, has become quite normal after the mine disaster.

Profile of Marinduque

Marinduque is a small island with a population of 200,000 living in an area spanning 959.2 hectares (source: Province of Marinduque 1996 Socio-economic Profile). As the crow flies, it is located 170 kilometres south of Manila and lies cradled by Luzon's Bondoc Peninsula to the northeast, and the island of Oriental Mindoro to the west. A daily ferry connects Marinduque to Lucena on the main island of Luzon, on which Manila is located, and four times a week Philippine Airlines flies a return trip to the national capital. The island has had electricity since 1981 and now even boasts direct-dial telephone services. There are no local media: newspapers are flown in from the national capital and the only radio station that covers the island is based in Lucena. The largest towns are Santa Cruz (57,000 inhabitants) and the provincial capital Boac (55,000), followed by Mogpoc (29,000) and Gasan (27,000). More than half the island population is employed in coconut, rice and corn farming, and fishing.

Local theatre traditions

Before the copper mine spill made international headlines, Marinduque was best known for its colourful outdoor theatre pageants during Holy Week, which yearly attract thousands of visitors. Known as *Moriones*, this semi-religious theatre tradition is related to the *Moro-moro* (van Erven 1992: 31–32). It has roots in pre-colonial rituals, the Christianization campaigns of Spanish colonial missionaries, and Moro attacks by Muslims from the south. Theatre scholar Nicanor Tiongson (1992: 15–16) glosses the word *Morion* as 'helmet', referring to the headwear of the Roman soldier Longinus (or Longhino), the hero of the *Moriones* play. Longinus is the soldier who pierced the side of the crucified Jesus

Christ, guarded his tomb, and was the first to witness his resurrection. In the Marinduque version, Pilate tries to buy his silence, but Longinus, spontaneously converted to Christianity after Christ's revival, instead runs through the town to tell everyone about the miracle. Pilate orders his soldiers to capture the renegade, who is eventually beheaded, a tragic conclusion which the *Moriones* theatrically express by empaling Longinus' wooden mask on a sword and lifting it up for the crowd to see (Tiongson 1991: 77).

Teatro Balangaw

Eli Obligacion, a self-styled local cultural organizer in his mid-forties, grew up in Marinduque's rural interior, where his mother, a housemaid, raised him on her own. She always took him to see the *Moriones* and he remembers locals telling stories about 'strange creatures' such as spirits, dwarves and evil sorcerers. Many Marinduqueños still wear amulets and frequently report dwarf sightings. Thus, the canal next to Eli's house is popularly believed to be haunted, but he himself prefers to regard the island's magical dimension as a positive force. This is why he has named his community theatre group *Teatro Balangaw*: '*Balangaw* means "rainbow". Rainbows appear here periodically, right on this spot. A rainbow represents harmony of colours, many beliefs, many kinds of people. It symbolizes what we are and what our purpose is: bridging differences between people.'[7]

After graduating from high school in 1970, Eli Obligacion migrated to Manila along with so many other young Marinduqueños. He could not afford to go to college and, due to martial law, universities were closed anyway. He found a job as a waiter, spent a year in a drug rehab centre after being caught with a small amount of marihuana, and finally landed a job at the Norwegian Embassy, where he would remain for the next fourteen years, working himself up from messenger boy to office manager. In his spare time he performed in musical productions at Manila's Metropolitan Theatre and frequented discos and race tracks. Tired of Manila's fast-paced mix of work and play, he quit his job and returned to Marinduque in 1990, using his savings to build a wooden house on a plot of land his mother owned.

In 1991, a performance of an Orlando Nadres play in Boac by a visiting theatre group from Tayabas, a town near Lucena, inspired Eli Obligacion to form a theatre group of his own, together with three former school mates. Teatro Balangaw's first production, *Mara Unduk*, a dance drama about the island's mythical origins written by Obligacion, was performed on the eve of the annual Boac *fiesta* in December 1992. Fifty students from Marinduque National High participated. The following Easter, Teatro Balangaw spearheaded a politically sensitive revival of the *Moriones* tradition in the island capital. Although *Moriones* were still being performed in Mogpoc and Gasan, Eli Obligacion explains that in Boac they had been replaced by a *Sinakulo*, a change in tradition that had been imposed by local politicians after they had seen a performance in 1973 by a visiting troupe from Bulacan: 'It had been the first ever show on the islands to use sound and lights and they were so impressed that they wanted to make it into an annual event, financed with public funds.' But Obligacion felt that this *Sinakulo* was too expensive and not indigenous to Boac. He wanted to revive the *Moriones* instead. Local politicians, the bishop, and Congresswoman Carmencita Reyes resisted the idea, but Teatro Balangaw went ahead anyway.

The cast for Teatro Balangaw's controversial *Moriones* production included young high school students who had participated in *Mara Unduk*, some older women acting as a background chorus, and three people who had been involved in the old Boac *Moriones* productions from before 1973. But due to political pressure on community leaders, only 350 people participated instead of the 1,000 participants who had initially signed up. Balangaw's revival of the *Moriones* play lasted two hours and took place at the traditional performance site, on the banks of the Boac River. It demonstrated that community theatre could be an effective medium for increasing people's awareness and for critically engaging them in their own local culture and history. The following years, Teatro Balangaw would create several other historically inspired musical theatre productions and continued to annually perform updated versions of its modernized *Moriones* play during Easter.

The PETA–Balangaw connection

Teatro Balangaw's association with PETA and the Marinduque branch of the Philippines Rural Reconstruction Movement, an NGO that initiates grass-roots developmental projects and environmental awareness all over the Philippines, dates back to 1996. A national consortium of people's organizations, to which both PETA and PRRM belong, was planning to hold its second national festival in Marinduque that year. For this occasion, Trina Malaga, a Mindanao-born PRRM organizer who had been working in Marinduque since 1993, asked Eli Obligacion to write a play about a local hero during the 1896 Revolution. He wrote a script entitled *Mis Lagrimas a Ti* ('My Tears for You'), which Ernie Cloma then came to workshop for four days with members of Teatro Balangaw. Impressed with their energy and skills, Ernie Cloma invited the group to participate in PETA's annual Youth Theatre Festival at Fort Santiago in December 1996.

Since its foundation in 1992 Balangaw has gradually become more community oriented. By April 1997, with the exception of Eli Obligacion, the original founders were no longer active and the majority of the members were now senior high school and early college age. Most of them worked part-time to supplement the subsistence-level incomes of their families. Consequently, most of Teatro Balangaw's activities take place at the weekends. Conscious of the limitations of the musical theatre mode in which he himself tends to write and eager to respond as concerned artists to the Marcopper mining disaster, Eli Obligacion invited Ernie to come help his theatre group create a realistic piece on this issue.

The copper mine spill

Marcopper Mining Corporation came to Marinduque in 1967, bringing electricity and about 1,000 low-paying jobs to the island. All high-level jobs were reserved for expatriates and Filipino engineers, living in a secluded, fully serviced bungalow compound near the mine on Mount Tapian. Almost from the beginning, activists sounded the alarm against the damaging impact of the open-pit mine on Marinduque's environment and the danger of situating it on an earthquake-prone faultline. Copper mining requires rocks mined from the pit to be crushed to extract their copper. The remaining rock pieces, called tailings, and the water it is soaked in, contain a residue of toxic heavy metals, such as cadmium. These waste materials were first dumped in an artificially dammed pond until, in 1978, a new copper deposit was discovered underneath it and Marcopper decided, with the permission of its major stockholder Ferdinand Marcos, to dump the debris through a pipeline and a causeway constructed of tailings into Calancan Bay on the island's northern shore. The new pit's waste water was drained through a tunnel into a small stream connected to the Boac River. It was this tunnel that collapsed on 24 March 1996, flooding the island's two main rivers and its coastal waters with highly contaminated liquid and some 4 million tonnes of tailings. UN investigators later established a 'total loss of the use of the rivers for livestock, fishing, laundry, bathing, and agriculture, reduced access, and increased health risk due to immersion' (De Mesa 1996: 24). The disaster cut off fourteen *barangays*[8] from the outside world and affected the livelihood of some 20,000 people, including hundreds of fishermen, who have not been able to catch much of anything since then. 'And there are close to a hundred residents along the river in whose blood toxic levels of heavy metals have been detected,' says Trina Malaga.[9]

Preparing for the workshop

Ernie Cloma arrived on the morning boat from Lucena on Sunday, 27 April. He was accompanied by a young MTTL trainee named Gabo, who would document the proceedings, and Dessa Quesada, who has been with PETA since 1981 and over the years has built up a vast international experience as a performer and workshop facilitator. A few days before coming to Marinduque she had returned to the Philippines after an extended stay in Japan, where she had been working with Filipino migrants and a Japanese Philippines solidarity network.[10] She explained that PETA workshops are usually taught by a team of two, with a third person documenting: 'It is our principle of working: collaborating even in teaching, breaking through the authority of the all-knowing teacher or theatre artist's guru mystique.'

Budget and participants

Eli Obligacion had a total budget of 15,000 Pesos (US$ 375) to pay for production materials, local transport, food, lodging, Manila–Marinduque roundtrip fares for Dessa and Ernie (who were lodged at his house), and for lunch for the participants. The Amoingon Elementary School did not charge for the use of their class room. The majority of the twenty-five participants were teenage members of Teatro Balangaw, with a handful of others coming from barangay Buenavista's youth group and two from PRRM, who were five years older than the other participants. PRRM island coordinator Trina Malaga had seen the powerful impact of Nestor Horfilla's community theatre back in her native Mindanao and wanted her staff to acquire similar theatre skills to enhance the effectiveness of PRRM's educational campaigns.

Ernie and Dessa prepared a syllabus for a 'Level 2 – Repertory Guidance' workshop, which included advanced acting exercises and playwrighting and which was designed to culminate in a full production. As they always do, the PETA team planned its activities according to the specific needs of the host. Eli Obligacion wanted to train his group in realism because they had mostly been doing dance and musical theatre. Ernie and Dessa therefore emphasized improvisational acting exercises during the first two days, the syllabus for which they divided into modules. For each module they scheduled more exercises than needed so they could instantly drop, substitute, or vary any of them, according to the responses of participants and the dynamics within the group.

Day one

Monday morning 28 April. At 9 a.m., after everyone has trickled in, Ernie, Dessa, Gabo, and Eli introduce themselves and succinctly explain that they will be working for five intensive days creating an original production that deals with the current concerns of the Marinduqueños. Ernie urges the participants not to worry if some of the early exercises may seem childish; soon enough, he promises, the process will be raised to their intellectual level. 'I always begin by setting the group's attitude in that way,' Ernie comments later over lunch: 'It is crucial to tell them what to expect, not necessarily exercise by exercise, but more like "this morning we will do this." You can't really impose a process on uninformed people.'

Dessa and Ernie take turns, like a well-oiled machine, while they run a series of limbering and voice exercises that playfully invite the participants to touch (shoulder to shoulder, back to back) and loosen up body and mind. Next, the participants introduce themselves by saying their names accompanied by a sound and action, after which they do a popular folk song and dance. This playful way of getting acquainted with each other continues with a musical chairs-type game and an 'Animal Concert,' which Ernie begins by describing an animal which the group has to guess and then act out with a sound. Subsequently they work in groups of four cats, four tigers, four peeing dogs, four mice, and four chickens, ending the exercise in a cacophonous joint recital.

The group is now ready for the expectation check. They look for a place in the room where they feel comfortable and identify a partner far removed from them with whom they establish eye contact and communicate non-verbally about (1) what they can contribute to make the workshop successful; (2) what they want to learn from it; and (3) what the problem is that bothers them the most. They then take two steps towards their partner and repeat the same movements again. Next, they walk all the way up to their partner and verify verbally whether what they had wanted to communicate has come across correctly. Then they take 30 seconds to find similarities in each other's movements in an attempt to find common ground in expressing, through movement, their response to the three questions. They practise for a few minutes and then five pairs perform their dances simultaneously while the others form an audience. Ernie tells the spectators to join those pairs that they feel most affinity with. Three larger groups again try to extract commonalities from each other's movements to create a joint dance. When the exercise is over, the participants sit down in a circle and explicitly verbalize their expectations: they want to learn writing, singing, dancing, acting, and generally want to become more confident. The main problems they see on the island are the dismal public transportation system and, of course, the mining disaster. Everyone then agrees to create a theatre show about Marinduque's conservation. With everyone energized, Dessa and Ernie seize the opportunity to explain what they have planned for the rest of the week.

Structure of the Marinduque workshop

- *Day 1*: release exercises and spontaneous improvisations, followed by exercises in scene and story building.
- *Day 2*: advanced acting exercises plus a lecture on production mechanics.
- *Day 3*: creative writing followed by an extended exposure trip to two up-river *barangays* that have been severely affected by the mine spill.
- *Day 4*: raw improvisations based on the material gathered in the exposure trip and then determine a basic scene structure for the play.
- *Day 5*: polish the script and intensive rehearsals.
- *Day 6*: run through, performance in the Boac town plaza, and an evaluation.

Ernie concludes the workshop summary with general remarks about the need to be alert, cooperative, disciplined, and sensitive. He and Dessa then divide the participants into five groups, each of which will be responsible on any one of the days for time keeping, cleaning the space, and for communicating problems that might exist among the participants to the artist-teachers. These so-called 'O-A-O teams' are also supposed to report back at the end of each afternoon, assessing how that day's activities have enhanced the group's thematic orientation (O), their artistry (A), and their organizational skills (O). By forcing small teams to thus reflect on different aspects of the process right after they have undergone it, the participants gain deeper insight into the workshop dynamics and start to feel ownership, rather than only passively consuming whatever the PETA facilitators dish up. After an action song and an exercise requiring the participants to express a feeling by first individually and then collectively moulding themselves into a sculpture prompted by an emotion-evoking keyword (e.g., love, pain, attraction), the group breaks for lunch at noon.

Over lunch, the workshop team briefly reviews the morning session and previews the exercises they have planned for the afternoon. At 1.30 p.m., Dessa and Ernie resume with a name game and a creative movement activity as a warm-up before embarking on an expanded acting exercise adapted from Boal's oppressor-oppressed series. After focusing on their breathing, the participants think for a minute of a situation when they felt most oppressed and then start talking to themselves, adding movements and acting in their own space. Each of them then take individual turns to perform a 10-second moment of oppression drawn from their own experience, usually personal recollections of being cheated or unjustly disciplined by parents. Next, as a contrast, they are asked to express a memory of the moment they felt most loved or loved someone else.

The acting exercises are taken up a level when the participants are asked to step out of their own personalities into fictional ones. They pretend to climb a mountain, jump on a train, touch each other's ears, tiptoe, pull each other's hair, and roll over like a ball. After thus individually exploring the expressive arsenal of their body, the work becomes more concrete when they are asked to prepare to attend a birthday party and add speech to their mimed movements. They are instructed to think of a gift, brush their teeth, wash up, and get dressed, while Ernie urges them to focus on details of gestures and facial expression. After the exercise, Ernie gives feedback on the quality of their acting: 'Sometimes you obviously miscommunicated to one another, others misread what the gift was. This was because your movements, actions, and facial expressions were not clear.' In the video we can see how Ernie explains that if the participants want to give their characters more emotional depth, they should draw on their emotions. If they do this, they will feel what Ernie calls the 'f' (for feeling), which will make their acting more convincing. He coaches them to pay attention to these details during the next exercise, in which he asks them to act in pairs as if they belong to opposite social classes, first silently 'feeling' the role, then adding gibberish, and finishing with an intelligible dialogue between partners playing each other's social opposite. The higher class puts down the lower one and then they reverse through a verbal conflict. Before they do the improvisation a second time, on the video we can see how Ernie urges the participants to 'take it more slowly as (they) go down' when they exchange status with their partner, an instruction that might cause someone unfamiliar with ongoing feudal Philippine rural power relations to wonder about the apparently simplistic class dichotomy this exercise explores. All the side-coaching is intended to make the acting more precise, something the PETA team will continue to accentuate throughout the week.

Also included in the video is a physical transformation exercise. Dessa first demonstrates the principle by shaking hands with Harold, then walking away from him, leaving him frozen with his hand in the same handshaking position. She then walks back into the designated acting area as another character, now kneeling with her face against the hand, which through her changed posture suddenly appears to be slapping her. Dessa holds her face in pain while Ernie replaces Harold by playing a dentist pulling a tooth from her mouth, and so on. Eventually the transformations lead to the moment that is also included in the video, when Ernie plays a doctor who diagnoses haemorrhoids and whose hand hold a prescription, which is then transformed into children clapping hands through Harold's intervention.

Other acting exercises that afternoon graduate from mime via gibberish to comprehensible dialogue. In one such activity, the participants act out certain situations in pairs, being allowed to say only one word each: 'Go!' and 'No!' They invent a father–son conflict, a fight between lovers, and a discussion between brothers, which compel them to say the two words with varying intonations: either pleadingly, seductively, or angrily. A second activity requires a larger group to invent characters and a plot for a short drama of which the setting is stipulated by the facilitators (e.g., a market or a funeral). They are only allowed to use five nonsense words for their dialogue: 'Plick', 'Plock', 'Toing', 'Tuga', and 'Swak'. They take a few minutes to huddle and basically direct themselves. The resulting improvisations invite dramaturgical tips from Ernie and Dessa regarding blocking and general *mise-en-scène*.

Lighter playful theatre games and action songs always follow heavier, more elaborate improvisations and acting instructions. In 'Dual Motion', for example, a pair acts as one person, taking turns talking. In a more complex and hilarious variation, 'Expert Hands', the pair continues to act as one character, but person A folds her hands behind B's back, while B's hands stick through the arms of A. Thus, B's hands make the appropriate gestures for A's improvised monologue. They conclude the afternoon's work with an extended version of 'Plick, Plock, Toing', this time with comprehensible instead of nonsense dialogues and each group presenting the drama they improvised earlier in as many different theatrical styles (e.g., dance theatre, musical, naturalism, cabaret) as they can think of. This variation, called 'Forms, Forms, Forms,' is to expose the group to forms different from the musical theatre they have grown so accustomed to.

Day two

The second day begins with stretching and voice exercises, after which a new 'O-A-O team' is assigned. A leg wrestling exercise follows: parallel pairs, their heads in opposite direction, lie on the floor with their inside legs locked together. They must try to push their partner's leg down. This is followed by a tribal war, in which four tribes in four different corners first create their own dance and chant. While Tribe One does a chant to thank the Creator for a bountiful harvest, Tribe Two hunts in the forest. The remaining two tribes are warriors and have created a war chant and dance, which they perform as they attack Tribes One and Two. The exercise offers a good physical workout and provides the facilitators with the opportunity to talk about different kinds of conflict in society.

More serious acting follows the warm-up games. The group jogs around in a circle and, after a 'freeze!', acts out a silent conflict, pretending to be civil on the surface with a tension-filled subtext underneath. For example, two participants play rival women at a cocktail party. They are in love with the same man and really want to scratch each other's eyes out but cannot because they have to behave. Subsequently, after feedback on their acting, Dessa works on clarity of expression in a sculpting game. She gives the participants 10 seconds to find a pose, first of a beggar, then of a prostitute, a cop, and a priest, coaching them as to their character's feelings, age, facial expression, physical features, and vocal particulars. After first doing the exercise on their own, she then asks them to interact with an imaginary someone, constantly coaching them to clarify posture, gesture, characterization, and story.

After each extended acting exercise, which that morning also includes a guided fantasy or 'Travelogue', Dessa and Ernie review with the group what they have learned, explaining such basic concepts as blocking and stage levels. Before lunch, they also work on dramatizing a story with a beginning, middle, and end. The only ingredients Ernie gives each participant are a situation, a character's profession, and the phrase 'One day I'll be famous'. Four volunteers get 10 seconds to prepare with their backs to the group and then all four at once act their piece during one minute. The spectators closest to them have to guess what their story is about. At the end of the morning session, each group receives a two-page scene from a modern classic of Filipino drama, which they have to read over lunch. In the afternoon, they will have to apply the elements of storytelling and acting they have learned that morning to the scene they have been assigned, working in groups of two or three, with one of them acting as a director.

The afternoon begins with a warm-up game which Ernie calls 'Alex Bangcayo Brigade,' after an infamous urban guerrila unit. He learned it at a victim of war kid's refugee camp in the heart of Davao, Mindanao during Cory Aquino's war against Muslim separatists:

> I remember, we were playing and suddenly a helicopter came over and all the children scattered in panic. In their version of the game each group decides among themselves which five people of the opposing team they will kill. When one of the kids they have targeted steps into the no man's land she or he will get shot. The first group to eliminate their five victims wins, but it is pure chance, because the other group decides the order in which they will step into no man's land. They tossed for the right to start. When I returned to Manila, I didn't play it that way. I called it 'Embrace Me', using the same principle, only less violent: before they start, each team selects which five from the other team they will embrace.

Next, Ernie summarizes the plots of the plays from which they have selected scenes for the different groups to work on, instructing the participants to pay particular atention to characterization, movement, gesture, intonation, and setting. For example, *Babungan Lata* ('Tin Roof'), by Agapito Joaquin, is about poor settlers who canot pay their taxes. The scene selected from this play, which can also be seen in the video, involves the tax collector's confrontation with an impoverished mother and her angry son.

Each group first gets half an hour to break their scenes down into smaller units in which they try to detect the objectives the characters are trying to achieve. The idea is to gather as much information regarding character, conflict, and dramatic setting from the text as possible. Then they rehearse their scenes for about an hour anywhere in the primary school compound. Dessa and Ernie move from group to group to provide directorial assistance. At the end of the afternoon each group performs their scene. Harold and his group, as we can see in the video, act their scene from *Babungan Lata* outside, behind the workshop space.

In the feedback, many participants say they found the difference between the earlier release and acting exercises and this kind of actual performance quite big. They also discovered that in order to really get into their roles, which were quite far removed from their own life experiences, they needed to memorize the lines. As a result, many of them became so focused on remembering their speeches that they forgot to interact with the other actors.

Preparing for exposure

From the performance critique, Ernie segues to dramaturgical instructions for the following day's exposure. The aim of the exposure trip, he explains, is to find out first-hand what the effects of the Marcopper disaster have been on the environment and on people's lives:

> You should look for elements of drama wherever you go. You might become attracted to a particular character in the place that we are visiting. Go talk to them, ask for their story. We will put it into drama. What is the main conflict in their story? Will it centre on a couple or on the entire *barrio*? Or are we going to focus on the mountain and what happened to it, environmentally? You will see that your stories will be composed of different episodes, a beginning,

> middle, and end, from start to finish. But you can also start in the middle and work your way back, or tell it from different perspectives. Whatever you decide to do: the conflict and character must be clear.

Production mechanics

The afternoon concludes with an informal lecture on theatre production. Ernie and Dessa explain the different responsibilities of a production manager, a director, an actor, a choreographer, a musical director, a designer, a light and sound designer, a technician, a publicist, a fund raiser, and a front-of-house staff, noting that sometimes in community theatre all these tasks are done by one or two persons. They single out the stage manager's responsibilities as most crucial because that person coordinates the behind-the-scene activities before and during the show. Edwin Mironez, an energetic 19-year-old from Mogpoc, volunteers for this task. Dessa and Ernie conclude the day by convincing the group that it is indeed possible to create and block scenes, compose different characters, learn lines, songs, and choreographed steps within the remaining three days, even though a professional company usually takes between four and six weeks for the same process.

> ### Day three: Exposure
>
> On Wednesday morning the group leaves at 7.30 a.m. to visit two inland riverside communities, Sitio Ogbac and Binunga, which have been devastated by the mining disaster. The two PRRM participants in the PETA workshop have secured permission for the visit from the village leaders. The trip, by borrowed bus, takes about an hour, partly over badly damaged dirt roads. The participants are divided into two groups and before they embark on their exploration, Ernie gives them some final instructions on how to conduct their interviews. He tells them to be sensitive and not just record people's stories but also smells, sounds, and visuals. In addition, he asks them to bring back an object from the site: a stone, a broken plate, or an old can; anything that might carry some symbolic meaning.

> The participants work in pairs, one conducting the interview and the other taking notes. Ernie finally reminds them that they are collecting raw materials for a theatre performance that should benefit Marinduque. They should, therefore, not forget to invite the people they interview to come to the show on Saturday.

The field trip turns out to be a rewarding experience with the villagers more than willing to talk. As they eat their lunch in the bus on the way back to the primary school, the participants enthusiastically exchange stories they heard. Back in the workshop venue, Dessa first takes them through a movement exercise called 'Follow the Leader', for which she uses a tape recording of 'Bathala', a popular environmental awareness song by Joey Ayala. Divided into groups of four and spatially arranged in the shape of a diamond, one person in each group invents movements to the music, which the other three are supposed to follow. Rotating to the top of the diamond, each participant gets a chance to choreograph a dance.

> ### After the exposure
>
> The rest of the afternoon is devoted to creatively processing impressions from the exposure trip. Each participant makes a visual arts collage on a large sheet of paper, using newspaper clippings, colouring pencils, and the symbolic objects they have brought back from the exposure site. It gives them a chance to reflect on the experience. They each take turns explaining their art work to the rest of the group and then get half an hour to compose collective collages in four groups. As they present these, the germs of some stories emerge. They get another half hour to work out the story line of these embryonic plots and then present them, with a beginning, middle and end, to the others in the form of dramatic improvisations. One of these features an old man, Luis, who talks about how many fish he used to catch in the Boac River and how sorry he is for his grandchildren, who will now no longer be able to

experience this. Another story is about Mang Roger, a Marcopper employee who remembers how one day his supervisor, engineer Cruz, warned him way before the disaster happened never to drink from the local pump nor to build his house near the low-lying areas, because the soil and the water there were already contaminated.

Day four

Feeling the time pressure, the group has agreed to start an hour earlier. They begin their warm-up at 8 a.m. The creative work of that day begins with a brainstorming session about the theatrical form they want to use for their production. Since they have to perform in the open air and will not have money for a good sound system, realism, which works best in intimate indoor settings, may not be so appropriate. The group decides to compromise and to alternate realistic scenes with some music and dance numbers to cater to the Filipino hunger for theatrical spectacle. They each sign up for a writers pool, a music pool, a movement pool, and a design pool to divide the artistic responsibilities for the show. They proceed to discuss a possible script outline and soon agree that the play should start with the opening of the mine back in the 1960s and the recruitment of local workers, followed by the disaster and the effects on the inland communities. The performance should end, they feel, with some kind of people's protest. They want to use Joey Ayala's song 'Bathala' to weave together the different components, but, Dessa explains, 'We insisted that they also put in something local. That's how they came up with the idea to put in three different versions of the *putong*, the traditional Marinduque welcoming song, to accentuate the three different moods of the play: peace, lament, and defiance.'

The group covers a lot of ground that Thursday morning, sketching the contours of what will become the eventual scenario. They determine that Mang Roger, two village children, and a clairvoyant, Lydia, will become their main characters. Their research had revealed that a child had been hospitalized after eating fish from the contaminated river and Lydia, they explain to the PETA team, is an actual person living in the bush near the Malindig volcano. She roams around the island warning everyone about a mythical Golden Calf that lies buried in the mountains and which, when greedy people who dig for it reach its horns, will cause

Marinduque to disappear. 'This story fascinated me,' Ernie told me later in Manila, 'for it gave the story of the mine – digging for a golden calf – a metaphysical quality with biblical overtones, while still remaining true to the stories of the people that we had interviewed. We did use the actual words of Mang Roger and the children.'

Once the entire group has agreed on the order of the episodes, they begin to flesh them out, working in four separate groups. By lunch time, the dance prologue and the opening vignettes are already done. The rest of the day they improvise the remaining scenes, selecting the best bits for consolidation in a preliminary script. There is now intensive activity all over the school compound: outside some participants are writing a poem for the chorus under a picnic shelter, while others rehearse scenes inside or in some vacant corner at the back of the main venue. At nightfall, the group performs all the scenes they have created that day. While most of the actors go home, the writers continue working on the script until the early hours of the morning.

Day five

As usual, the day begins with a full body and voice warm-up followed by a recapitulation of the previous day and the assignment of a new 'O-A-O team'. Edwin, the stage manager, then chairs a production meeting, expertly talking the entire cast through the blocking and the set and prop requirements for each of the episodes. The rest of the morning is spent on improvising and mounting the scenes they had been unable to complete the previous day. After lunch, the group splits up to work in separate groups again. Ernie and Dessa now emphatically take charge as co-directors, coaching the actors on line delivery, reacting to cues, and timing entrances and exits.

At 3 p.m., the group travels by public transportation to downtown Boac to do a complete run-through on the stage of the covered basketball court, which doubles as the town's main square. However, an official basketball tournament, complete with whistle-blowing referees and amplified play-by-play commentators, makes rehearsing practically impossible. Ernie is not easily flustered: in the Marcos days he pulled off countless performances during black-outs, improvising stage lighting with car headlights, oil lamps, or even by burning dried waterbuffalo turds. So, while the basketball match goes on he and the group explore the stage, adjust the blocking, try out the opening dance with the fabric they have brought along, and walk through all the episodes. Afterwards, they sit down to listen to Ernie's director's notes, in which he hammers mostly on insufficient voice projection and concentration: 'You have a good message to give to your people, but if they can't hear you what's the point?'

Day six

About half the group has stayed overnight at Eli's house to continue preparing props and costumes. Over breakfast, before the video camera, Ernie looks ahead at what is still to come:

> Yesterday we did the blocking on the stage where we will perform, and even though they know the order of the play, they missed their lines and cues and their voices were too soft. So, today we have to really work hard on voice projection and scene polishing, plus of course production: we still don't have all the props we need. We will have a costume parade to see if what they have is appropriate for their characters. It may seem that the facilitators come out as always critiquing what they are doing, but we have to do that so that they will raise their aesthetics. We feel that they have the capacity. That's why yesterday we gave them an exercise, 'Ako ay magaling' ('I am good'), to give them more confidence, because there are at least four or five who are still quite inhibited.

Dessa opens the morning session with a thorough work-out consisting of a full body stretch followed by an elaborate series of vocal exercises specifically geared to improve voice projection and concentration. Then they rehearse the new scenes, try on the costumes, and do one more complete run-through before going to the basketball court. After trying to attach the backdrops, Eli realizes that the electric cables are not long enough to connect the PA system and the lone follow spot (which constitute the only available theatre lighting) to the power point. With less than an hour to go, they are forced to move the acting area down to the basketball floor. By 7 p.m. about two hundred people have gathered to watch the show, including a handful from the two *barrios* the workshop participants had visited for exposure.

The performance

The play, now entitled *Ginto sa Iilan, Putik sa Karamihan* ('Gold for the Few, Mud for the Many'), opens with a striking movement piece to express the Marcopper spill. Harold Miciano pulls a long yellow cloth, representing the tailings, through a tunnel of white material held open by two other actors with their hands and feet, after which the cast presents brief snap shots of what is to come. First we see a family packing up in a panic to flee from the flood, then two children who get sick from the river, the clairvoyant who announces further disasters, and a farmer whose crop no longer grows. The entire cast then dances to 'Bathala' to conclude the prologue.

The first full scene takes us back to the past: Canadian Marcopper officials are being welcomed to the island as saviours with a traditional *putong* ritual. A chorus, which accompanies all the scene transitions, then imitates the sound of bulldozers and drills before reciting a stanza about local people being kept in the dark about the environmental damage caused by the mine. The next scene, about Roger being warned by engineer Cruz not to build on low-lying land, is taken almost verbatim from the exposure trip. It is again followed by the chorus, which now exhorts the audience not to believe Marcopper's promises to clean up and recompense. The chorus makes way for a strong solo by a priest figure, acted by Rommel Doria, whose pro-environment speech is rudely interrupted by angry Marcopper workers who urge him to stop his militant talk because they fear it will cost them their jobs. They gang up on the priest and freeze as the chorus comes back on to recite another stanza about a child who has lost his natural playground, which is immediately followed by a scene of two children playing on the contaminated river bank.

Thus, the Balangaw actors continue to string together realistic scenes interspersed with verses from their collectively composed choral poem. Many of the scenes feature disaster victims being fooled by medical doctors, mine officials, or local politicians. The clairvoyant, impressively performed by Jeanet Legaspi, provides the play's turning point by singing a lamentful *putong* about disease and suffering, while other members of the cast place candles around the stage.

The next three scenes are long solos, all based on verbatim material from the exposure trip. The first one, acted confidently by Laurence Sadiwa, features a fisherman named Luis who talks about how easy it used to be to fish in the river but that now he cannot catch anything any more. He can no longer pay the school fees nor indeed buy medication to treat his young son's fever. The second solo is for a visibly nervous Dennis Majaba, one of the PRRM participants. He plays a farmer named Cardo, who talks about his little daughter who died. In the third solo Rayleen Rey plays 'Lena', whose husband, a fisherman, died in a factory accident in Manila after he had to leave the island to find work.

Although content-wise the solos are moving, they are overly long and, with the exception of the first, not really acted strongly enough to hold up in the large basketball court. But the chorus manages to pick up the energy with a militantly sung *putong*, while individual actors step forward to tell the audience their personal resolutions to make a better future for Marinduque: one wants to become a human rights lawyer, another a social worker, and a third a doctor. Finally, the entire cast, holding pro-environment placcards and singing the national anthem, exhort the audience to unite and fight.

Evaluation

After the show, Ernie takes the microphone to tell the audience that the play they have seen is the result of a five-day workshop with members of Teatro Balangaw and artist-teachers from PETA and that they dedicate the performance to all the people of Marinduque. Melo Miciano, Harold's and Hajun's father, tells me he is proud of his sons and expresses the hope that they will perform the play in other Marinduque communities as well. Several unidentified local environmental activists comment that they equally enjoyed it and that they noticed that a lot of the factual information in the play was new to the audience:

> Many people from Boac town have never been up to the *barrio*. They know about it, generally, but don't seem to care. Looking around me I also noticed how people tuned in to the entertainment elements in the show, but turned off during the more serious parts. But this kind of theatre is good; it will draw people's attention, like fish to a bait.

While some audience members continue the discussion, the cast and facilitators sit down in a circle to evaluate the week's work. Each participant gets a chance to speak, but most of their comments do not go beyond expressing thanks and sadness that the workshop is over. Ernie and Dessa reaffirm their commitment to return to the island. Trina Malaga, the Marinduque PRRM coordinator, is clearly impressed with the effects of PETA's methods on the participants: 'I notice that their faces are bright and that the experience has built up their confidence; that it has challenged them to go further.' Eli Obligacion is equally pleased: 'Teachers had already told me that the young people in Teatro Balangaw had become more disciplined and responsible through our theatre. But it's incredible what the PETA team has managed to create here in only one week.'

Back in Manila, both Dessa and Ernie regret there was too much performance pressure on the participants. It would have been better, they agree, to create a simpler production for a low-key performance in the workshop venue or in the sites they had visited for the exposure. This would have allowed them to spend more time on genuinely empowering the participants, some of whom continued to be nervous or inhibited until the end. Dessa had noticed that before PETA's intervention Teatro Balangaw's artistic process had been quite top-down:

> Experience in improvisation and awareness of the creative process will give the actors the basis for evolving from here. Quite a number of them, especially those in the writers' pool, now look ready to take on larger responsibilies. They are the ones that would qualify for trainer's training in a Level Three Workshop, which will teach them how to create their own plays and start other youth groups here.

But the initiative for advanced training should come from the participants themselves and, unfortunately, to date no Balangaw members have applied. The group did, however, perform their Marcopper play in several other Marinduque communities and Ernie has returned to the island once for further consultations. In December 1998, Teatro Balangaw participated once again in PETA's annual festival, but the group continues to be overly reliant on Eli Obligacion's energy and resources.

Judging by the Marinduque workshop, then, PETA's BITAW method is a transparent and effective way to create community plays with youth groups in the rural Philippines. I have also seen it work well with different age groups in the big cities and, outside the Philippines, with Philippine migrants as well as with art academy and university students. Still, the BITAW is not some magic formula that will automatically yield positive results wherever it is implemented. Its success relies heavily on the personalities of the artist-teachers guiding the creative process. Their interventions are more likely to be effective when they possess extensive prior knowledge of the circumstances they are going to work in, when they have sufficient pedagogical expertise to design workshop syllabi and the didactic skills to implement them. But most helpful of all are flexibility, charm, and energy, qualities that are well-nigh impossible to learn.

Notes

1 Personal interviews with Ernie Cloma on April 28 and on 1 May 1997 in Boac, Marinduque, and on 5 May 1997 in Quezon City, Metro Manila.
2 Personal interview with Beng Santos Cabangon, Quezon City, 18 April 1997.
3 Personal interview with Maribel Legarda, Quezon City, 18 April 1997.
4 Personal interview with Nanding Josef, Philippine High School for the Arts, Los Baños, 7 May 1997.
5 Personal interview with Jack Yabut, Quezon City, 7 May 1997.
6 In November 1998 the Philippine Peso stood at 40 to 1 US dollar.
7 Personal interview with Eli Obligacion, Amoingon, Marinduque, 22 April 1997.
8 A *barangay* is a politically sanctioned neighbourhood association headed by an officially appointed democratically elected 'captain', who represents his area before the municipality.
9 Personal interview with Trina Malaga, Boac, 24 April 1997.
10 Personal interview with Dessa Quesada, Amoingon, Marinduque, 30 April 1997.

Bibliography

Broad, Robin and Cavanagh, John (1991) *The Philippine Challenge: Sustainable and Equitable Development in the 1990s*, Diliman: Philippine Center for Policy Studies.
Buenconsejo Garcia, Manuel (1994) *Social Problems in Philippine Context*, Manila: National Book Store.
Chant, Sylvia and McIlwaine, Cathy (1995) *Women of a Lesser Cost: Philippine Labor, Foreign Exchange and Philippine Development*, Quezon City: Ateneo de Manila University Press.
Cloma, Ernie and Fajardo, Mary Joan (1984) *Children's Theater Teacher's Manual*, Quezon City: PETA Publications.
Constantino, Renato (1996) *Fetters On Tomorrow*, Quezon City: Karrel.
David, Joel (1995) *Fields of Vision: Critical Applications in Recent Philippine Cinema*, Quezon City: Ateneo de Manila University Press.
Erven, Eugene van (1992) *The Playful Revolution: Theatre and Liberation in Asia*, Bloomington: Indiana University Press.
—— (1998) 'Some Thoughts About Uprooting Asians Grass Roots Theatre', in Jeanne Goodall and Jenny S. Spencer (eds) *Staging Resistance: Essays on Political Theatre*, Ann Arbor, MI: University of Michigan Press: 98–120.
Fajardo, Brenda and Topacio, Socrates (1989) *BITAW*. Quezon City: PETA.
Fernandez, Doreen G. (1996) *Palabas: Essays on Philippine Theater History*, Quezon City: Ateneo de Manila University Press.
Lumbera, Bienvenido (1990) *Tanghal: Towards a Filipino Stage Design*, Manila: Cultural Center of the Philippines.
Mesa, Max M. de (1996) 'And the River Stood Still', *Human Rights Forum* 1, 1 (July–December): 19–28.

PAHRA (1996) *Dark Stains Spreading on the Canvas: A Human Rights report on the Third Year of the Ramos Government*, Manila: Philippine Human Rights Information Center.

Pertierra, Raul (1995) *Philippine Localities and Global Perspectives*, Quezon City: Ateneo de Manila University Press.

Rafel, Vicente(ed.) (1995) *Discrepant Histories: Translocal Essays on Filipino Culture*, Philadelphia: Temple University Press.

del Rosario Castrillo, Pamela (1996) 'Karl Gaspar and the Mindanao Theater, 1970–1990', *Philippine Studies* 44, 1: 39–51.

San Juan, Epifanio (1994) *Hegemony and Strategies of Transgression*, Albany, NY: State University of New York Press.

—— (1995) 'On the Limits of Postcolonial Theory', *Ariel* 26, 3 (July): 89–115.

Schirmer, D.B. and Shalom, S. (eds) (1990) *The Philippines Reader*, Boston: Southend Press.

Severino, Howie G. (1996) 'A River Once Ran Through It', *I: The Investigative Reporting Magazine* (April–June): 19–27.

Sison, José-Maria (1986) *Philippine Crisis and Revolution*, Quezon City: University of the Philipines Asian Center.

Tiongson, Nicanor (ed.) (1991) *Tuklas Sining: Essays on the Philippine Arts*, Manila: Cultural Center of the Philippines.

—— (1992) *Dulaan: An Essay on the Spanish Influence on Philippine Theater*, Manila: Cultural Center of the Philippines.

Internet connection

PETA e-mail: peta@drama.com.ph

Chapter 2

Community theatre in the Netherlands

This chapter begins in 1977, the same year I left Holland for what unexpectedly became a twelve-year odyssey. A major portion of the story of Stut Theatre in my hometown, Utrecht, and indeed of Dutch theatre in general, therefore, by-passed me completely. In 1981, as a PhD student in the USA, I began my political theatre research, which after my graduation took me to the Asia-Pacific region. At one point, I had made up my mind to permanently settle outside Europe. But in February 1988, when I was almost broke in Manila and on the last leg of a long journey during which I had collected material for *The Playful Revolution*, I received an alarming call from my family and a job offer from Utrecht University. So, on 5 May 1988, the annual date the Dutch celebrate the end of World War II, I returned home.

1988 was one of those rare hot summers in Holland, with shirtless people catching rays seated on dangerously tilting kitchen chairs, or beer crates. Because I didn't have a place of my own, I was staying with a friend in Sterrewijk, a supposedly rough working-class neighbourhood just southeast of the ancient inner city. For weeks that June, the area was decorated in orange in support of the Dutch national team's campaign to become European soccer champions. Which it did, thanks in part to Utrecht-born soccer star Marco van Basten.

I had heard that people in Sterrewijk were occasionally

making theatre under professional guidance, but in the first few years after my return I was preoccupied with Asia and replanting my confused roots. In 1989 I let myself be talked into co-organizing a huge European tour for fifteen Asian performers and the two years after that I spent licking my wounds, teaching, and writing my second book. Since then, I have continued producing small inter-cultural theatre projects, either at the university or, on occasion, in cooperation with the Utrecht School of the Arts. It must have been in 1992 when one of the teachers there, Masja Knops, introduced me to Stut Theatre because, I guess, she was struck by similarities between their work and what I was reporting about Asia. In 1993, I saw my first Stut performance, *Hellend Vlak* ('Standing Straight on an Incline'). The second Stut play I saw was *Het Verdriet van de Volkswijk* ('The Sadness of the "Hood"'), in 1995. In the spring of 1996, I invited the group to participate in the global community theatre exchange that would lead to the book and video package that now lies before you. The Stut project I documented brought me back to terrain familiar from my high school days.

In 1964, when I was nine, we had migrated to Utrecht after my father had landed a job as an office worker for a printer's union. In the small southern village we left behind, our house had bordered on vast wheat fields in the back, perfect for kite flying right after the August harvest. In Utrecht, which seemed to me an intimidating metropolis but was, in fact, no more than a medium-size provincial city, we moved into a yardless two-storey upstairs apartment in Wittevrouwen, which back in those days was still solidly working class. After first attending a four-year secondary school nearby, in 1970 I transferred to another Catholic high school to prepare me for university. This larger institution, the Niels Stensen College, was located in a relatively new part of town called Kanaleneiland ('Canal Island'), so called because it is separated from downtown by the busy artificial waterway through which river barges ply between Amsterdam and the River Rhine. My best school friend, Jakko, lived there in the Loderlaan, less than 50 yards from the apartment of Feryal Seyrek, who participated in Stut's 1997 'Tears in the Rain' project. Feryal and her husband, who had migrated from southeastern Turkey to Utrecht in 1971 to work in the DEMKA steel factory, had moved from a smaller house downtown to a more spacious apartment in Kanaleneiland in 1974. And in the summer of 1974, Jakko and I pretended to be troubadours backpacking around the Mediterranean on a rail pass I had earned by working double shifts in Ben Brill's snack bar. In 1975, I became the first van Erven to go to university. A few months later – tired of cycling 30 kilometres a day to and from the new rental home my parents had moved to in the satellite town of IJsselstein, and eager to spread my wings, I moved into a student house at the edge of Sterrewijk. It must have been around this time that Stut playwright Jos Bours quit his part-time job as a teacher of Dutch at the same high school from which I had graduated only a few months earlier.

When Stut Theatre started its activities in 1977, the mainstream theatre in the Netherlands had still not quite recovered from the blow it had been dealt eight years earlier by rebellious young actors who had literally bombarded their older colleagues with tomatoes, rotten eggs, and, later, even smoke bombs to force them out of their self-complacency. While elsewhere in Europe such popular theatre companies as 7:84 in Britain, Lo Teatre de la Carriera in France, Dario Fo's La Comune in Italy, Grips in Germany and Els Joglars in Spain were at the height of their power creating a joyful theatre with a conspicuous regional cultural identity for the working classes (van Erven 1988), in Holland a similar impetus had led to the aesthetically oriented collective experiments of the Werktheater at one end of the spectrum (Ogden 1987) and to the heavily political theatre-in-education shows of Proloog and twenty-seven likeminded professional companies at the other.

The prolific Dutch political theatre-in-education movement lasted roughly from 1970 until 1985, reaching hundreds of thousands of people who had never seen live theatre before. Theatre historian Van Maanen calculates that during this period the twenty-eight companies produced more than 300 original plays, which were performed approximately 15,000 times (1997: 158). By 1986, however, all of these groups had disappeared, having fallen victim either to their own lack of artistic innovation, to internal ideological divisions, or to increasingly conservative Christian Democratic arts policies, which no longer wanted to waste the taxpayer's money on left-wing cultural activism (Erenstein 1996: 782–783). The vacuum they left was filled by an internationally renowned youth and children's theatre, and, less conspicuously, by community theatre.

Stut Theatre

Stut Theatre has identifiable roots in the Dutch theatre-in-education movement. In 1973, Stut's current artistic director and playwright, Jos Bours, had written an MA thesis on Brechtian theatre in Western Europe after completing an internship with one of the country's most successful theatre-in-education companies, 'GLTwee'.[1] In 1974, he was appointed internship coordinator for *VTU-Vormingsteater Utrecht* ('Educational Theatre Utrecht'), a new extension programme of the Utrecht Academy for Expression, the predecessor of today's Utrecht School of the Arts.[2] Typically, after preparatory fieldwork, VTU's student actors would collectively create and perform short educational pieces based on their research and give follow-up classes in schools and community centres of working-class neighbourhoods.

In February 1976, five VTU student actors were working as unpaid interns in schools and community centres of Pijlsweerd, a working-class area just north of downtown. Some of the local women asked them if they could make a play for them to celebrate the fourth anniversary of their rent-control committee. The students complied, preferring, however, to do this project outside the VTU framework. They asked Bours and his partner Marlies Hautvast, then a drama teacher in an Amsterdam youth centre, for help. However, when they saw how animatedly the women told their stories, the artists spontaneously suggested that the women become actors in their own play. At the time, Hautvast recalled in 1984, they did not yet realize they had made a fundamental departure from the typical theatre-in-education approach she herself had been trained in at the Utrecht Theatre Academy:

Looking back, it clarifies a lot of what we were trying to do, but during that period we, as intellectuals, were so busy doing all the thinking *for* the community residents, that we had no idea of the

kind of power that could actually come out of these people themselves. In hindsight, that request from Pijlsweerd was like hitting the
jackpot, because it was totally unique in those days.

(Bours and van de Hoek 1984: 10)

A little less than a year later, Bours, Hautvast and a handful of other
artists founded a volunteer group for stimulating community theatre in
Utrecht. Bours, the son of a mine official, and Hautvast, a farmer's
daughter, called their group 'Stut', after the device that supports the
ceilings of coal mine shafts. Jos Bours explains that they use the term to
symbolize the cultural support they want to provide for people at the
bottom of society: 'But back then, we also intended Stut to act as a
counterweight to the overly didactic theatre-in-education of that period,
in which intellectuals were doing all the analysing for the working
classes.'[3]

Intending to simply duplicate 'the' method they had distilled from
their first Pijlsweerd play, Stut returned to that same neighbourhood to
work on a play about a grass-roots campaign designed to convince city
officials to finance the renovation of the area's most delapidated houses.
The idea was that, through the play, the community residents could tell
the city officials how they felt about being treated by them as anti-social
misfits. The resulting 75-minute play, which would be performed eight
times, contained lots of confrontations with civil servants (played by professionally trained Stut actors), humour, and the unavoidable songs of
struggle. But despite the eventual success, the preceding creative process
had been far from unproblematic. The Stut artists had not realized, for
example, that during the first session the improvisation exercises they
had designed had forced the mentally unprepared participants to replay
painfully humiliating personal experiences, which caused many of them
to drop out. For the next project, about disabled workers, the Stut artists
decided therefore to start the process more playfully and, in general, to
behave themselves less as experts and more as partners. Aside from several people who returned from the house renovation play, for the new
project Stut also managed to recruit four new participants: actual disabled members of a neighbourhood action group. To break the ice, the
facilitators began the process with humoristic reconstructions of medical
examinations, using the information that came out of those to design
more specific instructions for a subsequent round of improvisations.
These then yielded more personal stories about, for example, work stress
leading to quarrels at home or the embarrassment of being stigmatized as
a loser by one's neighbours. Over time, Stut's initially rather categoric

view of 'the working class in the capitalist system' thus gradually gave way to psychologically more complex impressions of diverse inner-city residents. As a consequence of their more sensitive approach and egalitarian attitude, the participants now also allowed Stut to venture into more emotional personal terrain. The subsequent discussions and improvisations yielded a wealth of material from which the Stut team compiled scenes and songs that centred on the life of a worker who always used to criticize his disabled neighbour for exploiting the system until he changed his tune after becoming disabled himself.

Stut goes professional

The disability play was taken on a twenty-stop tour through Utrecht's working-class neighbourhoods. It revealed the contradictions and emotional dimensions in the lives of working people in a way that profoundly affected the community actors and their audiences. It also gave the Stut artists, who until then had been making a living as part-time drama teachers, the confidence to apply for a National Arts Council grant. Thus, from 1981 to 1983, Stut received an annual sum of 180,000 guilders (US$ 90,000), enabling the company to go professional. Working five instead of two days a week permitted the company to start new groups in other working-class neighbourhoods as well. By September 1982, Stut was actively assisting six community theatre groups, including a women's cabaret called De Schorre Krekels ('The Hoarse Crickets'). Most of these new initiatives had been the result of requests coming directly from the communities themselves, after they had seen the Pijlsweerd disability play.

In 1984, Stut published a self-study called Moed voor Morgen ('Courage for Tomorrow'), a reflection on what the company had learned from their first seven years of making community theatre in Utrecht's inner city working-class neighbourhoods. Socio-economically, conditions had only deteriorated in these areas, which had been constructed during the Industrial Revolution and which by the early 1980s had become decidedly run-down (Bovenkerk et al. 1985: 30). Between 1977 and 1984, the authors of Moed voor Morgen contended, Stut had found out the hard way that subcultural dynamics can vary considerably from one neighbourhood to the next, and, indeed, from middle-class leftist artists to a far from uniform working class. For example, in the *Bokkenbuurt*, a small self-contained community south of downtown, the local group which Stut had founded in 1982, disbanded after only three productions because, it was felt, the professional artists had tried to impose their progressive politics too much on the neighbourhood participants, who were mostly interested in comedy. Still, Bours and van de Hoek argued that middle-class artists and working-class people can successfully work together on community plays, because they themselves had working-class parents or grandparents and because they have demonstrated that they are not going to walk out on their community partners once more glamorous opportunities come along (1984: 45). Over the first seven years, then, Stut's main aim had been to create plays that reveal the complexities of working-class existence: 'Life at the bottom of society is clearly not uniform. People there adopt different survival strategies to confront their predicament and they are full of internal contradictions and external conflicts' (ibid.: 54).

No fool-proof methods

The authors of *Courage for Tomorrow* insist that there is no single fool-proof method for community theatre making. At best, Bours and van de Hoek argue, there are some general rules, attitudes, dramaturgical strategies, and techniques from which the facilitators can pick and choose to explore a particular theme or animate a group.

> The skills required for community theatre can only be learned in practice. The mix of sensitivity and tenacity, for example, that enables a facilitator to guide a discussion in a particular thematic direction and to provide the participants with a secure environment in which they can feel free to reveal the delicate tales underneath the surface of their existence. When participants have no particular theme in mind, rather than engaging them in a boring free-for-all discussion Stut begins almost immediately with improvisations – first playfully, then more seriously – on a number of different themes from which one will eventually be selected. Carefully guided improvisations,

then, are the basis of Stut's work. Because the participants are inexperienced actors, these improvisations need to be presented with precise instructions containing detail of characters, setting, and objectives that participants can relate to. The participants can then draw on their personal experiences for actions, gestures, and dialogues. 'This generates material to which people feel attracted,' explain the authors of *Courage for Tomorrow*, 'and, very importantly, while improvising they show things about which you can talk more easily afterwards than before; it creates mutual trust, also towards the facilitators, who show they are genuinely interested in them' (1984: 83).

The discussions after the improvisations usually yield enough starting points for a second round of improvisations, which then centre on more specific conflicts related to the general theme. Registering the details coming out in these improvisations is essential, Marlies Hautvast had learned by 1984:

> You dig much deeper into subjects than you would normally do. What may look like a superficial theme, turns out to contain a lot more underneath. All kinds of aspects and experiences affect people differently, or similarly without them realizing it. You use those deeper layers of experience when you prepare your assignments, because that is the material that you will be working with later to address your audience. Even though that point is still a long way off, you have to concern yourself with that from the beginning, because later you will benefit a great deal from everything you pick up now. Attitudes people adopt when sharing their experiences, the way they jump up to demonstrate something, the little signals of aggression when they remember something unpleasant. Those are the things you hear and see.

No single style

Certainly in the early years, Jos Bours worked more as a dramaturge than as a playwright. He placed characters and improvisation-generated dialogues into scenes, which, in turn, he ordered into a coherent dramatic structure that remained very close to the stories and opinions of the participants. Stut learned how to do this more effectively with each new project. For example, after a few plays with weak opening scenes, next time they resolved to start with a dynamic and emotionally charged crowd scene that efficiently introduced all the main characters and the theme. Other than that, Stut plays do not stick to any particular style, although they usually contain a good dose of humour and original songs that comment on an action or a feeling. Theatrical forms vary from fragmented collages and episodic plays with characters stepping in and out of their roles to directly address the audience, to more or less conventional domestic dramas. Yet, Stut plays always stress contradictions rather than easy solutions, tend to have more action than talk, and usually have more than one protagonist, so different genders and generations can relate to them.

Although situations, plots, and characters can be fictional, then, the actors fill them in, like empty shells as it were, with recognizable elements drawn from their own lives. 'That's why we work directly from an improvisation to a scene,' write Bours and van de Hoek: 'Because that way the actors remain close to themselves; they retain their own attitudes and not artificial theatrical ones; they retain their own language and not some theatrical speech.' Their theatre is never naturalistic, they hasten to add: 'We have given it accents and some stylization. We prefer to call it realistic, which, for amateur actors who act straight from their own experience, is a feasible task' (1984: 106).

Directing community theatre

Once a draft script has been distilled from the improvisational material, the facilitator changes gear and becomes a theatre director, who, when working in community theatre, needs to adopt a different attitude than in the professional theatre. Bours and van de Hoek: 'In community theatre people are what they act and act what they are. That is the basic principle the director needs to accept. You don't start from a text which actors then have to make their own. The actors have created the text themselves; they know how and why; they know what they want to play and what they want to tell their audience' (1984: 107).

Until 1987, Stut's productions were considerably less sophisticated than they are nowadays, because the dialogues used to be taken verbatim from the improvisations and because the company had a much smaller production budget. Bours basically placed the verbatim material in a dramaturgically coherent order, added a beginning and end, and composed a few songs together with political street band 'Rapalje', which in the early days always performed live behind the community actors, who sang the lyrics. In 1981, a special equipment grant permitted Stut to purchase its own portable lighting and sound equipment and since then has been able to present its shows under technically increasingly professional conditions. Professionally designed sets, however, would not come until the 1990s.

Funding

When Stut's first three-year grant period expired at the end of 1983, the Ministry recommended that the City of Utrecht take over the subsidy. But the Labour alderman for culture refused: he still remembered the Pijlsweerd housing play, which had so viciously attacked the local government. But an orchestrated disturbance of a public council meeting, with the vocal support of some eighty community actors, started a political process that resulted in a core funding from the Utrecht cultural affairs department, which grew from 100,000 guilders in 1984 to 375,000 guilders (US$ 182,000) in 1998.

The second half of the 1980s was a transitional period for Stut. First, in 1984, the Pijlsweerd theatre group folded after neighbourhood quarrels had also infiltrated the rehearsal space. 'That is when we decided never to work exclusively in one self-contained neighbourhood any more, but with working-class people from different areas,' explains Jos Bours (personal interview). He subsequently dug his teeth into a film documentary about workers of the Demka steel factory, which had closed down in 1983 and had created widespread unemployment and social friction in Utrecht. Subsequently, he and his partner worked for two years on a large musical production, *Carnaval der Lachebekken* ('Carnival of the Gigglers'), with which they celebrated their tenth anniversary in the 1,000 seat municipal theatre in 1987. It was followed by *Tussen Droom en*

Werkelijkheid ('Between Dream and Reality'), a project directed by new recruits Annemargreet Dwarshuis and Mieke Tolma, and *Spanje Retour* ('Roundtrip Spain'), a play about women from Sterrewijk and Oudwijk who leave their husbands behind for the first time in their married lives and go on an eventful bus trip to Spain. Meanwhile, Marlies Hautvast continued working with her community women's cabaret group, 'The Hoarse Crickets'.

Women's issues

The mid 1980s were a difficult period for working-class families, explains Hautvast:

> Particularly for women, who had tasted a bit of freedom through their activist work in the late 1970s, when things still seemed more hopeful. But when the factories closed down, their husbands stopped them from going to the women's cabaret, which they regarded as a useless club of lesbians. They wanted their wives to earn extra money for the household.

Jos Bours adds that this shift reflected a more general social disintegration process:

> Working-class norms and patterns that had been fixed since before World War II had begun to crumble. The previously undisputed respect for parents was making place for intense generation conflicts. The industry was falling apart, which resulted in changing role patterns between unemployed men and working wives and growing disillusionment among their teenage kids, who had always been promised good jobs as long as they did well in school. On top of that, newly constructed neighbourhoods on the outskirts and in satellite towns were drawing formerly close-knit communities in the inner city apart, and on the work floor the purely profit oriented piece production was replacing respect for working-class craftmanship.

But although they had to deal with increasing domestic pressure that forced several women to drop out, 'The Hoarse Crickets' also managed to bridge the working-class gender divide. Their performances for local chapters of the construction workers union were significant in that regard. Many of their husbands worked in construction, a sector frequently affected by industrial action in those days, and the women's skits

humorously dealt with strikes from the point of view of housewives struggling to keep their heads above water.

Many of the women participating in Stut's projects worked as house
cleaners, often without declaring their income on tax returns. In 1988,
Stut made a television programme about three such cleaning ladies for
the Humanistic Broadcasting Corporation. A mixture of drama and reality, it revealed how the lives of cleaning women are affected by their
work and those they work for. Depending on age and family background,
their attitudes ranged from laconical satisfaction derived from earning
extra cash to resentment about being treated as slaves.

Enter: the playwright

Until *Nest Smell* (1990), a project with runaway kids, the Stut approach
had remained pretty similar to what Bours and van de Hoek had
described in *Courage for Tomorrow*. But starting with *Meiden van Marée*
('Girls of Marée'), a play dealing with five sisters preparing the fiftieth
wedding anniversary of their parents, Jos Bours began to function more
as a playwright than as a dramaturge. For example, he now felt free to
invent a fictional family for the five female participants: 'In reality
they were not sisters, but they had so many similarities that they might
as well have been. They all came from a working-class background
and had all done cleaning jobs. Those who had moved up became very
judgmental of the others and those who stayed behind accused the
others of being stuck up. It was a challenge for myself to see how I
could make the text more complex without removing it too far from
the people.'

While Jos Bours took the freedom to fictionalize the material and fit it
into artistically more interesting forms, Marlies Hautvast looked for a
way to dig deeper into the material, which, she felt, their original improvisational approach no longer sufficiently permitted:

> In the discussions after the improvisations the participants would
> often say things that were much more complex than what they had
> been acting. Jos then tried to process that complexity and reveal
> those deeper layers in the scenes he wrote. What he came up with
> sometimes baffled them and at other times amazed them because it
> hit the nail right on the head.

Starting in 1991, then, Stut facilitators began to bring more of their own craft and artistry into the creative process. The initial improvisations continued to offer participants the chance to share experiences pertaining to a particular issue, while building trust and teaching the participants the basics of theatre. The director facilitates these early sessions, every minute of which is recorded on audio tape, while the playwright takes note of character traits, gestures, attitudes, and linguistic particulars. These details will come in handy later, when the director and playwright together shape the improvisational materials into an effective theatrical form that minimizes the distance between fiction and reality. Before he starts writing, the writer and director first filter the audio-taped materials for theatrically striking images and situations and expressions that well illustrate the contradictions between and within people. Bours states:

> Fictionalized texts can represent the experiences in a more interesting and profound way. It allows you to approximate a more complex truth by reconstructing these experiences on stage. Adding his own perspective, the writer can unravel deeper layers, structure the material, and develop a more theatrical form without creating a distance with respect to the audience or the actors. And the same goes for the *mise en scène* that the director designs.
>
> (Bours and Hautvast 1998: 13)

Changes in Stut's organizational structures

The increased artistic involvement of Stut's professional artists in the community theatre processes led to unsuspected complications. Two younger staff members seized the company's new direction as an opportunity to pursue their own ambition to establish a professional repertory ensemble composed of community actors. But Bours and Hautvast were categorically opposed to this idea, because they feared it would cut Stut off from its grass-roots constituency. When in 1993 the conflict threatened to escalate into a virtual coup by the younger artists, both sides agreed to replace the company's paper board by a neutral commission, which they asked to formulate a new constitution for the company. But the new board turned out to be less than objective and, without consulting Bours and Hautvast, appointed one of the younger artists as the company's new general manager. Bours quickly appealed by presenting himself as an alternative candidate for that position and with the decisive support of the head of the municipal cultural affairs department, who recognized that the proposed changes would destroy Stut's grass-roots character, managed to turn the situation around. Soon thereafter, the board stepped down, the two younger artists quit, and Bours was appointed artistic director by a new board headed by the director of the Utrecht Theatre Academy.[4] Frans de Vette, a veteran actor-director, agreed to become interim business manager.[5]

Even in the gravest moments of crisis, Stut never stopped creating new plays. *The Secret of Malou* (1992) was a Sterrenwijk project about mothers saying farewell to daughters moving out of the house. *Super Woman* (1993), directed by Berthold Gunster, was about working women who needed to organize their households in such complicated ways that their lives looked like veritable balancing acts. This show, as always scripted by Jos Bours, was presented in the round as in a circus, complete with a live orchestra, an MC, and the women dressed as acrobats. In 1993, Stut further produced *Hellend Vlak* ('Standing Straight on an Incline'), a play based on interviews with members of a Sterrewijk youth club.

Inter-cultural community theatre

After an extended leave-of-absence due to the internal tensions, in 1993 Marlies Hautvast returned with a ground-breaking inter-cultural project in the troubled neighbourhood of Kanaleneiland. It would be Stut's very first production with people of different cultural backgrounds and the start of many more. Marlies Hautvast had found an entry point through the area's social worker, Antoinette Arts, whom she asked for permission to talk to a women's neighbourhood safety group. She talked four Dutch, four Turkish, and one Moroccan woman into signing up for a play about their concerns. Marlies Hautvast recalls:

> The Moroccan woman came once, really seemed to enjoy herself, and then never returned because her husband did not want her to. We intended to do a short project, only for the women in the

neighbourhood. We ended up performing for 200 women from all kinds of ethnic backgrounds in the jam-packed community centre there. It was fantastic: there were twice as many women as the venue was allowed to hold. It was quite raw, but it worked like a charm right in that setting where it had originated. It would have required much more work if we had wanted to tour with it. We ended up performing it three more times, also in community centres and always for women only, because there were at least three of them who didn't want to perform for men.

The resulting play, a fragmented collage called *Circles*, showed how the women lived in their own settings, separated from each other in row after row of apartment blocks. It revealed how their minds are filled with recollections from their youth. At one moment, fragments of wedding rituals from all three cultures blended, each with their own music. Then the play cut to a Turkish woman sitting in her mother-in-law's flat in Kanaleneiland, and from there to a Dutch woman, sitting all by herself, far away from her own mother. At that point, both women started speaking parallel monologues in Turkish and Dutch, ending up speaking the same words, as if in some ritualized linguistic embrace.

The improvisations and discussions that led to *Circles* yielded enough material for several more plays. Later in 1993, Marlies therefore returned to the area to begin working on *The Day, the Night, and the Survival*, hoping to find a Dutch, Moroccan and Turkish woman willing to perform for men as well as women. The play, about two women on a symbolic journey through the wilderness, was written for Carla Pot, who would later also participate in *Tears in the Rain*, and Nazan Sahingöz, with Rabia El-Wali, who had earlier performed in *Nest Smell*, serving as a mystical Moroccan narrator. But a major problem developed when Nazan's husband unexpectedly forced his wife to withdraw from the production. 'I went to their house to talk,' says Marlies Hautvast, 'but his only argument was that whenever he entered a Turkish coffee house all his mates would tell him his wife was a whore.' Finding a substitute was not easy: new candidates first needed to consult entire families. After many weeks, they finally found Türkan. *The Day and the Night*, which squarely tackles Turkish–Dutch prejudices, premiered in 1994 and would be performed fifty times throughout the entire country. The success could not have come at a better time, one year after the lowest point in the company's history.

The next project, *Craftsman, Craftsman*, was a disappointment. Bours later realized he had overplayed his hand with a rather abstract script about three unemployed workers who had been given work placements as stage hands for a professional touring production of *Waiting for Godot*. While building the set they quote from Beckett's play, connecting his existentialist statements to their own predicaments. Although the actors themselves and a handful of spectators enjoyed the play, it was lost on the majority of the audience. It reminded Stut next time to stay closer to the cultural roots of Utrecht's working-class communities.

Measuring the effects of community theatre

In *Verdriet van de Volkswijk* ('The Sadness of the "Hood"') (1995), Stut and its community actors jointly explored discrimination from the point of view of the Dutch-born working class. The residents of Sterrewijk have long been represented by the Utrecht media and the well-to-do across town as slang-talking social misfits. In the initial improvisations, the Stut team gave the participants the freedom to vent all their prejudices, after which they collectively analysed them. They discovered an enormous diversity of opinion among the nine participating women. Jos Bours set the resulting play on the day of an international soccer match between Germany and Holland, an event which in Holland is always associated with World War II. The harsh anti-immigrant statements by some of the women, who feel discriminated by the city's social workers, are qualified by a fictional Jewish character and by Gusta, a German woman who had been participating in Stut projects since 1981. In the play she movingly recalls how, as a child, she used to be insulted as 'Kraut' and 'Nazi kid'. Although at least three of the participants dropped their extreme right-wing sympathies by the project's conclusion, Marlies Hautvast is reluctant to claim that Stut's community theatre can fundamentally influence people's politics: 'The potential for that change was already present in the group; maybe our process helped get it out. But there is no lifetime guarantee that people's thinking will be permanently affected by our work.'

Although Jos Bours and Marlies Hautvast describe themselves as middle-class leftist, they do not belong to any party and nor do they regard their work as political in the sense of increasing the participants' social awareness. 'That would be patronizing,' states Marlies Hautvast.

> As if we would be capable of telling them what life is all about. No, at best all of us achieve a more profound analysis of our own lives, by

sharing personal experiences and exploring factors that lead to them. I do think that the group process generates a deeper consciousness of the social dynamics that operate at a community level and if you present that to the outside world by means of theatre, it produces self-confidence in the participants.

An elaborate 1993 audience survey by theatre researcher Welmoed de Graaf underscores the positive community impact of Stut's work, as do remarks by actor Hans Loermans and his wife Leida, who have been involved in Stut productions since 1992: 'I often say, if not for Stut I'd have been the psychiatrist's most lucrative patient. That's what acting means for me. And the plays we do also give people something to think about. We don't give answers; we can't, but we do give people an opening to begin looking at things differently.' Turkish actor Talât Arslan agrees: 'It's a wonderful feeling, especially also afterwards when people tell you that they found your story so interesting and moving. Community theatre gets people talking to each other because it comes straight from life; it touches them, especially in our kind of neighbourhoods, where so many of these problems are a daily reality.'[6]

The positive impact of Stut's community theatre work is also beginning to interest politicians, who are increasingly at a loss as to how to deal with ethnic youth gangs and, in general, with the deteriorating social fabric in multicultural working-class communities. It has already led to the subsidized establishment of Stut clones in the northern city of Leeuwarden and Rotterdam, where the local company led by ex-GLTwee actor Peter van den Hurk, is rapidly gaining a reputation for its professionally produced multicultural community plays. Theatre artists in Nijmegen and Eindhoven, meanwhile, have also obtained *ad hoc* project funding to develop plays with working-class women, and artists in The Hague are currently exploring municipal funding possibilities to set up a Stut-like operation in their city as well.

Training community theatre artists

The increasing demand and the lack of professional training opportunities for community theatre artists have prompted Stut to start their own schooling project with extra support from the National Arts Council. Since 1997, therefore, the company has only been producing one major touring production a year, so it can supervise the creation of several smaller low-profile plays conducted by trainees. To reduce pressure and increase space for making mistakes, these localized projects are never taken out of the specific neighbourhood where they originate. Marlies Hautvast, who coordinates the schooling project, has not yet formulated a structured curriculum, but emphasizes the development of sensitivity and observation skills:

> We do train how to facilitate discussions. One exercise we did with the trainees is analysing interviews. We have hundreds of interviews with former participants in our archives. So one concrete question could be: read this interview with this Moroccan youth. Now, suppose you had to plan a follow up session, what points would you choose to flesh out further with this particular young man? They prepare it. Our criteria are: how do you get to know more about this human being? How can you dig deeper to find out more about why he thinks the way he does, what experiences have contributed to the formation of his opinions? Your starting point should be never to judge too quickly and to assume that there is always something new to learn about any person. I believe you can sensitize people, train them to do that; not in a week, but in an ongoing process.

In their twentieth anniversary season, 1997–1998, *Tears in the Rain* was Stut's major touring production. The company had also started developing a project about love and sex with older people, directed by new staff member Ingeborg Hornsveld and Jamal Hamid, a Moroccan student-director, was working on a small-scale project with four Moroccan young men.

CASE STUDY: STUT'S *TEARS IN THE RAIN*

The name 'Utrecht', historians claim, comes from the Latin word *trajectum*, meaning 'ford' or 'crossing place'. Apparently, in the year AD 47, Roman soldiers built a fortress here on the banks of the River Rhine, which in those days used to run where the quaint canals and wharves can be found today. The remnants of the Roman stronghold still lie buried at the foot of Utrecht's most impressive landmark, its 112-metre-high Dom Tower. It was built in the Middle Ages, when the city was religiously and politically at the height of its power. The protective moat that was dug just outside the old city walls remained the municipal limits until well into the nineteenth century. Starting in 1870, new houses were built outside the moat, to accommodate the population explosion that accompanied the Industrial Revolution, which reached Utrecht in the form of manufacturing enterprises and a major railroad hub (Bovenkerk *et al.* 1985: 32–33). Because of its central location in the country's transport infrastructure, the city always has had a larger than purely regional role, although in terms of national prowess and international allure it lags behind Amsterdam, Rotterdam and The Hague. Since its large steel factories closed down in the early eighties, Utrecht's economy has been dominated by trade, distribution, light industry, and service-related enterprises. After Utrecht University, which was founded in 1636, the Royal Dutch Trade Fairs and the international banking and insurance conglomerate Fortis are the city's largest employers. According to the 1998 *Utrecht Monitor*, overall unemployment rates have been rapidly declining since 1989 from 14 to 8 per cent (Anon 1998a: 27), because of above average local economic growth (ibid.: 59–62). But a differentiated scrutiny of these statistics per neighbourhood reveals that the majority of long-term unemployed, poorly educated Dutch-born and immigrant workers, live in working-class communities, which consequently also suffer much more than their share of associated problems such as crime, health, education, and relative poverty.

Socioculturally speaking, the city is emphatically mixed. Some 10.1 per cent of the population is of a nationality other than Dutch. Roughly 20 per cent of the city's total population of 234,000 are students in higher education, who constitute a vocal and culturally significant factor. If the employees of the multiple tertiary institutions are also added into the equation then it would not be exaggerated to call Utrecht a student town, a qualification that also explains the vibrant nightlife and the surprisingly sophisticated performing arts scene for a city of its size. There are at least twenty theatre venues of varying dimensions, at least three of which could be classified as large mainstream houses (750–1,500 seats). In terms of media, Utrecht has a small semi-volunteer local radio and television station, a more powerful and popular professionally run regional radio station – 'Radio M', a respected regional daily newspaper in the *Utrechts Nieuwsblad*, and is otherwise more than amply covered by the national public and commercial media.

Kanaleneiland

Kanaleneiland, on the southwestern edge of Utrecht, is an area of high rise apartments and family homes in rows constructed in the late 1950s and early 1960s in response to an increasing demand for more spatious middle-class housing with green around it. Beginning in the 1970s, however, Dutch families began to move out of here to newly constructed areas in nearby satellite towns such as Maarssen, Nieuwegein, and Houten. They were replaced by Moroccan and Turkish families, attracted to the spatious flats from cramped conditions in old inner city's neighbourhoods. By January 1998, of the 15,108 Kanaleneiland residents, 63.9 per cent were immigrants and the area statistically ranked amongst the city's highest in the categories 'unemployment' and 'poverty' (*Utrecht Monitor*, Anon 1998a: 30, 34). A likely place, therefore, for Stut to become active.

The beginning

The idea for the *Tears in the Rain* project in Kanaleneiland emerged from two earlier projects, explains Marlies Hautvast: *The Day, the Night, and the Survival* and *The Sadness of the 'Hood'* both featured parents who have trouble with their kids, although that aspect had not been the primary focus. Yet, we noticed that those were exactly the things people talked about most after the shows.'[7] In January 1996, Jos and Marlies therefore began calling around to community centres to check whether there would be an interest in an inter-cultural community play about parenting. The response was overwhelmingly positive. Even at that early stage, Jos recalls, he and Marlies were already thinking about a play in which parents from different ethnicities would make no bones about accusing each other of being the source of their problems:

> You know, Turks pointing to Moroccans, and Dutch parents to both. We knew it would be no use singling out only one group. We also knew that that would cause the greatest difficulties in the project, because there are very few self-help groups that genuinely work inter-culturally. There is only one integrated group working in Kanaleneiland: Turkish, Moroccan and Dutch women discussing ways to improve social safety in their neighbourhood. Marlies worked with them on *Circles* and *The Day, The Night, and the Survival*. In the best of situations people live side by side and tolerate each other. But for this project they would have to engage with each other more intensively and work together for more than a year!

Research

In the preparatory stages, Jos and Marlies always work as a team, comparing notes after an interview and then planning the next step. Thus, from January until the summer of 1996, they gathered information about inter-cultural aspects of raising teenagers in Utrecht's immigrant and working-class neighbourhoods. They first went in search of relevant organizations and institutions. A fortuitous conversation with Driss Elbenissi of the Multicultural Institute Utrecht (MIU) gave them access to the local Moroccan community.

Elbenissi had set up neigbourhood discussion groups for Moroccan parents and could provide useful information about Moroccan parenting styles, gender relations, and the suspicion Muslims generally have of theatre. He explained, for example, that Moroccan fathers tend to be less flexible in child rearing matters than the mothers and that teenagers take advantage of this shadowy terrain, which also exists between the Dutch and Moroccan cultures. Elbenissi was clearly enthusiastic about the Stut initiative, but warned them that finding actors would not be easy: 'the first generation does not speak Dutch and although parents of the second generation do speak Dutch reasonably well, they will need a lot of guts to get on the stage. Women won't at all: at the community level a Moroccan woman on stage is regarded as tantamount to a whore' (Bours and Hautvast 1998: 10).

The community theatre makers also went to talk to the municipal education department to find out about school drop-out rates and the involvement of Turkish and Moroccan parents in their children's education. A Turkish civil servant explained that Turkish parents put a lot of pressure on their children to succeed in school so they can have careers they can impress people with in Turkey. They use Dutch families as their yardstick, much more so than Moroccan families, which tend to look down on Dutch society as far too liberal. Marlies and Jos also talked with a Moroccan health information officer specializing in venereal disease and drugs. Jos was particularly struck by the grim picture this person painted of Utrecht by night: 'He hangs out in coffee shops and street corners and mentioned how shiny cars suddenly appear near a school's playground, offering 300 guilders to a kid if he takes a small packet of drugs across town. He told us that per evening 70,000 guilders worth of drugs are traded on the Vleutenseweg alone.' But Stut's informant also emphasized that less than 15 per cent of Moroccan youth are involved in this line of business.[8]

Until the summer of 1996, Jos and Marlies concentrated their research on the Moroccan and Turkish communities, because they knew considerably less about these than about Dutch working-class culture. Over a six-month period they visited virtually every migrant institution in Utrecht and put together an impressive collection of newspaper clippings. They worked their way down from local government and welfare institutions to Turkish parents committees in schools, where they recruited their first participants.

Recruiting participants

Finding the Dutch and Turkish participants for the project was relatively straightforward. The Turkish parents committee to which Talât Arslan belonged also provided another Turkish father, Mustafa Konus, and a Turkish mother, Sherife Akalin, both of whom would later drop out again.[9] The Kanaleneiland neighbourhood safety group became another important supplier of actors. Wil van Miltenburg, a Dutch mother in her early fifties, and Feryal Seyrek, a Turkish mother in her thirties, came from there. Jos and Marlies also invited several Stut veterans whom they knew were struggling with their own teenage kids. Hennie Freimouw, in her late thirties, used to live in Kanaleneiland before moving to another high rise neighbourhood in the city's northeast. She had been acting off and on with Stut since the late 1980s. Hans Loermans, in his early fifties, a talented actor, painter, and accordion player, had been working with Stut since 1993. He and his wife Leida, who accompanied him to every rehearsal, live in the Fruit neighbourhood, one of Utrecht's oldest working-class areas, just north of downtown. Carla Pot, in her late thirties, also used to live in Kanaleneiland until 1995, when she moved to the satelite town of Nieuwegein. She had acted in The Day, the Night, and the Survival and since then had found a part-time job as a childcare worker in the Galecop community centre in Kanaleneiland, the rehearsal venue for Tears in the Rain. She recalls how she first became involved in a Stut project:

Marlies was working with a group here at Galecop on *Circles*. Hennie was involved in that project as well and when she dropped out Marlies asked me to replace her. After thinking about it for a day I agreed and then found it fascinating to share experiences about marriage with women from other cultures. After that I acted in *The Day, the Night, and the Survival*, in which I play my own experience of always being good enough to substitute someone when they're sick, but being turned down whenever a real job opens up because I lack the necessary diplomas. Playing that experience on the stage helped me get over the hurt and gave me the confidence to do an accelerated degree in social cultural work.[10]

Four Dutch and four Turkish participants attended the first workshop session on 13 November 1996. Despite promises from Moroccan community organizers, Jos and Marlies had been unable to recruit any Moroccan actors. They knew it would be next to impossible to find Moroccan women but they had hoped to convince at least a Moroccan father and son to participate. They continued looking while the creative process got underway.

Unlike community theatre processes in other countries, Jos and Marlies never begin with get-to-know-you theatre games, because they are convinced these make working-class participants uncomfortable. Instead, they start improvising from concrete experiences right away.

The creative process

The sessions take place every Monday night from 8 p.m. until 10.30 p.m. in the Galecop community centre in northern Kanaleneiland. Before they begin their first session, Jos and Marlies serve coffee and tea, after which the participants hesitantly introduce themselves. The tension lasted five minutes, recalls Marlies: 'I asked them to sit in a circle and then they tried to postpone that moment of playing theatre with that strange Turk or Dutch bloke as long as possible by continuing to ask for more coffee. Talât broke the ice. It's worth gold when you have a spontaneous person like that with the guts to tell a childhood story that ends up moving everyone.' It provides Marlies with the opportunity to ask everyone to sing a lullaby and to paint the context in which those particular songs were sung. The exchange yields some lively recollections of absentee fathers, who in the Dutch case never had time to put their kids to bed, or in the Turkish case only returned to Turkey once a year.

The first real improvisation is for Talât and Sherife. Marlies tells them they have a son of 16, whom, they find out through a phone call from a teacher, has not been going to school for the entire week. They act it out, with Talât playing a macho father. In order to get them to move beyond stereotypes, Marlies gives them a follow-up assignment in which they have to talk with a trusted friend of their own gender about what really bugs them about their son. It leads to a lengthy discussion in which both Turkish and Dutch parents talk about how they deal with lying, disrespectful kids, and punishment. This subject is explored further in the second session on 20 November, when the childhood memories continue. This time, the Turkish and the Dutch participants surprise each other with tales of families with insufficient money to buy new toys and children who had to make their own. Most of the participants, who are already talking quite freely, feel they may have spoiled their kids to compensate for what they were never given by their own parents and that the price they now pay is loss of respect.

On the third Monday, only the women show up. Henny, Carla, and Wil begin the session with an improvisation about a 16–year-old daughter who no longer wants to go to school. 'From experience we know that these kinds of assignments are fun to act,' write Jos and Marlies in their self-study of Tears in the Rain: 'Given the chance to play an obstinate kid, parents often express all the things that irritate them about their children' (Bours and Hautvast 1998: 37). After the improvisation, the Turkish women comment that the father figure, which Wil played, was too mild. Marlies seizes this opportunity to ask Feryal to play her own introverted son next and Carla the gentle but firm mother to whom the son eventually opens up. Hennie plays an explosive Turkish father, who walks out when his son tells him he does not want to talk to him about his school problems. The improvisation leads to an animated debate in which the usually quiet Feryal becomes surprisingly vocal, revealing her contradictory feelings about how she would really like her son to be more independent and get a good education, but at the same time cannot help accepting his passivity:

> Last year I had an operation. Since then, a week before I get my period I always have a hard time controlling my temper. I feel bad then. I had a fight with my son. He bangs with his fist on the table: 'You always want to give me advice on this and that!' I tell him: 'You

shut up! You're not my husband and you're not my father!' I was so angry. I put on my coat and went outside. I closed the door and went to town. It was raining and I wept, but I thought, nobody can tell that I cry, because it rained so hard. I always have to cry because of my son.

(Bours and Hautvast 1998: 47)

It would inspire Jos to write one of the most moving speeches in the play and gave him the idea for the title, *Tears in the Rain*.

Throughout the early exploratory phase, the most important aim remains to dig up experiential material based on the participants' lives through cross-cultural improvisational examination of themes.

On 11 December, the group improvises on such examples of cross-cultural gossip as conservative Muslim women talking behind the back of a woman who likes to dye her hair and not wear a veil. Or, conversely, how similar community dynamics work in a Dutch working-class setting, when a woman who enjoys dressing in mini skirts is called a slut by others. Or how such issues affect Wil, who is the only Dutch woman living in a block of flats where the majority of the occupants are Moroccan. Perspectives on issues thus become more complex, revealing subtle differences in attitude towards religion and cultural traditions. The growing list of culturally non-specific common problems – such as the difficulty of dealing with their children's consumerist demands when there really is not enough money, compounded by the lures of petty crime – strengthen the bonding process.

A useful technique to dig underneath surface niceties is the so-called 'surprise assault', which Marlies introduces on 18 December. One participant is taken aside and receives privileged information which she can introduce unexpectedly during the improvisation. For example, several Dutch women are drinking coffee when Wil suddenly says that she has seen Carla's teenage daughter hang out with a Moroccan boy. Despite the tolerance they professed in previous workshop sessions, several of the participants now express all kinds of prejudices. To their own surprise, Jos and Marlies learn that Hennie's daughter is dating a Moroccan in real life. She tries to be open-minded about it but is afraid he has picked her daughter only because he believes Dutch girls are easy on sex. To explore this general situation in greater detail, Marlies invents a new situation on the spot: Mustafa is instructed to 'assault' Wil and Hans, whom she wants to try out as husband and wife, as their daughter's high school boyfriend. This improvisation and the subsequent frank discussion about discrimination and prejudice, intensified by the real-life love affair that brings everything literally close to home, spontaneously yield a very lively scene with juicy dialogues that will end up almost verbatim in the resulting play. Mustafa turns out to be just as hesitant and ambivalent as Carla or Hans: 'If my son came home with a Dutch girl, I wouldn't like it either. And if they did end up getting married, she would have to become Muslim' (Bours and Hautvast 1998: 67).

By the end of the year, Jos and Marlies still have not found Moroccan participants, despite following up countless leads. They therefore invite their Moroccan intern Jamal Hamid to come to work on the project as an assistant director. By the first session of the new year, Jos and Marlies have also found Jamal el Hassouni, an unmarried teacher of Arabic at a Kanaleneiland primary school they have gone to visit. They convince him to participate and he turns out to be a gifted actor, bringing along substantial stage experience from Morocco. A young Moroccan mother also shows up, but after a few weeks she disappears again without explanation. Because of these new participants, the 8 January session is dedicated once again to childhood recollections and an improvisation about a Moroccan daughter wishing to break free from brothers, fathers, and gossiping neighbours.

On 15 January, Jos and Marlies ask the participants to react to a newspaper article on increasing criminal behaviour among immigrant youths in Utrecht. Always ready to express an opinion, Hans blames Moroccan parents for leaving their teenage kids out on the streets too late. Both Jamals counter that most Moroccan parents are illiterate, have been raised in a dictatorship, and hence at home expect their kids to listen to their commands and, when they are out on the streets, to the cops. In Holland, Moroccan kids cannot handle the comparative lack of authoritarian control on the streets and in schools. The debate, which evolves from 'the' generic Moroccan youth to specific cases from all three cultures, soon becomes heated and jumps from incompetent Dutch teachers favouring foreigners to the difficulties of effectively communicating with one's offspring, regardless of culture.

Creating the actual play

On 22 January, Jos and Marlies propose to build the play around a love story between a Dutch girl and a Moroccan boy, seen from the parents' perspectives. All the participants agree and now the dynamics can change from improvisations followed by discussions designed to generate personal stories and potential dialogues, to a more explicit theatre process. Within a month, Jos writes a script and from that moment on Marlies becomes a theatre director. Although new material continues to be generated by a few additional improvisations for two new actors, Marlies will now particularly concentrate on polishing people's acting and blocking scenes.

On 5 February, the exercises are designed to help the playwright's imagination and, at the same time, improve the acting. After an a-typical warm up with a creative movement game and a voice exercise, Marlies assigns improvisations that require the actors to play in specific situations that she and Jos are thinking of using in the script. For example: 'you're a woman standing on a balcony who yells to a girlfriend on another balcony across a busy street'. Or, 'do the same thing but now the noise is so loud that you will have to attract your friend's attention non-verbally'. Or, 'a Turkish mother secretly puts her son's slippers in front of his bedroom door, so her husband will not know he hasn't come home yet. He catches her in the act'. From these mono-cultural situations, they graduate to inter-cultural encounters. When in one of these Hennie plays a Dutch woman ringing at Talât's door, she unexpectedly starts yelling at him in a racist manner that leaves him completely baffled. Afterwards she puts her arm around him apologetically, explaining she is going through a hard time at home and feels really relieved by the outburst. Talât is okay with it and a little later that evening gets away with a discriminatory joke about Moroccan illiteracy at Jamal's expense.

The following Monday there is no meeting due to a school holiday. This becomes the starting point for intensifying the creative input of the professional artists. They plough their way through all the materials they have been recording and transcribing since 13 November, preselecting a shortlist of 200 potentially powerful dramatic situations, striking theatrical images, and colourful expressions. They particularly look for material that reveals contradictions between and within people, such as domestic conflicts in all three cultures. Jos and Marlies also make an emphatic note to include a reference to the real-life suicide of a brilliant Turkish high school kid, which has recently sent shock waves through the Turkish community in Utrecht. Then the playwright can go to work.

When the 'list of 200' is ready, Jos and Marlies cut themselves off from the outside world for one entire day to brainstorm on a dramaturgical concept. They began with the opening scene, Jos remembers:

> Within seconds we knew that it had to be a situation with a lost child. We got that from Talât's story. A light opening scene, easy to mount, a few comical elements, all the characters come running out, and you introduce the theme: a child runs away and that has to do with bringing up kids. After that things became more difficult. Marlies sat down and I paced through the kitchen with my hands on my back. We always work at home on this; we can't stand having anyone else around us then. There can be endless silences, but also very frank dialogues, when either one of us thinks an idea doesn't work. In one day we thus come up with a scene sequence that does justice to the contents, to the lives and stories of the participants, and divides the roles fairly among them. And it gives me the confidence that I can write a play about it. After that I can sleep a little better and go to work. But before that for about three weeks I wake up at 5 a.m. It is a recurring ritual; failure anxiety.

On the brainstorming day, the playwright and the director also agree on formal elements. They decide, for example, that Talât should tell his story about the Turkish delight box as a solo to an imaginary son. The box, which to Talât symbolizes life's ambiguities, illustrates well the contradictions Jos and Marlies like to inject into their theatre: on the one hand, Talât wants to give his son new toys instead of the hand-me-downs he himself always used to get, but on the other, he would like his son to feel the satisfaction of making a toy from junk all by himself. Talât's story will also connect nicely to Feryal's, Carla's, and Hennie's similar experiences with their respective children. Jos and Marlies also take inventory of what they do not yet have. For example, they discover they really need to include a scene of a parents consultation night at the neighbourhood high school, because it will offer the opportunitiy to jux-tapose Turkish, Moroccan and Dutch attitudes towards school and raising teenagers bilingually. They therefore decide to try improvising such a scene on the following Monday.

The basic concept is now ready. The play will open with a crowd scene that will confirm the superficial notions people have of the 'other', but with a twist. When Feryal screams that she has lost her kid, Wil shouts that Turks should look after their children better. But when her husband then yells a discriminatory remark of his own, she tells him to shut up and help look for the kid instead. The Moroccan neighbours also join in the search. From that basic inter-cultural configuration, the play explores the inner lives and contradictory attitudes and emotions of dif-ferent characters.

On 19 and 26 February, Marlies facilitates improvisations for new scenes that Jos is considering to include in the play. He wants to see what they could look like in spatial terms and what they could yield in terms of spontaneous dialogues. The high school parents' consultation is one of the improvisations, Jamal hearing from friends at the mosque that they have seen his son walking hand-in-hand with a Dutch girl is another.

On 26 February reality catches up with art when Marlies has to throw her original rehearsal plan out the window to deal with recent developments in both Hennie's and Carla's household, where the teenagers are becoming increasingly hard to handle due to soft drug and alcohol abuse. This session is included in our video, with Leida filling in for Hennie, who had to cancel at the last minute. The video clearly reveals Carla's pent-up emotions as she alternates between playing herself and her daughter. The improvisation and the intense discussion afterwards inspired Jos with the idea to include a scene where Carla goes for a walk in the park to listen to the birds, something, she says, she always does to clear her head after a quarrel with her son.

When Jos has all the additional material he needs, he can start to write, a process lasting close to a month. He begins by going through the shortlist once again, paying particular attention to people's own words: 'I want their authentic language to ring through in the final text, so it should be singing in my mind constantly. I normally work at home. In the office it is impossible with the telephones ringing. From 9 until 11.30 a.m. I write down the ideas and the rest of the day I flesh them out. Around 3 p.m. I begin to slow down. Then I work for another half hour to prepare for the next day, so I will know where to continue.'

Presenting the script to the participants

On 17 March the script is all typed up, duplicated, and ready to be distributed among the participants. A young Moroccan man, Yamani el Khattabi, and a young Dutch woman, Mareille Roos, are attending for the first time. Jos and Marlies read the text out loud and invite comments. All the participants say they like the script, finding it both moving and funny. However, Sherife, who is still in the group at this point, is afraid she will not be able to learn all that text by heart. Marlies promises her it will be easier than she thinks, because they will learn most of their text during rehearsals; not at home in solitude. Both Hennie and Feryal, whose roles have been written very close to their real-life situations, express concern about their children's reactions. Marlies, who has made it clear all along that the participants can always demand text alterations, proposes that Jos change the names and situations to create more distance: 'After all, you have to get out there on the stage in all your vulnerability; not me.' On second thought, Hennie is cool with it the way it is: 'I don't think my daughter will mind and, besides, it will help me process the situation.' Feryal has more problems with it and so Jos and Marlies make an arrangement to go to her home and talk to her family.[11] As Marlies explains in the video, Feryal's reservations later resolved themselves naturally when she found a suitable moment to talk to her son and he, to her surprise, told her he did not have any problems with her talking about him in the play.

In retrospect, Jos is pleased with the cast's positive reactions, because he knew he had written a long, fragmented play and some of the participants do not read Dutch so well: 'It isn't just a play that develops from A to Z with a good guy and a bad guy and the lovers getting each other in the end. Still, at the first reading you only get gut reactions; they are too curious about where and how they appear in the text. You get more profound responses after they have started rehearsing.' Jos' playwrighting task is now all but finished. He moves on to the next playwrighting job and now only shows up occasionally for rehearsals: 'My responsibility then becomes more dramaturgical. Polishing scene transitions and maybe moving a few things around to make them more effective.'

For the next six months, Marlies' directorial craft takes centre stage as she teaches the actors to learn their texts and the necessary acting techniques to perform in a way that is transparent enough to show who they are as authentic people yet 'distanced' in the manner that they tell their story. This dialectical principle underlies the entire *mise-en-scène*, including the blocking and set design. 'This means that the audience gets the opportunity to empathize with the often contradictory feelings of the characters. But at the same time it urges them to intellectually engage with what is happening, because the characters either comment on their own actions or directly address the audience' (Bours and Hautvast 1998). In order to achieve this rather sophisticated level of acting, Marlies takes her time, never pushing the participants beyond their limits.

The rehearsal schedule now also intensifies. On Monday evenings, Marlies continues to work with the entire group on crowd scenes. She organizes additional rehearsals on other days to work with one or two actors separately. She always starts by having the participants first read the scene they are going to work on. Marlies then explains how it relates to other scenes in the play and discusses the emotional dimension of particular dramatic situations. She asks the actors to remember similar situations they may have experienced and how they then behaved. In this way, she extracts attitudes and emotional memories from the actors that can help them in the creation of their roles. The actors always first try to play the scene in their own words before getting back to the playwright's text. The characters they thus create are a composite of all kinds of experiences that live in them combined with the playwright's fantasy. 'But almost every participant has elements in the text that are very close to how they really are as human beings,' admits Marlies. 'Yet, you can't say of people that they are being purely themselves 100 times in a row in the same way. In order to present something personal, you have to practise a lot in order to call up that particular feeling again and again.'

Marlies is well aware that working cross-culturally clearly complicates this task:

Staging Dutch working-class attitudes and language is hard enough. So it has become very important to have Jamal Hamid with us. He works with the Moroccans in the group, directing their scenes while I coach him more on directing than on anything else, because he knows far better than me how his people express themselves. For example, the son in our play is rebellious but until the end casts his eyes down in the presence of his dad, because that is how Moroccan sons traditionally show respect. But the challenge is to also express what goes on inside of him. We've had no luck finding a Turkish director, so with the Turkish people we tell stories and demonstrate our cultural differences to each other.

Marlies dedicates the first two text rehearsals to the opening scene, because it requires everyone to be on stage at the same time. She first takes every actor aside to coach them on what to do and feel when Feryal screams she has lost her son. Marlies points out where the balconies will be and where the street and how the cast should enter running. She divides the scene into smaller units, rehearses these, and then reassembles them for several run-throughs of the entire scene, which thus acquires an almost choreographic quality.

From then on, Marlies works on one scene per Monday night rehearsal. These always begin with an extended chat over coffee rather than with a physical warm-up. Several of the participants have trouble remembering their lines or speaking Dutch, which convinces Marlies to put more original Turkish and Moroccan phrases into the dialogues. Through the context or a subsequent remark in Dutch these should be intelligible enough for anyone. Frequently, the rehearsals are spontaneously interrupted by an extended argument on a particular issue raised by a scene. Occasionally, Marlies also throws in a short improvisation when she wants to explore unfamiliar inter-cultural attitudes. For example, she has a Moroccan and a Dutch father meet to discuss the love affair between their son and daughter.

Before the summer break at the end of June, the group is ready to perform the first four scenes sequentially, complete with transitions. The crowd scene is followed by Talât's solo speech to his imaginary son, who has also run away once and whom he yearns to give all the attention he himself never received from his own father. The third scene, a conflict between the Moroccan father and his son, is more intense again and difficult to stage, partly because of the delicate subject matter and partly because Yamani often does not show up for rehearsals. His unreliability is more than compensated by Jamal El Hassouni, who is the first to know his text by heart and has a natural talent for the grotesque, which works particularly well whenever he gets angry with his son. With a bit of coaching, he also proves himself capable of more subtle acting when later in the play he has to poetically express his vulnerability as a confused and frightened father trapped inside a foreign culture. The fourth scene is the parental consultation evening at the school.

When they return in August from a backpacker's summer holiday in Turkey, Jos and Marlies learn that Yamani and Sherife have dropped out. Having no time for another tedious recruiting process through the community networks, they invite a friend of Jamal Hamid's, Mimoun Boujellad, and Türkân Günes, a relatively experienced performer who had also acted in *The Day, the Night, and the Survival*. Mimoun, a rather insecure 27-year-old waiter, requires considerable training, but in the end, with the joint support of Jamal and Marlies, he gets it together and manages to put a convincing 'Yamani' on the stage.

Throughout September, Marlies mounts the remaining six scenes, which centre on the parents' reaction to the love affair between Yamani and Mareille. The play was originally supposed to have ended with a final reconciliation between the Moroccan father and son, but a weekend-long rehearsal on 4 and 5 October yields a new final scene between Carla, Hans, and Hennie that the group insists on including because of what has recently happened at home. Carla's oldest son, whom we already knew smoked hash, had been getting more aggressive lately and the day before the weekend rehearsal, Hennie discovered that her daughter had wasted her very first pocket money on hash. Hennie was still livid when she came to the rehearsal: 'I flushed it straight down the toilet!' Thus a new final scene, that would also come to include Feryal and Türkan's statements about not knowing which culture to choose as guidance for their own parenting, was written and rehearsed in the last three weeks before the play opened. During this final period, rehearsals had been moved from the Galecop community centre to a community access drama studio, where the professionally designed set as well as some lights and sound had been set up. This way, the actors could get used to sound and light cues, entrances and exits, and performing under lights in the actual space with set and props. Stut always hires a professional crew to handle sound and light.

The performance

7 November 1997 is the big day. The Stut production staff headed by Elsbeth Reijmers has run an effective local publicity campaign through

direct mailing, radio announcements, newspaper articles and, most importantly, word of mouth. The premiere and two subsequent nights in the 200-seat auditoritum of inter-cultural theatre RASA are fully sold out. In the dressing room, Feryal gets a migraine attack, which some friends manage to massage away just in time for her to enter running when Türkan screams that her son Osman has run away. Although he is nervous, Talât then movingly presents his solo about how once he also lost his little boy, after which Jamal's outburst to his son – whom his friends at the mosque claim they have seen hand-in-hand with a Dutch girl in the downtown mall – causes hilarity among the Moroccan contingent in the audience.

After the parents consultation night at school, where we are introduced to a multilingual cross-section of teenage problems, the scene shifts to a confidently acting Hans, who is preparing to sketch his daughter's annual portrait on her birthday, but for the first time ever is unable to finish it because he notices something strange in her eyes. The next scene is again lighter: Türkan has Carla, Hennie, and Wil over for Turkish tea to thank them for helping her find Osman. While they joke around, the scene is intercut with a flashback of Feryal's son and husband fighting in silhouette, while the mother movingly delivers her 'Tears in the Rain' speech. Her softly spoken words are rudely interrupted by flashing lights and sirens announcing a fire in the local Moroccan youth centre. The two lovers, Mareille and Yamani, are now introduced. Their dialogue is full of foul-worded prejudices interspersed with tenderness. Mimoun/Yamani occasionally trips over his words when he curses the Moroccan teenagers who set fire to the centre and spouts his frustration because his dad has disowned him for dating a Dutch girl. Mareille, addressing the audience directly, recalls how she and her Dutch girlfriends used to be sexually harassed by Yamani and his mates when they were younger. But their verbal dance concludes joyfully as he lifts her up and she puts her head on his shoulder, a moment that predictably invites sighs from the audience. Next we get Talât's second solo speech addressed to his imaginary son, whom he wants to give the Turkish delight toy box he used to play with when he was a kid. But before he can finish an upset Türkan comes running in, carrying the newspaper that contains the article about the suicide of the brilliant Turkish high school student. Out of frustration she kicks Talât's box to pieces. In the more comical next scene, Mareille tells her parents that she is dating Yamani and that he is about to drop by to meet them. Hans leaves in disgust right after the Moroccan's arrival. The play then shifts to Yamani's home, where father and son reconcile. The finale is set on the bank of the Amsterdam-

Rhine canal, wheie Hans, fishing rod in hand, first meets Carla, who has come to seek comfort from the birds after yet another fight with her son, and then Hennie, Feryal, and Türkan, who confidently delivers the play's final speech about not knowing which culture to look to for guidance in raising her children.

Production budget for *Tears in the Rain*

Total expenses amounted to Dfl. 127,000 (US$ 63,500), Dfl 80,000 of which came from Stut's core funding and was spent on salaries for playwright, director, publicist, and set designer. The remaining Dfl 47,000 came from a special municipal fund for social renewal and integration (Dfl 30,000) and the rest from small private foundations. Of this Dfl 47,000, Dfl 32,000 was spent on items directly related to the production, such as renting the rehearsal space, materials for the set, costumes, props, and actors' expenses. Dfl 15,000, finally, was spent on publicity material (photography, newsletters, flyers, posters, and postage). Jamal Hamid's honorarium came from special project funding Stut receives from the Amateur Art and Cultural Education Division within the Ministry of Education, Culture, and Science to train directors of non-Dutch-speaking background.

Evaluation

Stut secured more than fifty bookings for *Tears in the Rain*, mostly in community centres and schools throughout the country, but also at two high-powered symposiums for urban social and cultural policy-makers. By the time the *Tears in the Rain* tour ended in December 1998, close to four thousand people had seen the show. Although they can never exactly predict the impact of their community plays, the comfortable pace of Stut's creative process clearly produced improved cross-cultural understanding, self-confidence, and artistic gratification among its participants. Working with a playwright whom the participants regards as one of the group also yielded a well-constructed play that inspired the actors, the director, and the production team to create a smoothly running, professional-looking show.

In terms of audience impact, Jos Bours may well be right in claiming that *Tears in the Rain* influences people to look at each other in a more humanitarian way: 'The only way to achieve that is to take people's experiences and feelings seriously and to give attention to all three sides, the Dutch, the Turkish, and the Moroccan. But it affects the participants the most.' Feryal confirms Jos' analysis: 'I did not only think of my problem, but also of the problem of Moroccan and Dutch people with children. Now I realize that people from other cultures also have many problems with their children. Anyone watching our theatre can get something out of it. It gives me confidence to tell my story on stage.'[12] Carla loved the reactions of the audience and says she could sense when her performance moved the spectators. Aside from the artistic gratification, she feels community theatre also has social benefits: 'This theatre makes you understand each other a little better and also why things happen the way they do in our neighbourhoods. It gives you confidence in your own identity and makes you realize, "Hey, we are also important! We're not marginal!" I tell you, community theatre is the next best thing to exchanging houses for a week with the mayor.' *Tears in the Rain* has made Hans realize that there are many cross-cultural similarities in the way parents suffer for their children: 'I believe the power of this kind of theatre is that it makes people think that they can do something about their problems by themselves, not by providing easy answers but by giving them a few other perspectives on the matter.'[13] Talât, who cheerfully participated in the process from beginning to end, eloquently sums up the benefits of multicultural community theatre:

> It gets people talking; it touches them because it comes straight out of our lives, straight out of the neighbourhoods where we live, where all the parents want the best for their children, regardless of whether they are Dutch, Moroccan, Turkish, or something else. You know, when you look around you see a wealthy country; that is why our parents came here in the first place. There are some things that Dutch people do well, so we tried taking Dutch parents as our example. But the thing is, you never know what really goes on behind those doors in all those Dutch households. And when you start putting some of that stuff on stage as well, then you no longer have to see them as ideal parents. You realize that you yourself do a lot of things right and that perhaps the best thing to do is to be open to other cultures and pick the good things out of each one and apply them the best you can in your own family.

Notes

1 GLTwee is an abbreviation of 'Greater Limburg Theatre-Two'. The name referred to the two provinces called 'Limburg', one in Belgium and one in the Netherlands. The Greater Limburg Theatre, jointly financed by the Dutch and Flemish governments, was founded in 1965. In 1970, it started a second-string ensemble for young actors, 'GLTwee', which specialized in theatre-in-education in the vein of Proloog and soon eclipsed the first-string ensemble in terms of productivity and popularity. Due to its alleged leftism, GLTwee lost its subsidy and folded in 1976 (van Maanen 1997: 156).

2 The Academy for Expression was founded in 1959 by drama teacher Wanda Reumer.

3 Personal interview with Jos Bours and Marlies Hautvast, Utrecht, 15 December 1998.

4 The director's name is Rien Sprenger, an important figure in Utrecht cultural circles and in Dutch drama education. From 1980 until 1982, he and his wife worked in Nicaragua, where they helped set up a community-minded national theatre school. Since then, the Utrecht School of the Arts, of which the Theatre Academy is a part, has been maintaining links with Central America through student and staff exchanges. The other board members of Stut are social worker Annemarie van der Werf and Mijndert Kok, who teaches at the Amsterdam film academy.

5 Frans de Vette joined Proloog after graduating as a director from the Amsterdam Theatre Academy. After three years, he became an actor with the less controversial theatre-in-education company Diskus from Rotterdam. In the 1980s, he worked for the Utrecht-based professional multicultural women's theatre ensemble 'Baobab'. Before accepting the Stut job, he also worked for the Nijmegen Playback Theatre, as a director of professional storytellers, and in educational television.

6 Personal interview with Talât Arslan and Hans Loermans, Utrecht, 12 February 1998.

7 Unless otherwise indicated, the direct quotations from Jos Bours and Marlies Hautvast in this case study were recorded during a personal interview in Utrecht, 1 July 1997.

8 Recent riots in Amsterdam, meanwhile, have prompted a national debate on the op-ed pages of the respected morning daily De Volkskrant (Kranenberg 1998; van Oort and Venema 1998). From this, a much more complex picture emerges than that of a poorly educated migrant generation naturally gravitating to street crime. Of the first generation of Moroccan migrants, van Oort and Venema claim, 35 per cent was illiterate and from relatively under-developed rural areas, while their Turkish counterparts were mostly literate and of urban origin. Other complicating factors they mention are a more pronounced Moroccan class and urban–rural divide, the high presence of a Berber-speaking cultural minority among Moroccan migrants, and the long separations of fathers from sons before families were reunited.

9 Sherife could not handle the performance pressure on top of mounting domestic tensions. After sharing her stories and participating in improvisations for several months, she would eventually be replaced by Türkân Günes, who had also acted in The Day, the Night, and the Survival. On 22 January,

Mustafa reported that he was assigned to irregular shifts and consequently could not commit to the forty-stop tour that Stut by that time had already booked for *Tears in the Rain*. He would not be replaced.

10 Personal interview with Carla Pot, Nieuwegein, 1 September 1997.

11 The quotations in this segment were all recorded on video in community centre Galecop, Utrecht, 17 March 1997.

12 Personal interview with Feryal Seyrek, Utrecht, 29 September 1997.

13 Talât Arslan and Hans Loermans interview, Utrecht, 12 February 1998.

Bibliography

Anon. (1998a) *De Bevolking van Utrecht per 1 januari 1998*, Utrecht: Bestuursinformatie Gemeente Utrecht.

—— (1998b) *Utrecht Monitor*, Utrecht: Bestuursinformatie Gemeente Utrecht.

—— (1998c) *Utrecht in Cijfers*, Utrecht: Bestuursinformatie Gemeente Utrecht.

Berlaer-Hellemans, Dina van and van Kerkhoven, Marianne (eds) (1980) *Tot Lering en Vermaak: 9 manieren voor 10 jaar vormingstheater*, Antwerpen: Soethoudt.

Bos, Karin (1992) 'Regisseur Berthold Gunster over nieuwe Stut produktie: Normen arbeiderscultuur passen niet meer', *Utrechts Nieuwsblad* (1 April).

Bours, Jos and van de Hoek, Peter (1984) *Moed voor morgen: Buurttoneel uit volkswijken van binnenuit met hulp van buitenaf*, Den Haag: WVC.

Bours, Jos and Hautvast, Marlies (1998) *Tranen in de regen: een Werkverslag van A tot Z*, Utrecht: Stut Theater.

Bovenkerk, Frits *et al.* (1985) *Vreemd Volk: Gemengde Gevoelens*, Meppel: Boom.

Carnet (1994) *Performing Arts in the Netherlands and Flanders*, Amsterdam: Netherlands Theatre Institute.

Desloovere, Martin (ed.) (1994) *Community Theatre: een verkenning*, special issue of *Theater & Educatie*, 2 (fall).

Dieho, Bart (ed.) (1979) *Theater op de Bres: Vormingstheater in Nederland en Vlaanderen*, Amsterdam: Espee.

Erenstein, Rob (ed.) (1996) *Een Theatergeschiedenis der Nederlanden*, Amsterdam: Amsterdam University Press.

Erven, Eugene van (1988) *Radical People's Theatre*, Bloomington: Indiana University Press.

Hollenberg, Inez and Klinkenberg, Rob (1980) *Mickery in Amsterdam*, Amsterdam: Stichting Mickery Workshop.

Kranenberg, Anneke (1998) 'Marokkaanse jongens moeten veel zelf uitzoeken', *De Volkrant* (20 November): 7.

Lit, Gerry van der (1998) 'Scheiding zwart/wit is een feit', *Utrechts Nieuwsblad* (5 May).

Maanen, Hans van (1997) *Het Nederlandse Toneelbestel van 1945 tot 1995*, Amsterdam: Amsterdam University Press.

Mat, Joke (1996) 'Hier Geldt het recht van de sterkste', *NRC-Handelsblad* (23 December).

Meijers, Constant (1998) '"Constant" and "Toneelbestel op de helling"', *Theatermaker* 9–10 December 1998 and January 1999: 4–5.

Mesters, Bas and Müller, Henk (1998) 'Ze Zouden toch teruggaan?', *De Volkskrant* (4 April).

Meyer, Dennis (ed.) (1994) *Tomaat in perspectief: Theatervernieuwing in de jaren '60 en '70*, Amsterdam: International Theatre & Film Books.

—— (1997) 'Nederlands Jeugdtheater: openstaan voor buitenlandse invloeden', *Theatermaker* (June): 49–52.

Muus, Philip (1996) *Migration, Immigrants and Policy in the Netherlands*, Amsterdam: Centre for Migration Research.

Ogden, Dunbar (1987) *Performance Dynamics and the Amsterdam Werkteater*, Berkeley, CA: University of California Press.

Oort, Roemer van and Venema, Tijno (1998) 'Meegebrachte Achterstand fnuikt Marokkanen', *De Volkskrant* (30 December): 9.

Prins, Eva (1998) 'Zeven Steegjes speelt eigen historie', *Utrechts Nieuwsblad* 3 June.

Roos, Mark (1995) 'Engagement met psychologische ondertoon: Stuts *Vakman! Vakman!* levensecht toneelstuk over afgestompte werklieden', *Utrechts Nieuwsblad* 31 March: 15.

Schwab, Dave and de Vries, Annette (eds) (1995) *Zoeken, vechten en houden van: zeven gesprekken over multicultureel theater*, Amsterdam: Scarabes.

Snelders, Gerdie (1992) 'Toneel is aan de bewoners niet besteed, maar als Stut speel, loopt de buurt uit', *De Volkskrant* (12 November): 17.

Somers, Maartje (1993) 'Supervrouw weegt de ideale man', *Het Parool* (9 May): 38.

Sue, Sandra (1995) 'Antilliaans Volkstoneel: wie heeft er van mijn bordje gegeten?', *Contrast* (23 November): 35–36.

Velden, Eric van der (1992) 'Stut Theater warmer en rijker dan menige beroepsvoorstelling', *Utrechts Nieuwsblad*, (16 November).

—— (1993) 'Supervrouw tot poezig leeuwinnetje getemd', *Utrechts Nieuwsblad* (5 April).

Venderbosch, Maarten (1998) 'Kanaleneiland gaat vast weer vooruit', *Utrechts Nieuwsblad* (31 January): 23.

Internet connections

STUT@knoware.nl

<http://utopia.knoware.nl/users/stut>

Chapter 3

Community theatre in
Los Angeles

The first time I saw Los Angeles for real was in the summer of 1978, when I was 23 and passing through in a beat-up VW bug, on my way from Tijuana to San Francisco. I had just spent three adventurous months south of the border, travelling by bus, boat, and train through Baja California, Guadalajara, the Yucatan, Belize, Guatemala and back to the US via Mexico City. All I saw of LA that first time was the cliché: the clogged-up freeways, and a cluster of skyscrapers surrounded by yellowish clouds in the distance. I passed through Los Angeles twice more during the mid-1980s and did not really get more thoroughly acquainted with the city until the summer of 1995, when I received a good taste of the top end of the latino theatre world at the South Coast Repertory's Hispanic Playwrights Project in Orange County and of the text-based avant-garde at what turned out to be the final edition of the Padua Hills Playwrights Festival. I was also introduced to Sally Gordon, who was then a part-time instructor at Cal State. She invited me to a performance of *La Mujer Hambrienta* ('The Hungry Woman'), which she had collectively created with Latina women from Northeast LA. In May and June of 1997, I returned to document one of Sally's new community-based theatre projects. Whereas in 1995 I had lived in Santa Monica, this time Rod Prosser and I were invited to stay with one of the project participants, who lived in racially mixed, predominantly working-class, and some say not altogether safe, East Hollywood. Sally's partner Beto, a Salvadoran refugee, lent us a second-hand pick-up, which was no luxury, given the mess that is LA's public transport system.

Confidently basking in the glory of his recent re-election and as yet unembarrassed by public knowledge of his sexual exploits, President Bill Clinton visited California on 14 June 1997 to deliver a long-awaited speech on racial conciliation. Typically perhaps, the event was scheduled to take place in the attractive confines of one of the state's more prestigeous institutions of higher learning: the University of California at La Jolla. Clinton's address coincided with a heated debate over a new law, Proposition 209, that was intended to dismantle affirmative action for California state employees, including university personnel. At the same time, a new proposal banning most bilingual instruction in California's public school system was being drafted to complement Proposal 187, which had excluded illegal immigrants from such public services as health care. All these measures, purportedly to prevent non-tax-paying undocumented aliens from profiting from facilities paid for by upright tax-paying citizens, only resulted in further tightening the noose around the neck of the ever expanding non-English-speaking underclass. For, just as with the ineffectual war on drugs, neither suppressive legislation nor ultra hi-tec infrared surveillance cameras on the US–Mexico border are going to prevent hundreds of immigrants from daily pouring into LA. Undoubtedly the city's economy would quickly go down the drain if they did.

It would be pretentious to try and formulate yet another definitive description of Los Angeles. The city's size, its local politics, its real estate speculations, its multiple ethnicities, its class divisions, its media density, its entertainment industry, its increasingly diverse Spanish-speaking populace, its colourful Mexican-style murals, Chicana lesbianism, the Rodney King beatings, the O.J. Simpson trial, the Northridge earthquake, and countless other issues and speaking positions have already served as starting points for book shelves full of scholarly studies on this eleventh largest city in the world and the more than 16 million Angelino/as who live in it. Hence, to speak with the editors of the multidisciplinary essay collection *Rethinking Los Angeles*, 'it is no coincidence that Los Angeles is held by some to be the prototypical postmodern city' (Dear *et al.* 1996 xi). Their depiction of their hometown seems as good as any:

> Casual observers, visitors and residents alike, catch little of the city's underbelly. They are instead persuaded by the glossy, utopian images of the burgeoning World City – a collage of prosperity, fantasy, and play: the corporate glitter of a downtown citadel; the sunshine, the surf, and mountains; the city as a giant agglomeration of theme

parks. Beneath such images is a cityscape more reminiscent of a Third World nation, a dystopia that is increasingly polarized between haves and have-nots, in which neighborhoods increasingly resemble combat zones as warring gangs struggle for turf supremacy. Here, the air, earth, and water are perpetually being poisoned. Here, public responsibility for basic human services, including shelter, education, and health care, are being abdicated.

(ibid.: ix–x)

Trying to look with a bird's eye view over the five counties that constitute Greater LA, say, from one of the scenic outlooks coming down from the San Gabriel Mountains on the Angeles Crest Highway, the futility of all these otherwise fascinating attempts to intellectually pinpoint LA hit home. They sound spot on but there is so much more to it all, so many more communities and subcultures they overlook and stories they do not tell; yes, even Mike Davis' uncompromising *City of Quartz* and Rubén Martînez' poetic *The Other Side*.

Theatre in Los Angeles

Limiting the scope to the theatre scene in Los Angeles, a slightly sharper picture emerges, but even here the editors of *Rethinking Los Angeles* remind us that,

(T)here is no need to go downtown to enjoy the principal entertainment and cultural events of the postmodern city. There are alternative major theatre districts in Pasadena, Hollywood, Long Beach, Orange County, and elsewhere. Art, music, and other forms of cultural expression flourish in the formal museums and performance halls scattered throughout the region, as well as informally on the sidewalks of East Los Angeles, South Central and elsewhere.

(Dear *et al.* 1996 12)

As one might expect, virtually all theatrical activity in LA is at the very least affected, if not overshadowed, by the looming presence of the film and television industry. Most professional actors who come to southern California regard LA's stages as platforms from which to launch into the major film studios. Hollywood even affects activist and community theatre, as Santa Monica-based street theatre artist Susan Suntree discovered to her dismay when she tried to find volunteers to perform in a play to protest against Steven Spielberg's construction plans in the

Ballona Wetlands, a unique swampy bird sanctuary, just south of LAX international airport:

> A dancer friend of mine and I decided to do a theatre piece about this issue. It was hard to get professional actors for this project. They were afraid to lose their jobs. It was Spielberg versus street theatre. If he decides to harm you he can. Actors come here to be seen by agents so they can get jobs in films. Hollywood is a big, big industry here. You can't get elected mayor if you don't have the backing of Hollywood. Riordan, who succeeded Tom Bradley in 1995, got zillions that way. It isn't just that those moguls won't give you any money; none of their friends will give you money either.[1]

This same corporate world has been expanding its financial interests in LA's vast theatre industry since the Reagan–Bush years, when state and federal governments began to gradually withdraw subsidies from the arts. The 2,000-seat Ahmanson's theatre is a prime example. Matthew Bourne's controversial homo-erotic production of *Swan Lake* had a hugely successful run there in June 1997. In the same period, the 3,197-seat Dorothy Chandler Pavillion across the plaza had programmed the LA. Opera production of Mozart's *Marriage of Figaro*, while the adjacent 760-seat Mark Taper Forum featured José Rivera's mainstream Latino play *Streets of the Sun*.[2] These three are arguably the most prestigeous among the forty or so commercially owned larger venues in Greater Los Angeles with a seating capacity of 500 and over. The area further comprises thirty-five medium houses of 100 to 499 seats and at least 125 so-called 'equity waiver' houses with less than 99 seats.[3] The 1995 *Southern California Theatre Guide*, where I found these figures, also lists some eighty registered theatre companies in the area, only a handful of which have a Latino, African-American, Asian-American, or multicultural profile.

Community theatre in LA

Latino theatre in Los Angeles is not exclusively Chicano or Mexican-American; it includes Central Americans and even migrants from further south, such as playwright Milcha Sanchez-Scott, who is partly Colombian but set her most famous script, *Roosters*, in a semi-rural Mexican-American community. Then there are young chicano performance groups, such as 'L.A. Teatro', the Latino Theatre Company based at the Plaza de la Raza Cultural Center, the Bilingual Foundation of the

Arts (BFA), the Latin Theatre Initiative at the Mark Taper Forum, and
The Hispanic Playwrights Project at the South Coast Rep in Orange
County (van Erven). And then there are those who work at the grass
roots. Heavily funded, such as Cornerstone, who recently collaborated
with Peter Sellars on a big musical production with Latino community
residents from East L.A (Korteweg); or ill-funded.

To survive, theatre activists are often forced to maintain a delicate balance between several worlds. Suntree, for example, finances her artistic
efforts on behalf of a healthier environment by teaching English at East
Los Angeles College, a two-year tertiary institution catering mostly to
mature-age immigrant students. Hector Aristizabel, an actor from
Medellín trained in the *creación colectiva* tradition of Santiago García and
Enrique Buenaventura, combines work as a drama therapist and as a primary school drama teacher with professional acting gigs and conducting
outreach workshops for 24th Street Theatre.

24th Street Theatre is a community theatre initiative of Robert Scales,
Dean of the University of Southern California's theatre school. Just like
the Yale School of Drama has its Yale Rep across the street, he wanted to
have a professional theatre nearby, where his students could do their
internships. To help him with this venture, he invited Jay MacAdams
and his partners, Stephanie and Jon White-Spunner, who had been running the respected Glorious Repertory at the Odyssey Theatre on the
affluent West Side. Scales found an abandoned garment factory in the
rough neighbourhood adjacent to the USC campus, worked out a deal
with the landlord, and then wrote a successful $30,000 grant application
to finance the building's conversion into a fully equipped theatre with an
exhibition space doubling as foyer. The 24th Street Theatre's mission is
quite different from Yale Rep, affirms MacAdams: 'It is outreach, youth
programming, and bringing schools to the theatre. That is our passion.'[4]

Funding and fragmentation in LA's community theatre

The 24th Street Theatre is relatively well-off with funding from
Cultural Affairs and a well-endowed private university. It has a
permanent venue to work in and enough income to pay a few
professionals. They are an exception; funding possibilities for
community theatre in LA are few and far between. Hector
Aristizabel manages to get small grants for workshops through

such welfare-oriented campaign organizations as 'Reach LA', which runs an AIDS Prevention scheme, and 'ArtReach', which tries to bridge the gap between senior citizens and primary school kids. He obtains school gigs via 'Performing Tree', which provides arts workshops for community centres and semester-long courses integrated in primary and secondary school curricula. But although some of the community artists know each other, given the long distances people have to drive to and from gigs, they hardly ever see each other, and, as a result, feel isolated.

Given the lack of interpersonal connections and the sheer size of the city, it is extremely hard to build communities in Los Angeles. Yet, Aristizabel is convinced that theatre can help: 'It is a group enterprise, a problem resolvent. When we create a play we create a community. It is about working together, not working against each other. Just improvising I need to be able to receive whatever you're giving me and take it somewhere, not obstruct you. If you block me, we cannot tell a story and grow together.' 'Soft' as this may sound, Aristizabel claims his playful approach even touches hardcore gang members:

> It has taken me eight years of this work to understand that their attitude is: 'You know, I can't afford to like you. I can't allow myself to like you, because you're just another fucking adult who is coming into my life and will disappear'. I try to make them aware that everything is set up for them to fail and become another statistic. Seven per cent of the LA population is African American, but they constitute fifty per cent of the inmates in this city! I tell them, 'We are building prisons for you guys; not universities. It costs $30,000 per inmate per year. But if you go to a bank after graduating from high school and you want a $10,000 loan to go to university, they don't have it!'[5]

Sally Gordon

Sally Gordon (b. 1940), a Boston native of mixed Ukranian-English ancestry, has also worked with 'at-risk youth' (as the welfare agencies term them). In 1989 and 1993 she conducted two extended projects in camps for juvenile delinquents from South Central, funded by the City of Los Angeles Cultural Affairs Department. But frustrated by the lack of official backing and recognition for her work, she currently practises her community theatre art as an employee of the privately endowed Hathaway Family Resource Center in the Highland Park area of Northeast Los Angeles.

Gordon, the daughter of an economics professor, grew up in France in 1949 and 1950 and in England from 1952 until 1955. She began her theatrical career in New York's Off-Off Broadway during the 1960s, occasionally directing in between acting jobs. Her income she supplemented by driving cabs and working in restaurants. From 1972 until 1974, she directed productions for a group called the Undercroft Theatre Company in the basement of a Manhattan church, discovering the thrill of performing for non-theatre audiences through an agency that reimbursed tickets for residents of half-way houses and drug-rehabilition centres. But the community theatre bug really bit her when she began to act and teach drama in primary schools for a professional children's theatre company operating around rural Maryland, Pennsylvania and West Virginia. Determined to build further on that eye-opening experience, Gordon moved to Los Angeles in 1975, where she first earned a living as a waitress, as a substitute teacher in the inner city LA public schools, and by teaching English as a Second Language to adults. Even in these educational settings she experimented with drama techniques to expand people's vocabularies. In 1977, Gordon founded The Firebird Theatre Company, which she profiled in her unpublished 1995 MA thesis as,

> a curious hybrid of children's and popular theatre that toured Southern California from 1977–87 with innovative adaptations of myths, folk tales, classical and original plays in its repertory. Most of the productions involved the use of live music, dance, masks, and some form of audience participation which eventually became the company's trademark. Performances took place at schools, museums, and libraries; at festivals, in theatres, prisons, and centers for senior citizens; and even in workplaces for physically and mentally handicapped adults. The company was booked into schools almost immediately by Performing Tree and ICAP (Inter-cultural Awareness program funded by Title I), two agencies in the area responsible for providing arts programs to young people.
>
> (1994: 10–11)

Shifting from popular to participatory community theatre

In hindsight, Gordon explains Firebird's increased politicization as a by-product of frequently performing in low-income rural and inner city schools, where most of the subsidized gigs were available and, as civil conflicts spread across Central America in the early 1980s, a growing number of Salvadorian and Guatemalan refugees resided. Firebird's experimentations with audience intervention came about somewhat coincidentally. When they were scheduled to start touring a Kabuki version of Grimm's fairy tale 'The Fisherman and his Wife,' the actors realized that the performance they had prepared was too short to fill a 45-minute class. Gordon therefore decided to invite some of the children on stage to try out different endings to the play, something she had learned from Robert Alexander's Living Stage Company in Washington, DC. From then on, Firebird continued working with second endings and audience participation, a technique she perfected through an intensive three-day workshop with Alexander in 1982.

The participation of Nicaraguan political theatre company Nixtayolero in the 1984 Los Angeles Olympic Arts Fringe Festival gave Gordon the final push to plunge into her own outreach work in the more dangerous parts of the city. She read up on Nixtayolero's philosophy as formulated by its director, Alan Bolt, learning how this company went into rural communities to create theatre with local people about social issues. She was particularly impressed with Bolt's emphasis on artistry, something which she has also always considered of tantamount importance in her own work.

Bolt's example of creating art in the revolutionary trenches, Alexander's audience participation techniques, and decreasing freedom in the Los Angeles school system caused Gordon to temporarily disband Firebird and to found the much more loosely organized Teatro de la Realidad in the Winter of 1984.[6] She joined a Central American solidarity group, travelled to Nicaragua as a Witness for Peace in the summer of 1985, and with a grant from the Ralph M. Parsons Foundation, began her first community theatre project. It was a ten-week programme of improvisational drama workshops for children aged 10 to 12 in an impoverished, predominantly Spanish-speaking part of LA. After the grant ran out she continued working there as a volunteer until she received another grant in the middle of 1985.

Being virtually untrained, Gordon learned by doing. She soon found out that art is simply not a priority among the much more urgent economic and social challenges LA's immigrant population faces. She learned four valuable lessons from her early community theatre experiments: (1) that not every participant is sufficiently equipped to sustain the process necessary to collectively create a full production; (2) that therefore the best approach is to first work towards the performance of a short piece in a process lasting no longer than a month or two and do so two to four consecutive times; (3) then create a longer, more challenging piece with the best and most reliable performers from the preceding smaller projects; (4) to pay the participants a small fee and treat them as professional artists.

In 1986, Gordon created several Central American solidarity performances with inner city youth. In the course of 1987, following what she thinks may have been an attempt by the FBI to misrepresent the company's connections with Central America, Firebird officially closed its books. That following summer, Sally Gordon travelled to DC to work with Robert Alexander in an advanced five-week workshop training programme for educators, social workers and theatre artists from around the country.

Robert Alexander's Living Stage

Deeply dissatisfied with the school system as we know it, Alexander has been trying to reform conventional western pedagogy through theatre outreach for children. His mission first started in New York City in the 1950s, followed by a successful high school project in Boston that caught the attention of Zelda Fichhandler, the founder of the legendary Arena Stage in Washington, DC. In 1966, at the height of the Civil Rights Movement, Alexander accepted Fichhandler's offer to become head of a professional children's theatre unit she was setting up in one of the worst parts of town. He assembled a technically skilled racially and gender mixed company of artists who could sing, dance and think on their feet. During three months, Alexander taught them how to improvise with techniques he had picked up from Spolin, Brook, and others. Then they started working in the area after school with local kids in high school recreation halls and community centres.

Already back in the 1960s, Alexander discovered that a gregarious well-connected community liaison person was indispensable for his work: 'This person would go into a neighbourhood and sit in a barbershop, a bar, a pool, and he would start introducing himself and say, 'We're Living Stage and we want to do work in your neighbourhood.'[7]

In 1984, the Arena Board bought Alexander an old two-storey night club, located in drug infested part of downtown Washington:

Instead of working in high schools classrooms and recreation halls, kids would now come into this magic space with sunlight pouring onto the dance floor. It was sixteen foot high, with five inches of foam rubber on the walls so kids could bounce off it without getting hurt. The colour scheme was red and yellow, which is sunny. The set consisted of 30 by 60 inch cubes and triangles and small bridges and a big ten-foot arch that you can hang on and ten-foot ladders and five or six thousand dollars' worth of sound equipment and good video cameras. There were no seats.

Typical Living Stage sessions begin with the 'guests' deciding a theme, followed by a musical jam – first instrumental, then verbal as well, until the kids and cast are all singing together. Dancing and playing can also be included in this welcoming ritual. Then, all of a sudden, an actor may jump up on a box and start improvising a verse to the music. A few moments later, another actor could start doing physical sculptures to express the emotional life of the words his colleague is inventing and so a scene emerges. The central character in the scene is always of the audience's age:

We would make this room that environment and the production people would keep moving the boxes around and that would go on for one hour with lots of changes, people would die, others would get born, the actors would come back as ghosts. Then we bring the improv to a crisis moment, the kid is gonna kill himself or the parents throw him out of the house, something, you freeze it and ask the audience: 'How do you want the ending?' And it was important for us, for them, that they would not propose endings that they thought would happen in real life, but that they started validating their dreams. First the dream then the reality. And then they would give the ending. And if somebody was very excited he could join the two actors in the scene.

In contrast to psychodrama, which tends to wallow in cathartic relief, and sociodrama, which draws its settings and characters from social reality, the Living Stage philosophy is based on the belief that the creative hemisphere of the right side of the brain can be exercised like any other muscle and that one can thus develop,

> the ability to step in someone else's shoes. For a moment or as long as you wish, you can imagine what it's like to be another human being or a plant or a river that's being polluted or a rose that's being sprayed with insecticide . . . It's important so that we can understand what it's like for another person to live a life that's different from ours. It can arouse our compassion so that we stop looking at life through our own very, very, very narrow focused lenses.
>
> (Alexander 1994: 7)

While obviously attracted to Alexander's method, Gordon finds him too hard on teachers and his technique less effective outside his secluded and securely funded space. In LA, she knows, the community artist has to produce measurable results in a relatively short time to satisfy the expectations of municipal politicians or the criteria of private foundations, who fund her projects. Besides, most adult community participants find Alexander's exercises too abstract or psychologically confronting.

Upon her return from Washington, in the summer of 1989, Gordon conducted a successful drama programme for approximately thirty young men at the Kenyon Juvenile Justice Center in South Central. In this project, in which she was assisted by an African American and a Latina actress, she drew heavily on Living Stage exercises. The following year she received an individual artist grant from the City's Cultural Affairs Department and used it to create a play with illegal Latino street vendors in the Hollywood/Pico-Union area. Within four months, she created a play with a group of thirty kids, teenagers, adults and a few older people. It dealt with the vendors' struggle to obtain legal status and the feud between two vendors to chair the Street Vendors' Association, a conflict which Gordon symbolically dramatized as the Aztec myth of The Five Suns. The process had its usual hitches, and an unusual one: the jealous husband of a recently remarried woman came to each rehearsal, constantly interrupting her improvisations, and eventually forcing her to drop out altogether. But the play, entitled *Donde caminan los dioses* ('Where the Gods Walk'), also provided a rare moment of satisfaction for the artist in Gordon:

> We had the gods walk through the streets of downtown LA to see what had happened to their people. When the Gods came on in their costumes, we had this Andean music. I swear to God, my hair stood on end every performance. There was this one scene about the breath of life for which I was trying to find the image so hard. So I got these yellow balloons to represent the sun, starting with small ones and then bigger ones and then we got the Sun God to put the breath of life into the largest yellow balloon I could buy, accompanied by Andean music. That was the most special moment of my entire life in the theatre. We put this huge balloon into the shopping basket of this real street vendor who was the heroine of the play. She came on wheeling this shopping basket through a wall of fire. She was incredible.

Donde caminan los dioses taught Gordon the benefits of creating a basic scene sequence to which the participants could improvise. She now finds fixed texts require too many boring rehearsals, lead to stilted performances, and allow no flexibility to work in inevitable last-minute replacement actors.

The lack of support from the CARECEN Central American Refugee Center that she had chosen as a performance venue was more than compensated by the relative financial independence through her individual artist grant, which gave Gordon complete autonomy. It enabled her to recruit someone to organize transport for the participants and to hire a few professional artists to raise the aesthetic quality of the performance. The project thus succeeded in giving the street vendors a voice, a human face, and a nominal improvement of their status. But one project's success does not automatically guarantee the next. In the second half of 1993 and the first part of 1994, Sally Gordon learned this lesson the hard way as she tried to conduct two simultaneous projects, one in the run-down Pico-Union district bordering on the infamous MacArthur Park, and the other in South Central. The Pico-Union project was an attempt to create a series of short open-ended plays with residents of a housing estate and present them in the vein of Boal's Forum Theatre. In hindsight, however, Gordon realized that Forum Theatre only works with actors thoroughly trained in creatively and quickly responding to 'spect-actors' (1994: 77). The venue she chose to work in, a community centre offered to her by the Pico-Union Housing Authority, was out of the way, and teenagers, fearing ridicule from their gang and tagging-crew buddies, hard to come by. Only four locals ended up participating in the two Pico-Union performances of *Un Cholo en las puertas del cielo* ('A Gangster at the Gates of Heaven'); the rest of the cast. Sally had to recruit among professional Latino actors she knew and participants from previous projects. The play was about a Latino teenage gangster, a *cholo*, who is killed in a drive-by and, disoriented, arrives at the Pearly Gates, which he thoughtlessly sprays grafitti on. An enraged Saint Peter wants to kick him into the lower depths but the *cholo*'s sister, also shot dead, intercedes on his behalf with the Virgen de Guadelupe, the Mexican version of the Holy Mother. Before she decides to admit him, however, she requests to review the boy's life, after which the play transforms into a dramatized collage of true stories told by the community participants. Instead of a neat ending, the Virgin and the *cholo* step forward to ask the audience whether they think he should be admitted to heaven and why they thought he had died at such a young age. In response, many spectators refused to accept communal responsibility for the boy's problems, laying the blame instead squarely with Anglos who discriminate against the immigrant labour force.

Gordon, who was clearly disappointed with the audience's reaction to *Un Cholo*,[8] harbours similarly negative recollections of the multiple-layered, year-long project she conducted for young gang members in South Central. During the first three-month phase of their work with the forty juvenile delinquents, Gordon and her two female colleagues ran warm-up and improvisation exercises for two three-hour sessions a week.

These activities, many of which Gordon and her team-mates adapted from Boal and Alexander, took place in the gym of camp Karl Holton, a closed residential reform school for young offenders, whose crimes ranged from petty theft to murder. They receive schooling within the fenced compound, which also has an old gym and occupies its residents with woodwork, ground maintenance, and kitchen assistance. The main purpose of Gordon's team was to build mutual trust and cooperation among the group (dominated by African Americans and Latinos) before venturing into improvisations. After three months, Gordon's team applied the same approach to a second group.

In January 1994, Gordon began the second phase of her South Central project at a special continuation high school for a group of about fifteen young men and women on probation.[9] She wanted to create an open-ended play with them based on their lives. In the process, she kept an eye out for the most reliable participants in the batch, four of whom she wanted to train so that they could act as co-facilitators in another ten-week drama programme with a third group of their peers at Camp Holton. Her ultimate goal was to prepare these trainees to independently conduct drama workshops at two South Central elementary schools. This last phase of Gordon's project, intended to consolidate the self-esteem and the newly found creativity of the participants by practising a professional skill in an educational environment, Sally Gordon regards as the most successful part of her work with juvenile delinquents.

Gordon feels that community theatre interventions with 'at-risk' youth are doomed to fail, because it is impossible to break down gang rivalries and so many youngsters are too psychologically traumatized to open up to artistic processes, which require high levels of trust and cooperation. The real problem is that they return to their old neighbourhoods, where it does not take very long to fall back in the old ways of life. Yet, Gordon believes her programme 'was important even though most of the young men have died or are probably now serving long-term sentences in jail. I hope some of them return every now and then to the memory they had of playing like children and feeling safe even though rival gang members were in the same room.'[10]

Anthony Cyriak, whose story about the gang-related murder of his brother
Max formed the plot for the play Gordon developed at the probation high
school in the project's second phase, has mostly positive recollections:

> When Max got shot I was only rapping and playing basketball.
> When I got involved with Sally's project it brought something out in
> me I didn't know I had, because of the violence I had been in. I dis-
> covered I could act and that I can express myself well verbally. I
> could help teach kids younger than me a different way than I have
> gone through. Afterwards, I ran some workshops myself at
> Manchester Elementary and some other places. It was nice. The
> kids understood, listened and had fun.[11]

Although he has not acted since 1994, Anthony, now a young father, is
trying to make an honest living, working in restaurants and writing hip
hop poetry. Periodically encouraged by Gordon, he is considering a college education.

Drama therapy and community theatre

While her projects in South Central and Pico-Union were frustrating,
Free Arts for Abused Children, an organization that gets professional
artists to donate time to teach kids, asked her to conduct a theatre workshop at the Hathaway Family Resource Center in Highland Park. It
meant the beginning of a fruitful but occasionally rocky collaboration
that resulted in Gordon's full-time employment as the Center's Arts
Facilitator in 1995.

Gordon's 'Life Scripts' programme has become a crucial take-off point
for her community theatre activities. A combination of Alexander influences and Life History (Perlstein) and Life Review (Butler) methods she
encountered studying drama therapy, she explains that her 'Life Scripts'
cycles last six to eight weeks and involve a great deal of visual arts:

> I may tell them to pick a piece of paper in a colour that expresses
> how they feel at that moment. Then they scribble on it, pass it on to
> a partner, who has to find images in it. What happens then is that all
> these experiences start pouring out, because some image will trigger
> a response. It is kind of a short cut to therapy, because things happen
> really fast. Another way would be instead of talking about a
> problem, to draw it – 'what is the biggest problem on your mind
> right now? Draw it!' – And your partner will draw a solution. You try

not to give advice. You could draw your body: what is in your heart, your groin, your head, etc. Trust building is a major part of this process. Then you begin a dialogue that everybody else can share in, which then leads to short theatrical improvisations.[12]

'Life Scripts' participants who demonstrate an interest in continuing to do drama are invited to participate in Gordon's community theatre projects, which, although still based on people's lives, move beyond therapy into the realm of art. Typically, these plays are made with additional financial support from an external grant and are presented as coproductions of Hathaway with Teatro de la Realidad. One of the first of such more artistically oriented follow-ups involved a group of Mexican and Central American migrant women frequenting the Hathaway Family Resource Center. For several months in 1995, Gordon collaborated with them on a play in Spanish based on their own experiences and those in their community. The women performed the resulting piece, La Mujer hambrienta ('The Hungry Woman') for friends, relatives, and neighbours in the Hathaway parking lot.

On 24 August 1995, I witnessed a repeat performance of La Mujer hambrienta for mothers and children at the nearby Monte Vista elementary school. The women proudly showed me the Aztec masks and goddess costumes they had made for the mythical prologue and epilogue of their play. With gusto, they then took the audience of forty through eight scenes of migration, macho abuse, and exploitation bracketed by a dramatization of the Aztec myth of an insatiably hungry woman, representing Mother Earth. The play thus traces the fire into the frying pan escape of a spiritually famished young woman named Soledad from the abuse of her husband in Mexico (played by the actual abused woman) to various instances of exploitation in Los Angeles. We witness her ill-fated attempts to find a job, friendship, and a home. Soledad obviously represented many Mexican and Central American women in LA who, besides food and shelter for themselves and their kids, yearn for respect and love.

Since that summer, Gordon has continued to develop educational plays on issues prompted by actual occurrences in the Highland Park community, such as the destructive effects of gossip (Chisme Caliente) and discrimination of the disabled (La Mariposa rosa). She also continues experimenting with Forum Theatre for young audiences in local high schools. Every summer since 1996 she has been directing artistically more gratifying large-scale theatrical events in the local park. These massive enterprises, which usually involve giant puppets, live music, and scores of community participants working alongside a few professional artists, are invariably held together by some legend or myth that encapsulates a more realistic community tale. Thus, the 1996 show about gang violence followed the narrative line of a 5,000-year-old Sumerian-Babylonian story about the struggles of the mythic king of Uruk, Gilgamesh, against his enemies. A professional African American actor played the lead with a Latino mortician in the role of Gilgamesh's friend Enkidu. In a naturalistically mounted prologue, these two, dressed in rival gang attire, encounter one another in the park, exchange insults and start a shoot-out. Gordon had talked four real-life paramedics from the LA Fire Department to carry the two dead heroes off on a stretcher, surrounded by a large group of actors and volunteers dressed up as Sumerians. In the play's epilogue, the two heroes make peace lying on their ambulance stretchers:

> In the original version of the myth, (Gilgamesh) fails in both his quests: to bring his friend back from the Underworld and to learn the secret of immortality. I wanted the audience to go on that journey with Gilgamesh, who travelled to the back of beyond to try to find his ancestor Utnapishtim, who was the only mortal to live forever. I wanted the young people in the audience to realize clearly that once you pull the trigger, there is no turning back.[13]

Frustrating victories

Gordon tries to infuse some sense of continuity in her community theatre endeavours. Her long-term vision is to develop an ensemble of community actors with whom she can achieve greater artistry. But four of the *Mujer hambrienta* participants, who had been part of *Chisme Caliente* and *Mariposa rosa*, dropped out of *Gilgamesh* due to a variety of complications, including a husband who threatened to leave his wife if she continued. Despite such setbacks, three other 'hungry women' rejoined the 1997 project that we documented and, since then, have also participated in the large-scale 1998 outdoor 'Isis and Osiris' show.

Gordon has to overcome many frustrations: professional artists who do not take community theatre seriously and deliver less than promised; unreliable volunteers; a social service agency as employer which proclaims to see the benefits of communal art but not the enormous energy it requires. A week or two before a premiere, Gordon can therefore sound utterly pessimistic about her work, arguing that, at best, it only has a therapeutic effect on an individual level. But the trainee concept she first tried out in the 1993 South-Central probation project has continued to pay off in Highland Park as well. Several women from *La Mujer hambrienta* now have steady jobs.

CASE STUDY: TEATRO DE LA REALIDAD'S *¡SAQUEN LA SOPA YA!*

Highland Park proper has a population of about 70,000 people, but adjacent neighbourhoods up to the Ventura Highway to the north, the Glendale Freeway to the east, I–5 to the south and the Pasadena Freeway to the west, are usually considered part of it as well, thus effectively increasing the number of area residents to 250,000. Approximately 70 per cent are Latino, half of whom are non-English-speaking recent immigrants. The majority of these are children, 18 and under, with young adult parents. Until about 1980 Highland Park had been a predominantly white middle-class district, but as married children moved out to newer housing conditions in the San Fernando Valley, young latino families started moving in from overcrowded, delapidated inner-city neighbourhoods, where most destitute recent immigrants first settle. In Highland Park houses are larger, better maintained, have yards, and, generally, provide a more attractive environment for raising kids. While it has its share of street crime and gang violence, these problems have not yet overwhelmed the community. And physically the place does not look destroyed in the way that the Pico-Union area or parts of South-Central are. Even though there are 'transitional neighbourhoods' with deteriorating apartment blocks and crack houses, they can still go either way, depending on whether new families shift to the area and fix up the houses, or more destructively minded folks move in.

Most of the shop owners in the area remain older white folk, in their fifties and over. Many of them are clustered in conservative church communities and, in varying degrees, are apprehensive of the Latino culture that is invading the area where they grew up and their parents with theirs. The mostly Protestant churches they attend are confronted with rapidly dwindling congregations, whereas the Catholic church is rapidly expanding. The Highland Park Ebell Club, a social institution for middle-class white women, is a cultural remnant of the neighbourhood's fading Anglo dominance. It has an auditorium with a beautiful wood-panelled proscenium stage on 57th Avenue, nine blocks south of the Hathaway Family Resource Center. They donated their space for Sally Gordon's indoor performance, the first time they had collaborated directly with Latino community theatre.

The Hathaway facility in Highland Park is located in a historical wooden house that until 1988 used to serve as a residential orphanage, also managed by the Hathaway Children and Family Services. This organization, which has been active in remedial childcare work around Los Angeles since 1919, also operates a residential facility for abused children on a farm donated in 1962 by film magnate Cecil B. DeMille. In addition, it runs a special education school and a number of walk-in family and childcare services. From 1988 until 1992, the suspended Highland Park orphanage was transformed into a non-residential resource center. In 1997 it was given its current name and, with a mixed staff of Latinos, Anglos and African Americans, now caters mostly to the Latino population of the larger Highland Park area, offering bilingual services, counselling, parenting classes, an after-school program, citizenship and ESL courses. From its reopening, it has also collaborated with Free Arts to bring in professional artists to work with its clients. This proved so successful that, with the help of municipal funding, it created the new staff position of Arts Facilitator, filled by Sally Gordon since 1995. As part of her job, Sally gives her six-week 'Life Script' cycles in the centre, teaches drama in nearby schools, and creates community theatre projects. These plays generate goodwill for Hathaway and have attracted the support of Latino councilman Alatorre (Sonenshein 1993: 181, 213, 208, 220, 259–60), a useful contact when it comes to subsidies and city contracts that provide the bulk of the parent organization's annual income.

Funding and politics

Pat Bowie, director of the Highland Park Center since 1992, believes in community empowerment for sustained long-term social development: 'If you really invest into a community and let them define their own needs and who they are, they have the ability to create their own solutions.'[14] Yet, she admits there is tension between this philosophy and the views of municipal politicians, who decide on grant applications, and, she knows, need to 'score' with quick fixes to social ills. Instead of prevention, they favour suppressive intervention. Apart from the Cultural Affairs Department, little other government funding goes to community empowering arts projects.

Recruiting participants and raising funds

In keeping with her ambition to form an ensemble of community actors, Sally secured the participation of three Mexican *Mujer hambrienta* veterans: Carmen, Maria, and Teresa. Maria, whose horrific life story had formed the basis for the 'Hungry Woman' play, brought along her teenage daughter, Alba. Teresa, who had recently been hired as a part-time staff member by the Hathaway Center after a successful stint as *Promotora*, would also run some of the exercises as Sally's assistant director.[15] As usual, Sally had difficulty recruiting Latino men, so she invited Javier, a Guatemalan political refugee, and Elias, a former Puerto Rican drug addict from New York, who had both worked in *Gilgamesh*, as had Alpha, a Filipina-American. Wanting to give these relatively experienced actors the opportunity to work more professionally, she hired two Chicano musicians, Michael Archuleta and Lorenzo Martinez, set designer Malcolm MacDonald, Chicana poster designer Dolores Guerrero-Cruz, and publicist Jerry Craig, who was later replaced after repeatedly failing to meet deadlines. To pay the professionals, including the two Chicano camera operators and a production assistant for our video, and the participants, Sally raised $10,000 from the Cecil B. DeMille Foundation and $3,000 from the Sidney Stern Memorial Trust.

Production expenses

Set design ($1,500); live music ($1,500); production assistance from two Cal State students ($500); public relations officer ($500); assistant director Teresa ($400); actors' stipends (12 x $200 = $2,400); poster/flyer design and production ($250); props and masks ($137.18); transportation ($47.40); stationery and postage for p.r. ($139.21); food and beverage for cast and crew ($303.89); childcare ($180); camera operators ($1,500); miscellaneous, including $286.80 for removing the piano from the Ebell Club stage ($312.66). TOTAL: $9,670.34. Sally's salary was paid directly by Hathaway and did not figure into this budget. The remaining $3,329.66 was used to fund later performances of *¡Saquen la sopa, ya!* and the next park production.

A few weeks before we began documenting, Sally had completed creating a play about teenage violence with Latino seniors from Franklin High, a secondary school with which the Hathaway Family Resource Center maintains close ties. It was a delicate process because one of the group's classmates had recently been killed by a Korean shopowner. Four teenagers who acted in this play, called *To Kill a Dove*, joined the project we documented: Gus, Daniel, Maryem and Susie. Susie's mother Blanca and aunt Sonia joined after first participating in Sally's 'Life Scripts' series in which they managed to therapeutically process the severe domestic abuse they had both suffered. As newcomers to community theatre, they struck us as the most interesting participants to follow more closely for the documentary.

Blanca, who earns a living cleaning houses, came to Los Angeles in 1983 after the bloody Guatemalan civil war had also started to disrupt life in her rural village, an hour's bus ride from Huehuetenango. She and her husband first came alone, leaving their two small children behind. They went the usual route: first by bus and train to Tijuana, then by foot across the border. After paying a *coyote* $500 to guide them into the US, he deserted them half-way, forcing them to hide a night and a day in the mountains near San Isidro. From there, they ran across the freeway. Blanca's sister Sonia came to LA with her husband in 1985. Her two daughters were born in the US. Her husband started becoming abusive in 1990 and she divorced him in 1993. In January 1987, Blanca and her husband went back to Guatemala to collect their children. Soon after their safe return to LA things started going sour.

The ethics of documenting

Despite its delicate nature, Blanca explicitly asked Sally to use her story of abuse, her daughter's incest, and the gang-related imprisonment of her teenage son as the basis for the new community play, the process for which she was well aware would be documented on video. Blanca, Sonia, Susie and the other participants gave written permission for filming, invited us to their home for periodic interviews, and, after the production, gave us clearance to use all material. In the meantime, they have seen and approved the resulting documentary and, as with the participating groups from the other five countries, I continue to stay in touch regularly. Even so, the presence of the video crew undeniably affected the process. Sally, who reduced her usual three-month process to one to accommodate our schedule, also suspects that our presence added prestige to her project and motivated her participants to work harder than normal. It definitely provided her community play with more publicity than it would otherwise have generated. However, although our presence may have provided an extra stimulus, I do not think it fundamentally altered the nature of Sally's approach.

Sally selected exercises from a large arsenal that floats around in her head. Many of the ones she used in this workshop were variations on Robert Alexander's; she wanted to see how they would work with a more advanced group. Others came from Boal, Spolin, or had been invented by herself for the Firebird actors to acquire a common theatre language and to give them material for their own outreach workshops. They were used as vocal and physical warm-ups, to focus the group and enhance its cohesion, eliminate stress from work or family, increase the performer's energy, teach basic theatre skills, stimulate the creative imaginations of the participants, and, ultimately, to generate improvised scenes for the play. 'By moving away from the inner focus on self to the outer focus of the surrounding environment and through the creation of a variety of characters,' Sally explains, 'these exercises help to expand the world view of the actors, and enable them to learn better how to empathize with others, which is what I think acting is all about, really.'[16]

The sessions took place on Thursdays and Fridays after work, from 5 to 8 p.m., and on Saturday afternoons from 2 to 5 p.m. With the exception of the first, which was held indoors, all sessions took place outside in the Hathaway Center's parking lot and playground lawn. Extra sessions were added as pressure mounted during the last week before the play's opening. Sally had a budget for art and craft supplies and to purchase food and beverages for the breaks; the women also sometimes brought home-made snacks to be shared by the group.

Week one, day one (22 May): trust building and theme extraction

After a brief introduction in which Sally stresses the openness of the process and the importance of being open to it in return, she begins with a 15-minute activity in which two actors work in pairs and learn three or four facts about each other, which they then use to introduce their partner to the group. This is a useful listening exercise – after all, acting is all about listening and responding – and does not put anyone on the spot: it is always easier to talk about someone else than about oneself. In order to get the participants out of the safety of their chairs, Sally then uses a variation on the categories game where the 'leader' can ask everyone wearing black shoes, for example, to change chairs; or those with only sisters or those who wear glasses; or who like jalapeña pizza; or who has children; or who is married or single. Lasting no more than ten minutes, it provides the group with the opportunity to get to know one another.[17]

The imagination and expressive capabilities of the participants are really put to work in the next exercise, which has been adapted from Robert Alexander. While Michael and Lorenzo play an upbeat Mexican tune, the actors walk fast and then freeze on Sally's command. Then they run, without colliding, and after the next 'freeze' start handling imaginary objects. The object should be suggested by the position their hands are in when they 'freeze!' In their minds they are asked to answer questions about the object's weight, material, colour, or origin. After another run and freeze, they invent another character for themselves and begin a silent dialogue guided by questions about family and profession. The activity enables the actor to very quickly make artistic choices and develop a character in a specific setting. It evolves into a group improvisation as the characters begin to interact with one another. After a 15-minute break, the group then lists what they consider the most urgent issues for themselves and for their community, which by vote they reduce to a shortlist of three: sexual abuse, domestic violence, and gang pressure on teenagers.

The final activity of the first day constitutes the start of the actual playmaking process. In a three-step exercise, teams of two (with the exception of the teenagers who insisted on working in an unproductive group of four) develop a one-page scene – a dramatic conflict based on fact or fiction and related to one of the three themes on the shortlist. They have to pay special attention to the age of the characters and the setting. The second step is to rehearse the script and the third to perform it for the others. This exercise yields two rough versions of scenes that will eventually be included in the final 'script': the gang-related troubles of Daniel at high school and the conflict with his mother over the *cholo* pants he bought with money she had given him for a haircut.

Week one, day two (23 May): fantasy exploration

Gus and Daniel are absent due to a high school baseball play-off game. Sally begins with a warm-up game. Jogging in a circle, the muscles are stretched by responding to the instruction to touch shoulders, feet, or reach for the sky. Those who lose their balance in the act, move during a freeze, are the latest to repond, or respond wrongly, are out.[18] Sally then starts a tape with romantic instrumental music and asks the actors to imagine they are kites carried off by the wind. As the music becomes wilder, Sally narrates, 'You're caught in a tree all tangled up and you're trying to escape – fight to get out. Now you are the children holding the kites – the wind pulls you up – how do you feel? Sad or happy?' After they have come back down to earth, Sally asks them to verbalize how they felt as kites.

Fantasy explorations like the kite exercise prepare the actors to work at increasingly higher levels of abstraction. The highest level, featured in the film, is an advanced Alexander technique called 'Inner Lives', which requires actors to express the soul of an object by means of sound and movement. Instead of the external manifestation, they should express its emotional life. 'You are the inner life of a new moon looking down on a pair of lovers', for example, prompts the actors to express the feelings of that moon. To help them, Sally asks the group what these might be. They suggest satisfaction, ecstasy, joy, love, or jealousy, because it is alone up there and cannot share in the pleasure of the couple below. Other objects are related to the themes on the shortlist: a gun in the desk of a high-school student, a house wall receiving an angry husband's fist, a wall being painted by a mural artist, a flower growing in the sidewalk, and a bullet entering the spine of a 9-year old.

Bluebeard

Because she likes myths and legends for their capacity to take community participants out of the naturalism of their own experiences, Sally deliberately introduces the story of Bluebeard, the archetypal domestic abuser. She hopes it might particularly inspire Blanca to explore the emotions and actions of a fictional character she can then later draw on for dramatizing her own story.

Sally's assistant Teresa first reads the story in Spanish and then the group casts itself in whatever role that strikes their fancy, dressing up with material from a box of fabric that Sally has provided. She considers dressing up as a creative act that enhances the willingness of the actors to move from the ordinary into the world of fantasy. The exercise also compels the group to practise dramatizing a plot, dividing it into scenes, and exploring the psychological and theatrical dimensions of the characters. The resulting performance is quite intense at times and afterwards Sally asks if anyone has discovered similarities between the Bluebeard story and their own. Blanca, who played Bluebeard, says she enjoyed dressing up and playing someone else but that she did not like her role. Like most of the women, she was critical of the young woman who fell for Bluebeard's charms: 'We women are stupid; we take the blame for things we haven't done. I identified with the girl, because I have been abused myself and I know what it means to be beaten up by a man. So while I played the man, I didn't want to cross over to the other side; I was still identifying with her.'[19] The discussion thus quickly moves to the real-life subject of how women are fooled by their internalized romantic ideals of men. Blanca: 'I must have been blind so I couldn't see beyond him. He was an alcoholic, used drugs, he beat me. And yet he remained my prince for sixteen years! I was afraid of being alone, of confronting life.' Most of the women relate similar disillusioning experiences with the men in their lives, which inspires Sally to ask them to improvise a short scene in which they juxtapose the fairy tale ideal with the reality about men, marriage, and family. Groups of two or three get half an hour to brainstorm, rehearse, and perform a scene. The exercise yields some usable sequences that eventually also find their way in ¡Saquen la sopa, ya!

Week one, day three (24 May): between the real and the surreal

The day begins with a 30-minute series of different walks, e.g. hopping, jumping, walking fast, backwards, crawling, walking joyfully, miserably, carrying a heavy bag, walking through autumn leaves, on the beach. The instructions become progressively more complex, requiring the actors to spacewalk on the moon, walk as giant 12-foot creatures and then as a limping, 125-year-old dwarf, making corresponding sounds and movements. Next, more abstract commands challenge them to be coals in a fire, butter melting in the oven, or wooden soldiers and rubber dolls. Reflecting back on the activity, Susie recalls how she imagined she was an old lady carrying a heavy bag with all her family secrets in it, an image that she will later develop into the play's final scene about a girl who carries her heart in a bucket.

The session continues with an extended discussion about the myth of the prince on a steed and about the US as paradise. Sonia summarizes the feelings of many: 'We came with the idea to work here for only a few years and then go home with all the money we saved to buy a house with a garden and set up a business of our own. But the reality is that we have to work hard, that we have to stay much longer than we want, and that there are drugs, gangs, cockroaches, and mice.' Sally then asks them to list some myths about family and the dark secrets it conceals. Without thinking twice, Sonia says: 'The myth that in my family there has never been sexual abuse and the myth that men are better than women.' The discussion eventually also expands to myths about children, who are to accept abuse and shut up, and about gangs offering the warmth and security that real families lack.

After the break, the group improvises ideal family myths juxtaposed with reality. Sally makes a circle with chairs: outside the circle is the myth in which the participants act out a family that goes to church on Sundays and afterwards harmoniously goes to the park for soccer and a picnic. Sonia plays the father, wearing one of Sally's hats; Blanca plays the wife and Susie the daughter. They themselves come up with a possible transition from ideal to real when Sonia, playing a man, starts flirting with another woman in the park and then goes home to find Blanca drinking coffee with a friendly neighbour, which causes Sonia to beat up Blanca in a fit of jealousy. This violence prompts Susie's spontaneous disclosure of incest, which, as Blanca later tearfully explains to the group, her husband first denied and only a year later would be confirmed by Susie's younger sister, leading finally to the man's arrest. They re-enact these painful moments once more, visibly unleashing intense emotions on the parts of Blanca, Susie, and Sonia, who continues playing the abusive husband.

To lighten the proceedings, Sally asks Teresa to step into the improvisation as some kind of fairy godmother who lends a hand to Blanca. Wielding her wand, Teresa grants Blanca the courage to tell her husband she is going to leave him. The intensity of the performance by Sonia, Blanca, and Susie inspires Maria and Alpha to relate their own stories of abuse. It also gives Sally the idea to use Teresa's fairy godmother character as a mediator between the surreal and realistic scenes of the play that is now taking shape in her head. The Saturday thus yields the germs for the powerful scenes that end up at the heart of ¡Saquen la sopa, ya¡: the money tree 'welcome to America' scene that opens the play, the ideal family scene, the soccer in the park scene, the incest scene, and the episode where the conservative priest blames Blanca for her divorce.

During this first week, Sally has instilled trust and sensitivity in the group, she has taught basic acting, and has prompted the group to explore three major themes that, in turn, have generated useful raw material for the play by means of carefully guided improvisations. Over the weekend Sally tries to think of ways to push the process beyond the raw nerve level of personal trauma into the realm of theatre art. Her other problem is how to update Gus and Daniel, who have already missed two crucial days. She is less concerned about Sonia, who will also be frequently absent due to night classes in college.

Week two, day one (29 May): fairy tales and teenage gangs

Today Sally plans to do improvisations with the teenagers, because Gus and Daniel have returned and have brought along their high school friend Maryem. As a warm-up, Sally has selected a mirroring exercise, which requires one of the participants to express with body and voice how he or she feels while the others imitate. After this short exercise, the participants choose a piece of brightly coloured tissue paper with which they create a dance, either alone or with some of the others. They are then asked to take hold of a length of wire and, with the paper, to sculpt their movements into a concrete image.[20] Accompanied by the musicians, who are constantly jamming and composing songs for the play whenever exercises do not require their direct contributions, groups of three create a movement piece to tell a fairy tale of their own invention. Alba, Alpha and Carmen come up with a delicate dance about a butterfly who flies too close to the sun. It will also find its way into the resulting play, as does Maryem's and Blanca's piece about a pure heart poisoned by a snake, and Elias' and Maria's story of a prince who liberates an oppressed princess. In this latter improvisation, Teresa appears once again as fairy godmother. Later, her character will evolve into a mistress of ceremonies who announces each new scene and mediates between the ideal world and the real. The teenagers, finally, create a dance about a boy who carries his heart in a bucket. It is virtually the reverse of the scene that will eventually conclude ¡Saquen la sopa, ya!, where Susie ends up playing Gus' original part and learning his lesson that you cannot numb your feelings forever if you have been deeply hurt once: you can only feel true happiness if you accept pain.

The tissue paper dance is designed to release the group's non-verbal creativity and to start out lightly on an oppressively hot day. After the break, Sally focuses attention on the teenagers, working with them and the others on improvising a scene in which a mother discovers that her son is involved in a gang. Before they start, however, Sally first draws out information about gangs. The teenagers are the real experts: they are confronted with gang culture everyday at Franklin High. The scene they create becomes one of the most hilarious in the play; particularly because of the convincing shouting matches between Maria as the fiesty mother and Carmen as the henpecked, jobless father. It also offers Sally an opportunity to dramaturgically connect the gang theme to the sexual abuse: Susie's brother, played by Gus, talks Daniel into joining his gang.

Week two, day two (30 May): cumulative improvisations

The warm-up consists of different tagging games borrowed from Clive Barker. One of these, 'Te-ak-ee-allio',[21] a rough native American wargame between two colour-coded tribes, playfully refocuses the group on the gang theme, which they continue to work on that evening. They redo the improvisation with Carmen as Daniel's abusive father, after which Sally suggests they delve into the father's past to try and find out why he has become the way he is. She only provides the group with sketchy instructions. They improvise a scene in the Guatemalan countryside a generation back, revealing that Dan's fictional father, who actually enjoyed learning as a boy, was forced to drop out of school to work in the fields. After the first version, Sally and the group try to get a more precise picture of the father and mother character. They conclude that he is probably one of those people hanging out on street corners trying to pick up a day's job and the mother someone working in a garment factory, getting paid by the piece. They never have time for their son and always order him around. Unbeknownst to them, he is being beaten up by gang members at school – a practice known as 'gang banging' – and sees how his buddy, played by Gus, makes easy money. Through this cumulative method of improvising, followed by discussion and a second round of improvisations, the group is able to improve their characterizations quite quickly. Sally lets the participants make their own creative choices, only stepping in when she sees them getting stuck in clichés. Thus she reminds Maryem that when Daniel confesses his gang banging problems, she should somehow try to express her dual loyalty in her acting: she is both his sister and Gus's girl. The day's session concludes on a lighter note with an improvisation of an ideal family with picture perfect kids and a gentle father who cooks and cleans.

Week two, day three (31 May): masks

The physical warm-up begins with the players standing in a circle and their right hand placed above their head, shaking it out as hard as possible. To exercise their voice they also let out a sound to show how they feel. The left hand, the feet, and finally the whole body are shaken out in this way. This is followed by a work-out of specific facial muscles in combination with emotions and sounds. Next, Sally asks the group to mould their face into a mask of fear, surprise, jealousy, anger and the like, changing features quickly to the beat of a drum. Later she asks them to add exaggerated body movements to the facial expressions – a useful preparation for acting with real masks. After a short sculpture transformation exercise based on the same principle, the actors, who are assigned a number, are told to become immigrants preparing to leave their respective countries, then immigrants fleeing across the US border, and finally immigrants in a detention center for illegal aliens. Sally plays the role of a stern immigration officer calling out numbers that allow each actor to take one step towards 'the other side', which represents freedom. She also subjects them to harsh interrogations, to which they have to improvise a response. Following this, the participants are asked to write short poems based on the feelings that the exercise evoked in them. They should first say the poem silently in their heads, expressing its emotions non-verbally with their faces. Then they are given fifteen minutes to write it down, after which they recite them out loud while two others try to express the poem's emotions by throwing their bodies into a sequence of strong sculptural positions. This exercise inspires Sally to create the two family sculptures behind closed doors that are revealed at the beginning of the play. Before they leave, the group decides on the title ¡Saquen la sopa ya!, an expression from Maria's native Puebla meaning literally 'let's take the soup out' and figuratively 'let's get rid of all the bad stuff in our community'.

Over the weekend and into the next week, Sally is thinking about the play all the time. Her main concern is that the bulk of the material the group has thus far created feels too heavy. Due to time pressure, she resolves to take some of the creative decisions herself, whereas she normally would like these to be taken by the participants. As a compromise, she consults frequently with Susie and Teresa and before the first session of the third week, they have a more or less fixed episodic scene structure for the play, alternating light moments with more emotional ones, fantasy with reality. Sally also wants to introduce a mischievous creature, known in Maya legends as a 'Nahual'. At the end of the play she envisions this figure, who always shatters illusions, to fight with the fairy godmother over Susie, who, fed up with the quibbles, finally pushes them aside and exclaims: '¡Saquen la Sopa, ya!' Then she'll take the heart out of her bucket, stick it on her breast and walk out.

Week three, day one (5 June)

Today's warm-up is another tagging game and some voice exercises, although Sally finds the conventional ones difficult for semi-literate or non-English-speaking participants. Instead of tongue-twisters, she has everyone speak out together at the top of their lungs about the most embarrassing thing that ever happened to them, followed by the meanest thing they ever did to another person, and the most courageous act they ever did. Then they sing some of their lines like an opera. The remainder of the Thursday rehearsal is taken up by fleshing out the scenes involving the teenagers. They practise the telephone conversation between Susie and Daniel, before he drives over to pick up her and Gus. The musicians meanwhile have composed some funky tunes to accompany the subsequent car scene that leads to Gus's armed robbery of Alpha's convenience store.

Week three, day two (6 June)

After playing 'hug-tag', the actors are asked to walk around silently and focus on their main character in the play. Rather than their own names, they will now give them another name and age. Thus Blanca becomes

'Josefina' and Susie becomes 'Perla'. Working in pairs, their partner then mirrors them, following whatever movement is made. From this exercise it is an easy step to sculpting the two immobile families behind the closed doors that Teresa opens after the 'Welcome to America' money tree scene, with which the play begins. Susie sculpts her family, paying special attention to positions of dominance and subordinance. Maria and Carmen jointly work on the other family, while an increasingly less timid Maryem offers suggestions as well. For the rest of the evening the group works on scenes that are still weak, like the one about the girl who carried her heart in the bucket and the one about the serpent who killed the pure heart. Also the interactions between Teresa as fairy godmother and Javier as the mischievous devil figure get long overdue attention. Before they call it a night, they also work a bit on the scene where Blanca/Josefina visits her son Gus/Angel in jail after he has been arrested for robbing Alpha's shop. With less than a week to go, they now have created all the scenes they need in skeletal form.

Week three, day three (7 June)

Most of the participants arrive at 10 a.m. to make the plaster masks for their fantasy scenes. Only Sonia is absent because of an exam at college and Gus because of a Saturday morning job at a fast food restaurant. The small stipend that Sally pays the participants cannot compete with those kinds of commitments. During the lunch break, Sally tells me that she is now reasonably happy with the balance between the symbolic and the realistic scenes. She is also glad that, having now chosen fictional names for their characters, the actors are able to distance themselves more from their personal realities, which, she argues, is what makes this theatre instead of drama therapy.

After a short warm-up, the afternoon session continues with more work on the final scene about the girl carrying her heart in the bucket. Sally gives Susie a lot of freedom to devise it. They also work intensively on the scene where Sonia, now back from her exam, is in jail as Perla's father Pedro remembering his own abusive past. Blanca powerfully improvises as the young Pedro and Javier, finally back after not showing up for several rehearsals, plays Pedro's fanatically evangelical dad. After mounting and blocking these two segments, there is too little time for a complete run-through, because the musicians have to leave for a lucrative Saturday night gig down in Orange County. Sally is visibly disappointed: she had wanted the group to see how the play runs from beginning to end and she herself had wanted to get a sense of where the strong parts of the play are, where it slows down, and where perhaps the musicians should cover up.

On this day, a conflict erupts between Sally and the professional designer, who has still not finished constructing the set. This has particularly affected the scene where Javier as Pedro's father needs to burn his son's feet while suspending him from a tree. Sally vocally critizes Malcolm while he counters that he has had to scramble all the time because Sally, he feels, constantly changes her mind. While it is true that Malcolm could have been present at more rehearsals, Sally expects the professionals she hires to put more time and energy than the actual hours they are getting paid for, because of the idealistic nature of the project and because she herself puts so much unpaid extra time into her projects. The reality is that some, like Michael and Lorenzo who reliably participated in all the sessions and obviously recognize the importance of Sally's brand of community theatre for Latinos, live up to Sally's high expectations, while others can or will not.

Week four: dress rehearsals and show time

In the days leading up to opening night at the Highland Park Ebell Club, Sally has scheduled two additional rehearsals on Tuesday and Wednesday. Since they were unannounced, the musicians and some of the actors cannot make it, and hence complete run-throughs are impossible until the Thursday night dress rehearsal. Blanca is starting to feel the pressure. It is her first time acting in public. Sally is also tense, sensing there is still a lot of hard work left to do if they are to have a good show on Friday. On Thursday night Malcolm's set is still not completely ready and Sonia has a math exam. Before the complete run-through, Sally quickly improves one or two scenes with a few subtle visual touches, such as a synchronized unfolding of napkins before the 'ideal' family's dinner. She then does a thorough vocal warm-up with the cast, knowing that the actors need to get used to throwing their voices across the rather spacious Ebell auditorium and will need to project even better for the Saturday afternoon outdoor show in the Hathaway's parking lot.

The run-through on the unfamiliar stage reveals a lot of practical problems that still need fixing. Particularly the pauses between scenes are way too long. Therefore, after they have acted all the scenes in sequence, Sally sits down and rather sternly gives the group director's notes. She reminds her actors to be alert for cues, exit in character, stay out of sight once off-stage, help each other get dressed if they have time, and not to mess with other people's props. She also gives each actor individual feedback and insists that everyone show up early on Friday so they can work on scene transitions with the musicians, Sonia, and the completed set before the audience comes in. She promises to have a few copies of the scene order available at strategic points backstage, so people can quickly check what comes next.

Friday, 13 June, the *Los Angeles Times* features two colour photographs and a nice article about ¡*Saquen la sopa, ya!*. The Spanish language daily *La Opinión* also has a sizeable announcement. And, most exciting for the participants, their favourite Spanish language TV station, Channel 34, has called to say they will send popular reporter Norma Roque to cover the Saturday performance for the 10 p.m. news. Sally has rarely had so much publicity for her projects and is especially pleased for the group: 'I wanted them to come away with the feeling that they have climbed Mount Everest. They have really stretched themselves as actors. Some of them are playing parts that are not even their own sex and they're doing stuff that is extremely surrealistic.'

The performance

At 6.30 p.m. the first people are let into the auditorium. The show is free and by curtain time at 7 p.m. about a hundred spectators have shown up for the event. Sally has also asked one of the Hathaway's clinicians to attend in case someone in the audience needs help after seeing the explicit incest references in the show. The actors are squatting behind the two doors in the now completed set; Teresa is waiting in the wings wearing her immigrant dress and carrying her suitcase; Javier is off stage on the other side wearing his *Nahual* mask; Michael and Lorenzo, dressed in ponchos, are ready to strike the first chords of *Historias de la gente* ('Stories of the People'), the rhythmic theme song they specially composed for the project. Then Sally walks out to welcome the audience. The show can begin.

The money tree scene, also included in the video, draws laughter when Javier devilishly steals Teresa's suitcase as his ironic welcome to recently arrived immigrants. The following dance falls somewhat flat due to the contrast between a sluggish, flat-footed Elias, who plays a prince courting a princess, played by a much more confident, light-footed Maria. But the loss of energy is made up by the subsequent tightly choreographed parody of the ideal family which is immediately followed by the heavy heart of the play: the relentless sequence from soccer and picnic in the park to the father's flirt, the abuse of his wife when he catches her drinking coffee with a neighbour, Perla's confession about the incest, the father's arrest, and the gossips in church blaming Josefina for having broken the sacred vow of marriage. Susie, Blanca, and Sonia perform remarkably strong in this difficult scene. Their emotions radiate out into the auditorium, but they are clearly acting now and not merely reliving their pain.

After the father's arrest, the play moves again to a lighter, surreal plane with two colourful fairy tale dances, one of a broken heart killed by a snake transforming into a butterfly and the other of a curious butterfly who flies too close to the sun and dies. From there, the play shifts back to the realism of Daniel's and Maryem's family. Daniel's mom, convincingly performed by Maria, first flies into a rage when she discovers her son has bought gangster pants with money for a haircut before she gives a piece of her mind to her unemployed husband, played hilariously undercooled by Carmen. The next scene, performed in half-masks, is the flashback to the husband's childhood in Guatemala, in which we learn he was forced to drop out of school because his father needed his help to till the land. Then we get the robbery of Alpha's convenience store by Gus and Daniel, who expertly mime driving a car on their way to a party. They are musically supported by Michael and Lorenzo, who fill in the gaps when scene changes are too slow and, at one point, even act out a confrontation with the teenage gangsters. Teresa effectively facilitates the scene transitions as a cheerful fairy godmother, but although her recurring confrontations with the *Nahual* are comical, some of her more rapidly pronounced speeches are lost on the audience. Once Gus is in jail for his armed robbery at stage right and Pedro/Sonia for incest at stage left, Teresa announces that the next scene will delve into the father's past. It turns out Pedro was severely abused by his own father. In Javier's interpretation he becomes an uncompromising evangelist who burns his son's foot soles whenever he finds him too insolent. Both the flashbacks thus indicate that abuse is often carried on from one generation to the next. Openness about dark family secrets and acceptance of pain as the inevitable price of happiness are also the final message Susie delivers in the delightful fairy tale scene that concludes the play. She plays a girl who carries her heart in a bucket because she does not want to feel life's pain. But when the king steals her heart, because, he argues, she is not using it anyway, she realizes she cannot do without, even though it is filled with pain. Regaining her strength, she confidently demands her heart back, sticks it on her chest, separates the quibbling *Nahual* and fairy godmother – who symbolize her inner struggle – and, screaming '¡saquen la sopa, ya!' throws open the two doors at either side of the stage, as the curtain comes down.

The Saturday afternoon show is weaker, possibly because the thrill of the first night is gone, the sky is grey, and the outdoor setting without stage lighting is less inspiring. But, in contrast, the audience of about 80 is more appreciative than the seemingly more introverted spectators of the night before. Upon Sally's invitation, on Saturday quite a number of people provide spontaneous and sometimes emotional feedback to the actors, some of whom have obviously gained so much self-confidence from the experience that they respond as if they speak in public everyday. Before they all sit down to a meal prepared by Hathaway volunteers, Sally huddles one last time with her cast. She has reserved a positive remark for each one of the actors. In response, Blanca is obviously glad it is all over, but acknowledges the support she has felt all along from everyone in the group: 'Never did I think I would be capable of doing a job like this, acting situations from my real life. I realize that it doesn't hurt me as much anymore, that I can overcome it, and that I can give a message back to my community. I can tell them, "if Josefina is recuperating, why not other people as well?" And that makes me feel good.'

In retrospect, Sally is pleased with the play they created and the way the two generations worked together. But if she had had three months instead of one, the participants would have been given more creative input and would have directed themselves more. The musicians were the glue of the performance; with more time, she would have liked to involve them more in the dramatic action of the play. And she would have tagged on a forum component, dressing up a spectator and, after coaching him or her for a few minutes, put them on stage in order to try and change some of the characters' lines and actions. But given the unpredictability of that kind of intervention, she would have needed more time to practise with her actors. Yet, the basic approach remains similar in all community theatre processes, she argues, no matter what the duration: 'I start with release exercises that warm up and stretch people's imaginations and develop bodies and minds as creative tools. Very early on the group determines the theme, which provides the guiding principle for the rest of the work. All the improvisational exercises, even the games, are inspired by this theme.

> Abstract fantasy exploration exercises further develop the
> creative imagination and the physical freedom needed to do
> character work and invent spontaneous dialogues with
> another actor. Fixed texts are useless. If you give people
> scripts it becomes really phoney and loses that natural spon-
> taneous quality. I must also point out that I would be much
> more gentle with first-timers than I was with this group, many
> of whom I had been working with for two years or more in
> "Life Scripts" and other community theatre projects. I knew I
> could do more abstract stuff with them and push them to a
> higher level.'

Aftermath

Immediately after the project's conclusion, Sally expressed concern that
some participants might fall into a vacuum after the intensely positive
experience of the *Sopa* project, which is indeed what happened to
Blanca. For a while, Susie did much better at school, but found out in
October that she was pregnant. She eventually gave birth to a little boy
in May 1998. Despite all this, she remained determined to finish high
school and go on to college. Her premature motherhood constituted a
sobering reminder of the limited power of community theatre to fundamentally change people's lives and social conditions.

On 11 September part of the group staged a 15-minute version of
¡Saquen la sopa ya! for more than 200 social workers and board members
of non-profit organizations dealing with youth at the community level.
They did most of Act II, which centres around Daniel's gang-banging
troubles rather than on the incest. Because the cast was excited about
performing for a large crowd and because of the time pressure, Sally was
able to tighten the play and to rehearse with concentration and discipline. As a result, their presentation looked very professional and was a
huge success in spite of the fact that most people in the audience could
not speak Spanish.

Sally tried to keep the *Sopa* cast together by organizing occasional
reunions before Christmas. They did a final performance of the play in
February 1998 and then most of the participants joined the cast for
Sally's next large-scale community theatre project, based on the Egyptian
'Isis and Osiris' myth. Maryem, Daniel and Gus as well as several other

teenagers from Fanklin High played major roles in this new play. Teresa, Sonia and Blanca also acted in it and at some point even Susie considered playing a mother with an infant. Although Alpha and Carmen eventually withdrew, Blanca's youngest daughter, Karla, danced as Spirit of the Nile River in a choreography of her own creation.

Sally Gordon's community theatre method gets deep under the participants' skin and consequently requires a great deal of trust, guts, energy, and determination on the part of both the facilitating artist and the group. Gordon's techniques, a mix of Alexander, Boal, Barker and other theatre educators, are undoubtedly effective, not least because of the integrity, commitment and sensitivity with which she implements them. At the same time, she demands a lot from herself, from the groups she works with, and from the organizations she works for. As a result, Sally Gordon, whose admirable reluctance to compromise is both her strength and her weakness, gets frequently frustrated when others do not meet her high standards. Such disappointments come with the difficult territory she has chosen to work in and the formidable challenge she has set herself to create a participatory and visually striking theatre that both satisfies her own artistic yearnings and allows the people she works with to speak their minds.

Notes

1 Personal interview with Susan Suntree, Los Angeles, 10 June 1997.
2 Howard Ahmanson made a fortune as a Savings and Loans banker, Dorothy Chandler was the wife of the LA *Times* publisher, and Mark Taper a major real estate developer.
3 The term 'equity waiver' refers to the practice of these small theatres to pay less than union scale wages to their actors.
4 Personal interview with Jay MacAdams, Los Angeles, 3 June 1997.
5 Personal interview with Hector Aristizabel, Pasadena, 1 June 1997.
6 Firebird was an officially registered non-profit organization with a Board of Directors. Teatro de la Realidad exists in name only and is not a legal entity. Sally Gordon applies for project grants as an individual and now through the Hathaway Family Resource Center.
7 Personal interview with Robert Alexander, San Diego, 9 June 1997. Unless otherwise indicated, all subsequent quotations from Alexander come from this interview
8 E-mail from Sally Gordon to the author, 4 December 1998.
9 Continuation high schools are specialized small schools that try to keep potential drop-outs and delinquents in school.
10 E-mail from Sally Gordon to the author, 21 January 1999.
11 Personal interview with Anthony Cyriak, Watts, 16 June 1997.
12 Personal interview with Sally Gordon, Highland Park, 15 June 1997.
13 Personal letter to the author, 13 August 1996.

14 Personal interview with Pat Bowie, Highland Park, 6 June 1997. Before joining the Hathaway organization, Bowie worked as a Peace Corps volunteer in Brazil and Paraguay, where she saw the beneficial effects of community arts for social change.

15 Since then, Teresa Ramos has become a full-time member of the Hathaway staff. In the *promotoras* program, women are trained as lay community health workers and, in turn, train others. The *promotoras* conduct neighbourhood health awareness promotion with Hathaway paying them a stipend for each presentation, which are usually held in their own homes. *Promotoras* inform people about health care, safety issues for children, birth control, drugs, and sexuality, issues that are otherwise difficult to talk about in the Latino community.

16 Personal letter, 14 October 1997.

17 I have seen variations of this game in the Philippines under the name 'Form a Line According to . . .'. See also 'Fruit Bowl' in Christine Poulter's *Playing the Game* (1991).

18 Gordon adapted this exercise from 'Up, down' (Sher and Verrall 1992).

19 Translated from the Spanish. Personal audio recording, Highland Park, 23 May 1997. Unless stated otherwise, all other remarks by project participants come from this source.

20 This is an art therapy exercise that Gordon adapted from Marion Liebmann.

21 Adapted from Clive Barker's *Theatre Games* (1977).

Bibliography

Acuña, Rodolfo (1986) *Occupied America*, New York: HarperCollins.

Alexander, Robert (1983) *Improvisational Theatre for the Classroom*, Washington, DC: The Living Stage Theatre Company.

—— (1994) *Healing Our Society Through Creativity: Understanding Your Birthright as an Artist*, Washington, DC: Living Stage Theatre Company.

Anzaldúa, Gloria (1987) *Borderlands/La Frontera*, San Francisco: Spinsters/Aunt Lute Press.

Barker, Clive (1977) *Theatre Games*, New York: Drama Book Specialists.

Boal, Augusto (1992) *Games for Actors and Non-Actors*, London: Routledge.

Bouknight, Jon (1990) 'Language as a Cure: An Interview with Milcha Sanchez-Scott', *Latin American Theatre Review* (Spring): 63–74.

Broyles-González, Yolanda (1994) *El Teatro Campesino: Theatre in the Chicano Movement*, Austin, TX: University of Texas Press.

Butler, Robert (1963) 'The Life Review: An Interpretation of Reminiscence in the Aged', *Psychiatry* 20: 65–76.

Chávez, Denise and Feyder, Linda (eds) (1992) *Shattering the Myth: Plays by Hispanic Women*, Houston: Arte Público Press.

Davis, Mike (1992) *City of Quartz: Excavating the Future in Los Angeles*, New York: Vintage.

Dear, Michael J., Schockman, H. Eric and Hise, Greg (eds) (1996) *Rethinking Los Angeles*, Thousand Oaks, CA: Sage Publications.

Erven, Eugene van (1996) 'When Sally Met José: Chicano Theatre in LA from Grassroots to Mainstream', *New Theatre Quarterly* 12, 48 (November): 356–367.

Gordon, Sally (1994) 'The Use of Theatre as Social Therapy in Three Community Settings: Los Angeles, 1985–1995', unpublished MA thesis, California State University at Los Angeles.

Huerta, Jorge (1983) *Chicano Theater: Themes and Forms*, Ypsilanti, MI: Bilingual Press.

—— (1994) 'Looking for the Magic: Chicanos in the Mainstream', in Diana Taylor and Juan Villegas (eds) *Negotiating Performance: Gender, Sexuality, and Theatricality in Latin/o America*, Durham, NC: Duke University Press.

Kanéllos, Nicolás (1990) *A History of Hispanic Theatre in the United States: Origins to 1940*, Austin, TX: University of Texas Press.

—— (1992) 'Hispanic Theatre in the United States: Post-War to the Present', *Latin American Theatre Review* (Spring): 197–209.

Kuftinec, Sonja (1996) 'A Cornerstone for Rethinking Community Theatre', *Theatre Topics* 6, 1(March): 91–104.

Landy, Robert J. (1986) *Drama Therapy: Concepts and Practices*, Springfield, ILL.: Charles C. Thomas Publisher.

Liebmann, Marion (1986) *Art Therapy for Groups: A Handbook of Themes, Games and Exercises*, Cambridge, MA: Brookline Books.

Martínez, Rubén (1993) *The Other Side: Notes from the New LA, Mexico City, and Beyond*, New York: Vintage.

Moraga, Cherrie (1983) *Loving In the War Years: lo que nunca pasó por sus labios*, Boston: South End Press.

—— (1986) *Giving Up the Ghost*, Los Angeles: West End Press.

Moreno, Jacob (1944) *Sociodrama as a Method for the Analysis of Social Conflicts*, Boston: Beacon House.

Osborn, M. Elizabeth (ed.) (1987) *On New Ground: Contemporary Hispanic American Plays*, New York: Theatre Communications Group.

Pearlstone, Zena (1990) *Ethnic LA*, Los Angeles: Hillcrest Press.

Perlstein, Susan (1981) *A Stage for Memory: Life History Plays for Older Adults*, New York: Teachers and Writers.

Poulter, Christine (1991) *Playing the Game*, Studio City, CA: Players Press.

Rivera, Tomás (1987) *. . . y no se lo tragó la tierra/. . . And the Earth Did Not Devour Him*, Houston: Arte Público Press.

Romo, Ricardo (1983) *History of a Barrio: East Los Angeles*, Austin, TX: University of Texas Press.

Sanchez-Scott, Milcha (1988) *Roosters*, New York: Dramatists Play Service, Inc.

Sher, Anna and Verrall, Charles (1992) *200+ Ideas for Drama*, Portsmouth, NH: Heinemann.

Soja, Edward W. (1989) *Postmodern Geographies*, London: Verso.

—— (1996) *Thirdspace: Journeys to Los Angeles and Other Real and Imagined Places*, Oxford and Cambridge, MA: Blackwell.

Sonenshein, Raphael J. (1993) *Politics in Black and White*, Princeton, NJ: Princeton University Press.

Spolin, Viola (1987) *Improvization for the Theatre*, Evanston, ILL: Northwestern University Press.

Torre, Adela de la and Pesquera, Beatríz M. (eds) (1993) *Building With Our Hands: New Directions in Chicana Studies*, Berkeley, CA: University of California Press.

Valdez, Luís (1990) *Early Works: Actos, Bernabé, Pensamiento Serpentino*, Houston, TX: Arte Público Presss.

—— (1992) *Zoot Suit and Other Plays*, Houston, TX: Arte Público Press.

Internet connections

Hathaway Family Resource Center e-mail: hfrc2@earthlink.net

Theatre Network Magazine:
<http:/www.interlog.com/~artbiz/>

L.A. On Stage:
<http://www.laonstage.com/>

Sally Gordon e-mail: sallyfbtc@aol.com

Chapter 4

Collective creation in Costa Rican community theatre

The Miami to San José flight felt like a celestial bull fight with countless July thunderstorms rumbling over the Isthmus, which our small jet was trying deftly to avoid. Finally, the confrontation could be postponed no longer: we dived straight through the thick black cloud cover over Costa Rica's Central Valley, the 1,200-metre high plateau in the middle of the country where the majority of its 3.5 million people reside. At the airport, we were greeted by Vicky Montero, a respected stage actress and cultural events organizer working for the Ministry of Culture, Youth and Sports. She drove us down to Puntarenas, the country's third largest city and once the country's proud port on the Pacific coast, where some three hours later we checked into a two-bedroom apartment with bunk beds: our home for the next four weeks. We would share it with cameraman Joaquin Salazar and sound recordist Francisco Esquivel Rodriguez, both employees of public television Channel 13. Many an evening, seated on the balcony, we would talk with them about Costa Rican culture, politics, and, of course, soccer against a dazzling backdrop of thunderbolts and lightning out over the Pacific. Never mind that the beach below us was littered with garbage, turds, and tree trunks, and that the region was suffering from a major dengue epidemic.

I had been to Costa Rica once before, travelling by Tica bus up from Panama City in December 1979 for a backpacker's holiday in the as yet hardly discovered coastal national park of

Manuel Antonio near Quepos. These were the golden years of Costa Rica, then a relatively stable investors' haven in an otherwise war-torn Central America. The following summer, my political innocence would gradually dissipate during a three-month trek through South America that took me from Colombia via Ecuador to Peru (where the Maoist 'Shining Path' guerrillas had just made its first violent assaults), Bolivia (where I was an unintentional witness to Hugo Banzer's coup), and via Argentina by train across the Andes to Pinochet's Chile. The journey opened my eyes to Latin American injustices behind the seductive picture postcard vistas. It also further kindled my interest in political theatre. Upon my return to graduate school, I began researching French and British radical people's theatre and started performing in campus productions of French popular theatre shows directed by Professor Dan Church. In 1984, when I was heavily into Dario Fo and had already met Teatro Campesino, the San Francisco Mime Troupe, and the Bread and Puppet Theatre, I played the title role in 'The Man who Became a Dog', one of Osvaldo Dragún's *Historias para ser contadas* ('Stories for Telling') in a Spanish-language production directed by the late Chilean poet Ricardo Yamal and a cast of Latin American expats. Fourteen years later, I was to find out that an Argentinian touring production of Dragún's legendary play arguably started professional theatre in Costa Rica and also laid the inspirational basis for its community theatre.

Alfredo Catania (b. 1934), an expatriate Argentinian director of television drama for Channel 13 and a former director of Costa Rica's National Theatre Company, had been part of the groundbreaking *Historias para ser contadas* tour of 'El Teatro de los 21' in 1961, the first time an independent theatre company had travelled all the way from Argentina to Mexico. Because a comprehensive, scholarly theatre history of Costa Rica does not exist, I have had to rely on oral histories such as Catania's, which suggest intracontinental connections.

Catania received his first theatre training from Frenchman Oscar Fessler[1] at the Santa Fe School of Theatre and, later, studied directing at the Buenos Aires National Academy of Arts. In the 1950s, he worked with 'Fray Mocho', the legendary independent theatre company that had mounted Osvaldo Dragún's first works back in 1957. Dragún's drama, a mix of absurdist and Brechtian styles, was a typical exponent of the progressive decade in Argentinian art that ended abruptly with General Onganía's *coup d'état* of June 1966 (Munck 1987: 160; Norden 1996: 38–39). Catania also worked for several years as a cultural animateur for the Directorate General of Culture, promoting community film, dance, music, and theatre in and around Santa Fe province. In the early 1960s, all these community and independent avant garde theatre activities were brought together under the umbrella of the Argentinian Federation of Independent Theatres (FATI). According to Catania, many companies practised a collective creation method that they had spontaneously stumbled on. He claims they only found out about Boal, García and Buenaventura much later at international conferences:

> We had a very free, open methodology. The themes emerged from the groups, which included doctors, lawyers, farmworkers, and students, all with their own concerns. The text was written on the basis of notes taken during improvisations we did after our field research. They dealt with lack of water or lack of food in certain areas. People were just following their instincts and their creativity.[2]

However, little of the work that Catania refers to has been properly documented and hence the dynamics of these pioneering community theatre encounters and the kinds of performances they yielded are now difficult to reconstruct. The 1961 *Historias para ser contadas* tour, nevertheless, suggests that numerous popular theatre initiatives were sprouting independently all over Latin America, for which some scholars have pointed to Bertolt Brecht's plays and theories as significant sources of inspiration (Riszk 1980: 132–133; Weiss *et al.* 1993: 152).

Before embarking on their groundbreaking journey, 'El Teatro de los 21' had corresponded with artist friends in Chile, Peru, Honduras and Nicaragua. 'But,' Catania insists, 'it was not as if we were booked by some theatre agency before we went to a particular country':

> We just went into university campuses to conduct workshops, like, for instance, the University of Guatemala City and the University of Léon in Mexico, places where we encountered like-minded people who had just begun to make theatre in Central America. We wanted to make community theatre with a social and didactic purpose. You

must also remember that this was a very romantic era. Fidel Castro had just formed his government and a compatriot of ours, Che Guevara, had joined him and would later return to Bolivia. There was, to put it mildly, a politically charged atmosphere all across the continent, prompted by disenchantment with the authoritarian rightwing forces on the one hand and a romantic attraction to collective action on the other. All this caused us to be people's theatre artists. We couldn't simply be actors, or, for that matter, even distinguish between our acting and theatre outreach. It was an integrated, constant state of being both.

South American exiles in Costa Rica's theatre

Although Catania had met some Costa Rican actors in Mexico during the 1961 tour, he never visited the country until 1967, when the Argentinan embassy in San José contracted him, his then wife Gladys, and his brother Carlos to conduct a four-month acting course in the second half of 1967. This initiative, inexplicably sponsored by a now supposedly repressive Argentine government (Munck 1987: 202; Norden 1996: 58–77), led to the establishment of Costa Rica's first official theatre school. It would first resort under the Ministry of Education and later under the Ministry of Culture, Youth and Sport, which was established in 1971 (Solís 1991–1992: 76; Herzfeld and Cajiao Salas 1971b: 29).[3] The increasing political repression in Argentina, meanwhile, prompted Carlos, Gladys and Alfredo to take up permanent residence in Costa Rica, first working for the new theatre school and later joining forces with Daniel Gallegos in a newly formed Department of Dramatic Art at the University of Costa Rica, the country's oldest tertiary institution, founded in 1940.

In *Traspatio Florecido* ('Flowering Crossroads'), one of the few comparative cultural studies anlyses to have come out of Central America to date, Rafael Cuevas Molina refers to the 1970s as the '*años dorados*', 'the golden years' during which Costa Rica's social democratic regime pumped relatively large sums of government funding into educational and cultural development projects (1993: 128–129). Historian and politician Vladimir de la Cruz argues that this openness to grass roots cultural action was a consequence of a strong leftist popular front, which had been gaining ground in Costa Rica after the victory of the Cuban Revolution: 'It stimulated political forces in this country and continued to develop until 1970, when the student movement got underway in a big way, as did new anti-imperialist movements, which combined to build a strong leftist block in this country.'[4] It seems likely, then, that South American ideas about promoting cultural democracy through collectively oriented grass roots theatre workshops fell into fertile soil among the first generation of students in Costa Rica's new university theatre departments.

Theatre history

Although the country had had an architecturally attractive National Theatre building in the centre of San José since 1897, it only really had one stable company, 'Teatro Arlequin', which produced a predominantly western repertoire for the San José elite (Herzfeld and Cajiao Salas 1971b: 27–28). Under Italian artistic director Luccio Ranucci, it had evolved in 1955 from a student theatre group at the University of Costa Rica and counted such later Ministers of Culture as Alberto Cañas and Guido Sainz among its actors (Solís 1991–1992: 74). They had the luxury of rehearsing four months for a mere two annual performances. Recognizing the social and artistic limitations of this approach, the Catanias therefore convinced Arlequin to sponsor a nationwide country and city tour of Dragún's *Historias* (ibid.: 77).

In 1970, 'Arlequin' actor-playwright Alberto Cañas was appointed as Costa Rica's first Minister of Culture. One of his first acts was to sponsor a provincial tour of classical Spanish pieces performed by a newly established National Theatre Ensemble. In 1974, Alfredo Catania, who had directed the University Theatre until then, succeeded Barcelona native Esteban Polls as Artistic Director of this company. He continued the policy of taking theatre to communities outside the capital. In 1975, one of his main projects was a touring production of *La Familia Mora*, a play about a conflict between landless families and big landlords written in 1974 by Costa Rican Olga Marta Barrantes. It was performed in 35 rural communities and attracted close to 15,000 spectators, many of whom were exposed to theatre for the first time (Perri 1975: 54).

In the mid-1970s, Catania formed two separate ensembles within the National Theatre Company: one composed of young actors was called 'Chayotera' (after a typical Costa Rican fruit), working mostly in the region; the other was a repertory company performing in the National Theatre, but which also conducted workshops in the big factories of San José. At the end of each year, both the repertory and 'Chayotera' got together for a joint production in the National Theatre. In this same period, one of the most renowned Chilean theatre companies, 'El Teatro del Angel', arrived in San José in exile. For more than a decade, this company, built around playwright Alejandro Sieveking and actress Bélgica Castro, would provide Costa Rican theatre with high quality professional impulses (Thomas 1986; Weiss *et al.* 1993: 158).[5]

In 1976, the cultural extension programme of the National Theatre Company was complemented by the outreach work of the newly formed National Theatre Workshop, the 'Taller Nacional de Teatro' (TNT). Under the initial direction of Catania's former mentor, French *action culturelle* veteran Oscar Fessler, the TNT's main objective was to train professional theatre artists in establishing sustainable community theatre groups. Fessler's emphasis was on process instead of production: 'the fundamental aim is . . . the cultural growth of the participants by liberating their means of expression, developing their capacity to observe and imagine, and finetuning their sensibilities and critical faculties' (Prado 1979: 13).

Luís Fernando Gomez, who was TNT's director in 1997, started his career as a 'Chayotera' cultural worker in the mid-1970s. Although it is unclear whether Gomez was indeed the first artist to go to Puntarenas to facilitate the workshops that led to the foundation of 'Aguamarina' in 1972, Catania remembers him going down there to train young community actors for the remainder of the decade:

> Like other 'Chayotera' *promotores* , he serviced two communities: one day a week he went to Puntarenas and the other day to Esparza, teaching acting, directing productions, and guiding the local groups through collective creation processes. Although he had read Boal and Garcia, whose books we had here at the National Theatre, we hadn't taught him a fixed methodology. We had prepared our *promotores* through seminars with sociologists and anthropologists and we had worked on group dynamics, theatre games, and improvisations. The *promotor* would start by asking questions about life in Puntarenas, the fishing industry, local factories, the concerns of the community. From improvisations they would slowly work towards a text, finally coming up with a performance, which would then be tried out and changed on the basis of audience reactions.

This same approach is still detectable in Aguamarina's work today and is not all that different from collective creation practices elsewhere in the region.

The Latin American collective creation tradition

On 26 July 1980, Magda Zavala, today regarded as one of Costa Rica's foremost feminist cultural commentators, interviewed Santiago García, who had founded theatre collective 'La Candalaria' in Bogotá in 1957. The publication of Zavala's interview in the influential theatre magazine *Escena* and the simultaneous tent theatre tour through Costa Rica of a 'Candalaria' performance constituted the country's first direct exposure to collective creation, which by then had become widely regarded as the engine behind the influential 'new' popular theatre movements of Colombia and Cuba. Less widely perhaps but no less significantly, collective creation was also being practised in Peru, Venezuela, Brazil, Ecuador, and Mexico.[6] Closer to Costa Rica, collective creation had also been nourishing the Sandinista revolution and was soon to become the major stimulus for a nationwide grass-roots arts and literacy campaign in Nicaragua (Klünder 1997: 22–26; Soto Larios 1998: 1–8).

Collective creation cannot be reduced to a single formula. As they should, most theatre groups who practise it have developed idiosyncratic techniques to suit their own specific and ever-changing sociocultural circumstances. Yet, García argues, there are some common elements such as music, carefully researched themes that correspond to the interests and the cultures of the people they perform for, simple but flexible production techniques that can be adapted to all kinds of indoor and outdoor venues, and lengthy creative development processes (Zavala 1980: 16). Both García and his colleague Enrique Buenaventura from Cáli's Experimental Theatre (TEC), further emphasize that collective creation is more than a playmaking method alone and requires a new kind of actor, one who is not someone's servile employee but, instead, a self-conscious socially responsible co-owner of the means of creative production (Buenaventura 1984: 17; Zavala 1980: 16).[7]

In the early 1970s, when 'La Candalaria' and TEC were exploring their own ways of collective playmaking, groups elsewhere in Latin America began to work in similar ways. For example, in 1968 professional actors from Havana had gone to work in the rural community of Escambray to create plays with local residents (Séjourné 1977). Also, throughout the 1970s and 1980s, ideas and methods pertaining to collective creation were being disseminated by the widely read Cuban theatre magazine *Conjunto*, edited by Guatemalan exile Manuel Galich. Many practitioners compared notes at the increasingly influential International Theatre Festival of Manizales in Colombia, which had started as a modest university theatre festival in 1968. Finally, numerous tours, workshops, and the exile of such seminal groups as 'El Galpón' from Uruguay and 'Libre Teatro Libre' from Argentina complemented an ongoing process of artistic cross-fertilization, which Cubans but above all Colombians such as Carlos Reyes, Buenaventura, and García dominated in terms of theorizing.

Many theoretical writings on collective creation are explicitly Marxist in orientation and unfortunately as verbose and schematic as the creative processes themselves are laborious. Furthermore, most groups that practised collective creation were composed of full-time, professionally trained artists. As such, their practice, status, and spirit were closer to radical people's theatre troupes in the vein of the San Francisco Mime Troupe than to community theatre. Rather than people's stories dramatized and performed by community residents themselves, most of their productions were either radically reconstructed existing scripts, or the original result of elaborately processed historical or political themes they themselves, as outsiders, thought were relevant to their popular audiences. More interesting for our purposes were the offshoots, the community theatre groups that sprang up spontaneously and concocted their own versions of the collective creation process to dramatize their local stories.

Hector Aristizabel, a Colombian community theatre artist now working in Los Angeles, used to be a member of professional theatre collective 'La Mojiganga' of Medellín in the 1980s.

We started from the idea that an actor is an intellectual, a person who studies literature, sociology, anthropology, psychology, which is something that doesn't exist here in the States. We specialized in traditional peasant theatre with masks, music, and a lot of acrobatics. We worked six hours a day for a year, sometimes two, to create a play. When we were sick of it, it was ready for performance. We used to do dialectical analyses of each single phrase in a text to get to its political subtext, but it became way too tedious.[8]

Márceles Daconte's account of the 'Candalaria' process indicates that *creación colectiva* is, in fact, much more methodical than either García or Buenaventura care to admit. First of all, Márceles Daconte dismisses the idea that collective creation never works with individual authors or identifiable directors. The difference is that an author working in collective creation should be prepared to collaborate with actor-members of a text committee and the director should work on an egalitarian, non-authoritarian basis with the other artists. A collective creation process always begins by establishing a general theme or selecting a pre-existing text, which are then extensively researched, discussed and analysed, if necessary with the help of outside resource persons such as specialized scholars and union organizers.

A typical feature of Colombian-style collective creation is the meticulous structural analysis that is applied to stories that have either been collected in the field or found in existing literature. All the major and minor conflicts are distilled from a particular tale and are then chronologically and causally arranged into a schematic order from which a central conflict is extracted.[9] Characters are subsequently placed into this scheme on the basis of the conflicting forces they represent and the contradictory motivations that propel their actions. The sum total of all actions, in turn, constitute a dramatic situation. This skeleton conflict provides the basis for a long period of improvisations in the second phase of the collective creation process. These improvisations can be verbal or non-verbal but in any case always distance themselves from the original plot through analogies invented by the actors.

During the second phase, the ensemble is divided in two groups, with half of the actors serving as critics of the improvisers exploring the dramatic conflicts and vice versa. This is the most dialectical part of the process, explains Márceles Daconte: 'One criticizes (the improvisation) for its formal and thematic aspects; that is, for its artistic effectiveness as well as its ideological impact' (1977: 95). The strongest scenes from this elaborate process eventually become the basis for a performance that is mounted in the third phase. For this purpose, the group splits up into different subcommittees specializing in either script writing, design, or music. As Márceles Daconte notes, these specialty teams are composed more on the basis of individual talents and skills than on egalitarian principles (ibid.: 96). The different components are then aesthetically polished by the subgroups and finally integrated and placed into a continuous scenario under the artistic supervision of the director. After this intensive rehearsal process, the show is ready for performance, evolving all the time by continuingly processing audience input.

Gerardo Bejerano, who now teaches acting at Costa Rica's National University in Heredia, remembers his fascination with Latin American collective creation techniques when, as a theatre student, he began to do community outreach for the National Theatre Company. He particularly recalls the inspiration of exiled collectives such as 'El Galpón' from Montevideo, who worked in San José for a while: 'We didn't study their methods as such, but we did try to distill a kind of creative grammar and work collectively. That definitely also became part of the method used by Aguamarina, although I don't know how much they knew about the origins of collective creation outside of our country.'[10]

Grupo de Teatro Independiente 'Aguamarina'

Danilo Montoya (b. 1957), remembers how an outreach workshop organized by a *promotor* from the Taller Nacional de Teatro inspired him and several other students from the José Martí high school in Puntarenas to found Aguamarina in 1972. Their first collectively created performance took place in the Ateneo Puntarenense on 4 October 1973:

> Twenty people came to see our show, which was called *Actualidad* ('Current Affair'), and which we had created collectively. It was about politicians who never deliver on their promises. Until that moment, there had never really been a theatre company in Puntarenas, let alone one that denounces politics. Some politicians felt threatened; others, from the left, wanted to send us into the communities to win votes for them. But we wanted to have the freedom to denounce what we thought was wrong without being dictated what we could and could not criticize.[11]

With the basic techniques they had learned from *promotor* Fernando Gomez, the young Aguamarina actors began evolving their own creative method. According to Montoya:

> One of us suggested we create a play about deforestation. He then began improvising a tree who feels the pain of being cut down, while someone else played the rain. Some things didn't work; we threw those out. But that's basically how our system works. Later, we added the research bit and divided the work. One of us researched the government's responsibility for deforestation, how many acres were affected; others went in other directions, and then we would get

back together again to report, discuss, and decide what elements to explore further in our play. Improvisation was the basis of everything.

After 1973, the National Theatre Company sent another theatre worker to Puntarenas, who saw Aguamarina's second show, *Tarde comprehensión* ('Belated Understanding'), and found it too long and repetitive. He taught the young actors not to overburden their scenes with information and, generally, helped them to direct more effectively. Aguamarina then entered *Tarde comprehensión* for Costa Rica's first government-sponsored national community theatre festival in San José. The play, which criticizes the church and the middle and upper classes for ignoring the poor through the story of a young kid looking for his estranged father and his drug-addicted brother, impressed Catania, who therefore continued to send *promotores* to Aguamarina. In 1976, he also invited Danilo Montoya, along with community actors from other regions, to come work at the Taller Nacional with Oscar Fessler, who taught them advanced improvisation techniques. When he returned to Puntarenas Montoya applied what he had learned in the collective creation of a new work: *Puerto 7020*, which was about how people from all walks of life pass the buck and refuse to take responsibility for social problems. The fisherman, the dock worker, the grass-smoking unemployed youth, the physical education teacher, the prostitute, and the priest all conveniently designate society at large as the guilty party. Aguamarina, which performed the irresponsible characters as marionettes, entered the play in the 1977 national community theatre festival, this time winning first prize. 'That play caused us considerable trouble locally,' remembers Montoya:

> A phys ed teacher got mad at us because he thought we had satirized him. Then the press jumped on us as well, creating a stir, but it also increased people's interest in our work. People in Puntarenas always complain that the national government never really cares about them. But we argued that we, *Porteños*, also let it happen to us. So we try to do something about it, challenge people to fight a bit more for their rights. And we're always open to people's input. A people's committee once came to us when we were mounting a play. They showed us slides and gave us information, which prompted us to change the play that very same evening.

Marvin Lara, Aguamarina's current artistic director, joined the group at the end of 1975, after first participating in an extracurricular theatre workshop at the high school he was then attending. After first observing the process leading to *Tarde comprehensión*, he was assigned to do the lights for *Puerto 7020*. The following year, 1978, Aguamarina composed a new comical show from left-over material of previous improvisations. Entitled *Así es la Cosa* ('That's the way it is'), it consisted of four 15-minute plays called *El Sueño de un Nica* ('Dream of a Nicaraguan'), *¿Porque será?* ('Why is it?'), *Superman* and *El Diablo de Dios* ('Devil of God'). *Así es la cosa* was performed more than 300 times up and down the Pacific coast. In 1979, Aguamarina created *El pescador* ('The Fisherman'), a play about the failed attempt to form a fishers' union, which won another national festival award (Montoya). The reconstructed collective creation process for this performance, in many ways typical for Aguamarina's grass-roots work, is documented in detail in the case study below. In 1980, Aguamarina helped students of the José Martí high school create a play adaptation of the novela *Vida y dolores de Juan Varela* ('The Life and Pains of Juan Varela'), written in 1939 by Costa Rican author Adolfo Herrera García (Ovares and Rojas 1995: 127–130). The production won the first prize at a national school theatre festival and, as an additional bonus, provided Aguamarina with several enthusiastic new young members.

From 1981 until 1983, Aguamarina created no new productions, preferring instead to develop the performance skills of their new recruits. In 1982, they entered another version of *Juan Varela* in a new community theatre event on the Caribbean coast, the *Palma de Oro* ('Golden Palm') Festival in Limón. After winning first prize, Aguamarina returned its cheque to the organizers, arguing that competitions for money only unnecessarily alienate the participating community theatre groups from each other. Ever since, the *Palma de Oro* budget has been spent on food, lodging and transportation, equally divided among the participants.

Performing in prisons

In 1983, Montoya received a grant to study for three months under Alejandro Sieveking of the exiled Chilean Teatro del Angel. When he returned to Puntarenas he found employment as a counsellor in San Lucas prison island. The deplorable conditions he found there, particularly for mental patients kept in the same cells as hardened criminals, inspired the next Aguamarina production, *Crónicas de un desajusto* ('Chronicles of the Maladjusted'). *Crónicas de un desajusto* is based on the cases of three individuals – Romulo, Tricky and Jova – who were actual detainees at San Lucas. During the research process, which lasted several months, the actors looked for commonalities in the interviews they held with prisoners and the archival material they had managed to lay their hands on. They then created composite characters from elements they had found in this material. Tricky is a petty criminal who has become so used to life in prison that he can no longer live outside. Jova, the mentally ill character, is released but does not want to leave Tricky, who, ironically, is the only person to have ever shown him genuine affection. Romulo, who shares a cell with the other two, has raped his own daughter and Tricky puts such a guilt trip on him that he ends up hanging himself, a gruesome ending that attracts a fictional television news crew to denounce the prison conditions. Danilo and Marvin, who returned to San Lucas to reconstruct several scenes of *Crónicas* for our video, told me that the actual performances before the prisoners were often tension-laden. As far as I could judge from their performance inside the cell, they must have been theatrically powerful, too, and may indeed have contributed to bringing about long overdue prison reforms for mentally ill inmates.

In the second half of the 1980s, Aguamarina began to lose steam. Membership had always fluctuated between ten and twenty. Whenever they had needed new members, Montoya and Lara would simply conduct a few workshops at a local high school and afterwards invited the most eager students to join them. Marvin Lara believes that all community theatre groups eventually experience recruitment problems: 'During membership dips we have to make a big effort to look for new people and remotivate the older ones. So, in 1986 the five remaining actors went to perform in Mazatlán, Mexico, to reinspire ourselves. But instead of returning stronger, one of us, Oliver, also left.'[12] And even Danilo Montoya, under increasing pressure from his family, was contemplating leaving.

In 1989, after Aguamarina returned from another trip to Mexico, Montoya's mother died and he decided to permanently withdraw from Aguamarina. With their founding director gone, some of the remaining Aguamarina members wanted the group to change direction and explore text-based theatre, but after one unsatisfying experiment, Marvin Lara, an adamant believer in collective creation, was elected as the group's new artistic director. His first project was a project on HIV/AIDS entitled *Sin Alternativa* ('No Choice'). It was a delicate process, he remembers, not only because of the theme but also because of the fragile group dynamics:

We began the work late in 1990 and wanted to premiere it at the next *Palma de Oro* Festival in Limón in September 1991. But the subject was complicated and we had to do a lot of research. We also needed to recruit and train a lot of new members. It was my first serious work as director, so I felt quite a bit of pressure. I had directed shows before, but these had only been small outreach workshop showcases. Now I felt pressure from Danilo and from Jimmy Castro, who had wanted to take the group in the direction of more conventional text-based theatre. When they left Aguamarina, they argued that the group had completed its cycle and would be better left to die. But I disagreed and wanted to continue. So I struggled with that until the first performance in Limón. It was really a special occasion, and Jimmy and Danilo made the effort to come all the way out to the Caribbean coast to support me.

After the festival in Limón, Aguamarina continued performing the strongly didactic *Sin Alternativa* in San José, Monteverde, in the islands in the Gulf of Nicoya, in Cartago, in Alajuela, and all over Puntarenas. But their stay in Limón had also given them an idea for a new project. Close to where they had been staying, a girl had hanged herself from a tree. When they returned to Puntarenas, they began researching documented cases of suicides and mental disease. They called the resulting play *Pídele al tiempo que vuelva* ('Ask Time to Turn Back'), a surrealistic play about a man who is under so much pressure from his family, his work, and financial contraints that he decides to commit suicide. But his soul remains alive, capable of hearing the commentaries of his family and colleagues, who eventually convince him he has made a mistake.

In 1993, Marvin Lara somewhat surprisingly agreed to direct *Hágase la mujer* ('And the Woman Was Created'), an existing comedy written by Juan Carlos Campos from the Dominican Republic. 'We found the subject important and the script more powerful than we could ever create it,' he explains his choice to work on a text-based project. Indeed, judging by the unpublished script Lara gave me, the play is a delightful comedy featuring an outspokenly feminist Eve who does not put up with Adam (and God's) machismo and walks out on Paradise. Left alone, Adam then realizes that the conservatively ruled Paradise is not such a pleasant place after all and walks out on a baffled God as well. Thinking about it, even God has to agree with them and abandons the place, vacating it for Lucifer, who now pretends to be God. As the play closes, Lucifer is overheard sugarcoating the preceding paradisical revolt by retelling it as an allegorical story of an apple and a snake. Aguamarina's new interest in supplementing its collective creations with productions of relevant high quality scripts written by lesser known Latin-Caribbean writers was further confirmed in 1994–1995, when they produced the Dominican political satire *Se Busca un hombre honesto* ('Wanted: An Honest Man').

In March 1996 Aguamarina returned to collective creation with *Leyendas y Tradiciones Costarricenses* ('Costa Rican Legends and Traditions'), a project with which the three remaining core members, Marvin Lara, Gerardo Arias, and Eduardo Martinez wanted to train a promising batch of newcomers: two housewives, an electrician, and four high school students. They performed the resulting play, which contained such spectacular features as stilt-walking and fireworks, at Aguamarina's 25th anniversary, which coincided with the seventh edition of Aguamarina's own *Chucheca de Oro* community theatre festival, held in and around the Puntarenas municipal cultural center from 11 through 13 July 1997.

The issue they wanted to bring across with *Leyendas*, according to Marvin Lara, was not to dismiss new technology or to stop people eating junk food:

> I eat hamburgers too, but I also enjoy eating *roscillas*, *canela*, and *gallo pinto*. We should not forget the good things of our heritage when we embrace the superficial cultural stuff imported from outside. We want people to see that we have a lot of valuable local stories as well as rich culinary and other cultural traditions. We wanted to reconstruct these and show them to the public.

The four legends Aguamarina decided to dramatize were *La Careta sin bueyes* ('The Oxcart Without Oxen'), a Costa Rican version of *La Llorona* ('The Weeping Mother'), *La Segua* ('The Horse-faced Woman'), and *La Tule Vieja* ('The Curious Spinster'). 'The Oxcart' is set during a cholera epidemic around the war of 1856 and features an agnostic farmer who refuses to lend his oxcart for a religious procession and is therefore cursed by the local priest. The oxen turn into birds and Pedro, the farmer, is doomed to spook around with his cart for eternity. *La Llorona*, a legend known throughout Central America, is about a pregnant woman who is abandoned by her lover, drops her newly born baby in a river, and then goes crazy. Her wailing can reportedly be heard by remote waterfalls. *La Segua* is about a seductive woman who flirts with a man and then transforms her face into that of a horse. *La Tule Vieja*, of which a scene is included in the accompanying video, is about an inquisitive woman who wants to know what dogs see when they howl at night. A quack, capitalizing on her gullibility, sells her a bottle that allegedly contain a pregnant dog's teardrops which she should put into her eyes at midnight during full moon. She follows his instructions and sees the ghosts of the deceased parade through the streets. She faints and is eventually carried away by stilt-walking candle-carrying souls of the deceased.

Aguamarina framed the four legends in a domestic situation set at the beginning of the twentieth century, when a father, Rosendo, sits down to tell stories after dinner. After he has narrated one about witches in straight story-telling fashion, the four main stories are subsequently dramatically presented on stage. At the end, the performance returns briefly to Rosendo's family, after which the actors step out of their roles to dole out traditionally prepared Costa Rican snacks and conclude the show with a firework display.

Leyendas y tradiciones costarricenses was set to open at the *Palma de Oro* Festival in Limón, but when that event was cancelled due to lack of funds, Aguamarina premiered it at the Puntarenas Casa de la Cultura in September 1996. They later performed it six more times, including the show we filmed in July: 'We can't afford to do *Leyendas* too often,' explains Gerardo, 'because we have to pay for the fireworks for each show out of our own pockets.'

Over the course of a quarter century, Aguamarina must have touched the lives of thousands of Puntarenenses, including spectators and all the community artists who, at one time or another, have been directly involved in the productions. It still attracts its biggest crowds at outdoor performances in basketball courts, on the beach, or in the market, while considerably smaller crowds attend its indoor shows at the Casa de Cultura, a municipal facility that includes a 250-seat theatre auditorium, an exhibition hall, a small museum, and a library. Marvin Lara is aware that the group's popularity unavoidably fluctuates over time:

> In the 1970s and early 1980s, when there were twelve community theatre groups in Puntarenas Province alone, many people knew us. Now only a portion of Puntarenas still knows us. We have to cover a large territory, for Puntarenas is very big. We have audiences in Barranca, El Roble, Fray Cassiano, and my own neighbourhood, Barrio El Carmen. When Danilo was still with us, our themes were more directly related to Puntarenas. Now, our themes tend to be more national or even universal: suicide, AIDS, political honesty, traditions. We should maybe mix our themes better and identify ourselves more with Puntarenas.

Finances

In 1998, Aguamarina was still struggling to find a new internal equilibrium. Over the course of two decades, the city itself has also undergone drastic changes: most of the local factories have closed down and many people have moved to new settlements closer to the mainland, away from the sandy point on which the old downtown is located and where most of the fisherfolk still live. Finances are a continuing worry for Aguamarina. Other than occasional material support for *Chucheca de oro* through the regional office of culture, the company, which has always had a predominantly working-class membership, receives no subsidies. Marvin Lara, who has been struggling to keep Aguamarina afloat together with his friends Gerardo Arias and Eduardo Martinez, admits that they cannot indefinitely continue to pay for production expenses out of their own pockets:

> Materially speaking, I have nothing. I want to keep on giving to the theatre, but I can't afford not to also take care of myself. If tomorrow I have nothing to eat or nowhere to live, no one will tell me, 'hey, you've given twenty years of your life to the theatre, now you can come live at my place for free.' It doesn't work that way. I do some computer programming on the side and I have a little silk screening business together with my brother. But during our *Chucheca de oro* Festival, for example, I neglect that work and then don't make any money.

Before he and his friends take a back seat, Marvin Lara is determined to train a self-reliant next generation of Aguamarina members, indeed a noble aim in a country where the professional theatre seems mostly in disarray (Bonilla 1992). According to playwright Samuel Rovinski, who has also lived and worked in Mexico and Venezuela:

> Artists formed by the popular theatre movement of the 1970s are now forced to survive in the commercial theatre, whose audiences and tastes have declined. The current theatre scene here in San José lacks spiritual roots in the communities, because the state withdrew its support and left culture to be determined by market forces, something which, by the way, you see happening all over Latin America.[13]

Cultural historian Rafael Cuevas Molina agrees with Rovinski and Catania that community theatre groups such as Aguamarina and Teatro Cariari in Limón represent a sorely needed counterweight to the increasingly powerful neoliberal forces in Costa Rica:

> Before the mid-1980s, the Costa Rican used to never display his material possessions because it was considered bad taste. It used to be in good taste to demonstrate that all Costa Ricans were 'igualiticos', equals. The society now values a person who has succeeded in the marketplace. This has led to a moral deterioration that puts a value on material accumulation no matter how and has caused an enormous expansion of corruption at all levels of government and an increased consumerist mentality.

Cuevas argues that this change in mentality evolved more rapidly in Costa Rica than in other Central American countries because, statistically speaking, in Costa Rica rural and urban youth have comparatively equal access to mass media (by means of a largely unregulated nationwide cable network) and quality education, whereas this contrast between city and countryside is much more pronounced in other Central American countries (1993: 130–132; 143–144). The downside, Cuevas thinks, is that the media present the United States as the highest cultural standard: 'For the Costa Rican middle and upper classes Miami is the cultural Mecca. For a painter to have an exposition in Miami or to sell something there is the highest he could ever hope to achieve and this attitude applies to the entire Caribbean basin, including Venezuela and Colombia.'[14]

Aguamarina, which has helped to form sustaining amateur collectives in other communities around the province of Puntarenas, consciously tries to combat Costa Rica's increasing consumerism and social carelessness by creating relevant performances through a transparent collective creative process that is documented in the case study below. Gerardo Bejerano, theatre lecturer at the National University, therefore, considers the group of great cultural value to his country: 'They have continued to work from a community base for over 25 years, never losing touch with their people. And because they are a little isolated from the Central Valley, they have maintained an identity of their own, continuing to manage their group without outside interference.' Yet, with the current core group about to hand over responsibilities to an immature new batch, the group's future looks by no means secure.

CASE STUDY: *EL PESCADOR*

Sonia Villalobos is one of the few Costa Rican Members of Parliament who returns to her home town when the weekly sessions terminate on Thursdays. She is a great admirer of Aguamarina. When she brought the prestigious National Sports Games to Puntarenas in 1995, she therefore put the theatre collective in charge of organizing a parallel cultural festival that included a huge parade through all the *barrios* of the city. More than 5,000 people from all over Costa Rica attended and saw Aguamarina perform their anti-macho production *Hagase la Mujer*. According to Villalobos: 'They have played a very important role in this community, also because they have sustained for so long. Many groups spring up all over the place but after a short while they lose interest and then disappear again. Aguamarina is now already a generational enterprise.'[15] But historian Arabela Valverde qualifies Villalobos' assessment: 'True, they are recognized and popular. But people here are not so cultivated and the masses are not so interested in theatre. The *Porteños* are quite expressive and live life simply. They live with their front doors open and sit in the doorway to converse with the passers-by. The rich and the poor mix socially. They may go dance on Fridays and Saturdays, but few people go to the cultural centre to see a theatre performance.'[16]

The Casa de la Cultura, a converted prison and army barracks in downtown Puntarenas, took fifteen years to complete. The original idea was born in the pro-community arts atmosphere of the 1970s, but due to the city's neglect by national politicians the complex was not opened until 1992. Miguel Gomez, Jr., the owner of the local Imperial Hotel, headed the fundraising committee, and Danilo Montoya, Aguamarina's founder, became the centre's first volunteer theatre coordinator. Today, the regional director of culture, Aguamarina, and the other local theatre group, 'Vías', determine the Casa's programming, but all agree that it is hardly the happening place it should be. Still, it provides both 'Vías', which offers a more conventional theatre fare for a middle-class clientele, and Aguamarina with a convenient rehearsal space and a reasonably equipped venue for their performances. But Aguamarina does its most effective work outside the Casa, at the socially and culturally much more diverse community level.

Profile of the city and province of Puntarenas

Greater Puntarenas, named thus because of a protruding point (*punta*) of sand (*arena*) on which it is built, includes the new urbanizations of Barranca and El Roble and has a total population of 100,000 people (*Análisis Situacional* 1997: 138). It lies 130 kilometres from San José on the Pacific Coast. The city proper, including downtown and its adjacent neighbourhoods (Cocal, Barrio El Carmen, Pitahaya, Chapernal and Aranjuez), has close to 20,000 inhabitants.[17] The harbour function, which the city already had before the country obtained independence in 1821, caused the population to be multicultural from the start. All over the country, indigenous Costa Ricans had mixed with the Spanish colonizers (Hall 1979: 42–50), but as the country's main port Puntarenas also attracted Europeans and other Latin Americans. The largest influx came from nearby Nicaragua, which to this day continues to provide the majority of Costa Rican immigrants. The first Chinese began to arrive in the 1860s, followed by a larger group around the turn of the century. Today, they form a significant local economic force, owning many small grocery shops called *pulperías* and restaurants, although they continue to be culturally unintegrated.

The coffee barons, who have been dominating the nation's economy and politics since colonial times (Stone 1975; Vega Carballo 1980: 79–94), also used to have Puntarenas firmly in their grip. They financed the railroad, which came in the 1870s, first connecting Puntarenas to Barranca and Esparza, later to the capital on the Central Plateau, and finally all the way to Puerto Limón on the Caribbean coast (Hall 1979: 125–129). During the summer months, from November until March, this new infrastructure brought many well-to-do families down to Puntarenas, making it the country's most popular seaside resort until World War II. Miguel Gomez, Sr. (b. 1910), whose Spanish immigrant father started the Imperial Hotel, fondly remembers the old summers: 'Back in the old days, the big ships stayed at large and would be unloaded with smaller launches. On the weekends, we used to have beautiful outdoor dances near the pier. Even the working man used to dress up. The great orchestras used to come down to Puntarenas during the summer. No scandals like you have nowadays.'[18]

To profit from the port and the fertile hinterland, industry began to develop in Puntarenas around the turn of the century, but by the 1970s the local factories could no longer keep up with better equipped foreign competitors. The port permanently lost additional business after a big fruit pickers strike in the mid-1980s, which caused the major banana companies to abandon the Pacific coast. And the national economy as a whole ironically suffered from the end of the civil wars in Nicaragua, El Salvador, Honduras and Guatemala: suddenly Costa Rica became an expensive instead of a stable and secure place for foreign investors. Arabela Valverde explains: 'Labour now is more costly here, because our system of social security is so much more expensive than that of other Central American countries. The neoliberal government tries to get rid of it, but people won't allow it.' However, she points to the new port facility at Puerto Caldera as the number one cause of the local economic crisis. San José-based entrepreneurs managed to have a modern deep-sea port constructed there in the late 1970s, drawing away a substantial portion of the import and export trade from the technically outdated Puntarenas. The competition from Caldera, from where big trucks can reach the capital much more quickly than from Puntarenas, also eventually caused the closure of the railroad to Limón in 1991.

Despite a big Taiwanese grant to reconstruct the old pier for tourism, in July 1997, when we began documenting Aguamarina's way of working, Puntarenas continued to face many social problems. Its principal economic activities remained fishing and fruit farming while the local industry was composed of a cement factory, a tuna canning plant, and several small ice manufacturers. The official unemployment figure hovered around 6.4 per cent, but did not reflect substantial underemployment caused by short-term contracts and temporary suspension of fishing activities due to internationally imposed quotas. The hardest hit were undoubtedly the small fishermen and their families, the target sector for Aguamarina's *Pescador* ('Fisherman') project.

Creating The Fisherman play

After the 1997 *Chucheca de Oro* Festival was over, Aguamarina embarked on an accelerated, intensive project about local fisher folk. To train their four new teenage members, veteran artists Marvin Lara and Eduardo Martinez would take them through a reconstruction of the collective process that in 1979 had led to the creation of the *El Pescador* play. In a condensed 4-day version of what usually takes several months, the group wanted to let the young actors undergo a more genuine collective creation process than they had experienced with *Leyendas y tradiciones costarricenses*, for which Marvin, Gerardo, and Eduardo already had done most of the creative work before they came in.

Collective creation seems to work best when participants are equally experienced as researchers and actors. When we documented Aguamarina's work, that parity did not exist and, as a result, the older actors, all in their thirties, dominated the proceedings. Gerardo and Eduardo have known Marvin for many years, are good at improvising, and have a strong enough personality to disagree and suggest their own alternatives to Marvin's proposals. During the week, they also frequently meet in a café after work to informally discuss an idea for a new improvisation or a change of scenario. That is why they found it important to improve the research and improvisational skills of the youngsters and to increase their confidence by means of the process we were invited to document.

Step one, selecting a theme

Before we arrived in Puntarenas, Aguamarina had already decided to reconstruct some of their better known earlier works for our video. After we made clear that we were more interested in filming their creative method than in the group's history, we all agreed that a newly created play about the current conditions of fisher folk in Puntarenas would best suit both our purposes. So, although we did film the *Leyendas* performance in its totality, selected scenes from *Crónicas de un desajusto*, and a reconstructed process of the AIDS play *Sin Alternativa*, we concentrated our efforts on *El Pescador*. This meant, of course, that the theme was already determined before we started. However, Marvin explained that the usual procedure is to select a theme from various competing proposals:

> Before our first plenary meeting, we have a period in which each member of the group superficially researches a theme they're interested in, in order to generate provisional interest among the other members. If you don't have a theme, you simply participate in the evaluation. Then those who feel most strongly about presenting a proposal conduct more research and return with folders, handmade documentation, or anything else that can serve to reinforce their idea. The objective is to sell the idea to the others in the group, convincing them that it has indeed theatrical potential and is relevant for our community. Generally, this period lasts a month and then we decide by majority which subject we are going to tackle. Once we have voted, we put the best of the other proposals aside for a future occasion.
>
> (Lara interview)

Gerardo Arias Elizondo, who had made the original proposal for *Leyendas*, provides a more concrete time frame for Aguamarina's meticulous theme selection process:

> First I did two weeks research, which in the case of *Leyendas* meant mostly looking for books. Then, after everyone has agreed on the theme, we all conduct further in-depth research, which in the case of *Leyendas* took several more weeks. Depending on the subject, we go out to interview people on the street, see how they live, or sometimes we invite resource persons to come and give a talk. For the AIDS play, *Sin Alternativa*, for example, we invited a local street-corner health worker. Or we individually do research in the library, as was the case with *Leyendas*. This preparatory phase can last up to two months, after which we pick up our regular Saturday afternoon rehearsal rhythm again for the improvisations.[19]

The participants

Gerardo, who is a coordinator of the local swimming pool, is unable to get off work for the fishermen's project. Gretel and Cynthia, both housewives with small children, cannot come either. Such absences are quite common, explains Marvin Lara: 'There are times when we have to give a bit of money to an actor who can't afford the bus fare. At other times we have to change the rehearsal schedule so that people can come because they are working, or they have to study, or they have to look after their kid or a little sister.' So, together with core member Eduardo Martinez, a librarian who now works as the regional director of culture, he begins the investigation process with the remaining participants: Gerardo's teenage sons Ivan and Paulo, Araceli, a high school student Marvin has worked with before in Barrio El Carmen, and Cindy, another high school student.

Monday: step two, exposure and interviews

After the theme is selected, the next step is going to the very place where fishermen live and work, to gather first-hand information on what constitutes the life of a fisherman. So, on Monday morning, 14 July 1997, Marvin and Eduardo huddle with Paulo, Iwan, Araceli and Cindy in a makeshift waterfront shelter in Barrio El Carmen, an area just north of downtown where many fisher families reside. Both Marvin, whose father runs a small grocery store, and Araceli, whose father is a factory worker, live in this neighbourhood. Marvin reviews a list of questions that each actor has prepared and then, similar to what Ernie Cloma did before the exposure trip with the Marinduque youth in the Philippines, he coaches them on interview techniques and fieldwork research strategies. That morning, their research will centre on how fish is being bought and sold, what life is like out at sea, and how wives deal with the extended absences of their husbands. They gather their material from interviews with a fisherman seated on an empty drum near the wharf, from a group of workers unloading an industrial trawler, from employees in wholesale fish markets, and from fishermen mending nets on the streets. They learn about the economics of fishing, about the devastating effects of El Niño which changes the water temperature and thereby affects the habitat of fish, about Asian industrial trawlers that fish in Costa Rican waters and saturate the local market with their product, about alcoholism and womanizing, about the struggle of the small fishermen against the big ones and the difficulties of organizing them into co-operatives.

After lunch, all the actors take turns to report in detail what they have learned from the morning's interviews. The objective is to construct as complex a picture of the lives of Puntarenas fisher folk as possible. From this discussion, details will be extracted that can later add to the richness of their play. In their reports, the actors focus on the things the fisher folk they spoke to have in common, noting details of character, particular ways of talking, walking, and gesticulating. As it turns out, people in Barrio El Carmen manage to live quite well off their fishing. Many people own more than one small boat and some even own a car. But in other *barrios*, like the cryptically named '20 de Noviembre' area where they will conduct interviews the following morning, people are considerably worse off.

Marvin has invited former Aguamarina member Jimmy Castro to join them for the afternoon sessions. He is an experienced improvisational actor and although he is now an office clerk he has also worked as a fisherman himself: 'I went to fish because I was out of work and here in Puntarenas, the easiest job to find is fishing, because everyone knows someone who fishes, or owns a boat. Fishermen have a strong sense of solidarity: they help each other at sea or on land. If someone dies, for instance, they collect money for the funeral.'[20] This Monday afternoon, then, Jimmy serves as a resource person and contributes useful anecdotal information. He talks about how one day the boat he was on lost power and drifted all the way to the Ecuadoran coast, where they were finally rescued. Marvin, who also still regularly goes fishing with his mates, remembers how one day when they were hauling in the net, it got caught in the propellor: 'Now the captain wasn't going to dive in; the newest recruit always gets to do that. So I had to to do it; also, I guess, to prove myself for the others. And there were sharks and everything, but I went in anyway and untrapped the net.' And Jimmy immediately counters with a tall tale of his own: 'I once had to do that too. 3 a.m., dark as hell. But I dove in and found myself face to face with a hammerhead shark at twenty arms' length. Another thing is that fishermen are very superstitious. They tell lots of horror stories. Some *lanchas* are even considered haunted, you know. Thunderstorms don't really bother them, but *mangeras* scare them. These are like little mini-tornadoes that suddenly appear out of nowhere and raise the waves sky high.'

Besides sharing his personal experiences as a fisherman, Jimmy also corrects factual information in the young actors' reports. For example, he adds that many fishermen nowadays want their kids to study rather than follow in their father's footsteps, an element that is later included in the script. He further questions Cindy's judgemental conclusion that all fishermen are womanizers and alcoholics. He does not deny that they drink, but then explores some of the possible causes for their behaviour. He describes how they have to stay out at sea for several weeks in cramped conditions, how they always talk about soccer and politics, and how religious they are. He also provides valuable technical specifics about how to mime hauling in nets and explains the difference between a small *panga*, which never leaves the Gulf of Nicoya; a medium *lancha*, which goes no further than 20 nautical miles and usually stays out for less than two weeks; and the large *lanchas*, which can stay away for as long as a month and sometimes travel as far south as the Galapagos Islands.

The discussion thus continues until dark, jumping from such technical details as the number of hooks there are on each line and how coloured flags mark net position, to the most lucrative kinds of fish, the tiered exploitation by middle men and wholesale traders, and the corrupt politics involved in obtaining bank loans and fishing licences. Before they go home, Marvin recapitulates the most salient aspects of the information they have gathered on this first day. Normally speaking, he explains to me, this seminar-like processing of the research material lasts three or four Saturday afternoons. 'And we only work three to four hours per Saturday; so time can fly by really fast. It is really a collective education process, too.'

Tuesday morning unfolds pretty much the same as the Monday: Marvin, Eduardo and the youngsters travel by public bus towards the mainland and then walk a few hundred yards inland to get to the '20 of November' neighbourhood. Here, they start the interview process right away, obtaining more detailed information about the way Taiwanese and South Korean trawlers operate and how they underpay local workers.

There seem to be few enforced labour rights for fishermen. Cindy strikes gold when a fisherman tells her a dramatic tale about an experience he had back in 1988 when due to bad weather his boat ran out of fuel and he and his mates were left out at sea for five months. All they ate was the fish they could catch and all they drank was rain water. Their families had already paid for a funeral mass when they were finally discovered near Japan and managed to fly home via Hawaii.

Tuesday afternoon: step three, from scenario sketch to improvisation

In the afternoon, the actors report back once again with Jimmy providing additional information. Their accounts inspire Marvin to draw puppets in particular configurations on a notebook page. These sketches, which Marvin sometimes makes spontaneously during the discussions and at other times draws at home during the week, constitute the rough contours for the improvisational scenes that the actors will subsequently get in to: upstage left Marvin has drawn two fishermen in a *lancha*, downstage right two women who wave goodbye, upstage right the local fish buyer awaits the arrival of boats, downstage left a fish merchant is on the phone to a big time wholesaler in San José. Obviously inspired by Jimmy's Monday afternoon remark about fishermen nowadays preferring their sons to get a good education, he also draws a solitary puppet, scribbling the word 'study' next to it.

Marvin explains the subsequent procedure: 'Different actors can try to fill in the four basic dramatic situations I have sketched. Each actor is free to make suggestions, which the others are then committed to trying out. This improvisational phase can last many weeks, until we have exhausted all options. We usually begin improvising on the same day as the interviews, because the material is still fresh in the minds of the actors then. If we wait a week, the things that may seem obvious today won't be so simple any more.' The cumulatively structured improvisations form the heart of Aguamarina's collective creation process and take up most rehearsal time. The sessions are always preceded by a 20-minute body and voice warm-up.

Together, the actors distil a basic plot from Marvin's sketches: two fish-ermen go out to fish in the smallest type of boat, a *panga*. There will be a scene at home with the wives, another scene with the fishermen having a discussion about politics, soccer, and women out at sea, a scene where they return to port and sell their catch, and a final scene in which the exploitation is illustrated through a cellular phone conversation of a middle man with a big fish exporter in the capital. These plots constitute the parameters for a first round of improvisations with Cindy and Araceli acting as the fishermen's wives and Eduardo and Paulo as fishermen who go out to sea. In a second round, their roles are taken by other actors, and so forth. According to Marvin:

> If someone has an idea how to do a scene differently, they get up to explain it and then cast themselves and others for another improvi-sation based on their alternative idea. Thus, there is a lot of space for a scene to grow, layer upon layer, gradually building up over weeks if necesary. If there are different versions of one scene, the group dis-cusses which one is the best. The same principle we apply to the creation of characters. Every actor will take turns playing a particu-lar role, expressing what they have captured from their research, from their interviews. They deposit their interpretations into a data bank from which we can extract the best work from each actor and eventually accumulate one single, composite character. The actor who will be cast in that role, can draw on those elements that all have agreed are most significant for representing that character. And if two people want to play the same role, they both get the chance to act it, after which the group decides. If they can't come to an agreement, the director has the final say.

Marvin intervenes whenever he sees an improvisation get stuck or when some of the younger actors imitate the preceding improvisation too closely. This is particularly the case with Ivan and Paulo, who are clearly overwhelmed by the gusto with which Jimmy and Eduardo act. Cindy and Araceli, meanwhile, do not have other actresses to alternate with. As a result, their work remains superficial. Their main challenge is to convincingly act mature wives. To improve their improvisations, Marvin therefore insists that they go back to the original impressions they gath-ered in Barrio El Carmen and the 20 of November area. To give all the actors more structure, he asks them to jointly work out a general plot. The group reviews the preceding free-for-all improvisations and selects the most important issues these raised. They conclude, for example, that

Eduardo's fictional character talked mostly about 'family' and 'soccer', whereas Jimmy's main point had been to express the fisherman's psychological state of constant worry while out at sea. Both Marvin's, Ivan's, and Paulo's emphasis had been on exploitation. Cindy and Areceli, finally, had dealt mostly with the financial problems they faced as fishermen's wives at home. Tightening the scenes this way eases the actors' trouble to invent dialogues in the next round of improvisations.

Wednesday morning: step four, consolidating the scenario

On Wednesday morning, Jimmy comes in with the proposal to add a scene about the son of one of the fishermen. He wants to include something in the play about kids being forced to drop out of school to contribute to the family's income. He suggests to have the son come home from school with the news that he has been awarded a scholarship to study abroad while his father is checking his fish hooks. Marvin likes the thematic aspect of this idea but is not convinced that the scene works best where Jimmy wants to put it. Eduardo suggests the possibility of a flashback when the two fisherman are out at sea. They try both options and everyone agrees that Eduardo's is dramatically more effective.

From that point on, the group decides to consolidate the scenes they have created so far, so they can begin to polish their acting. Eduardo and Jimmy are now definitely cast as the two fishermen, Paulo as Jimmy's son, Ivan as fishmonger, Marvin as a wholesale merchant, and Araceli and Cindy as the fishermen's wives. The men work on the mechanics of buying and selling fish on the wharf, price levels, diction and typical slang expressions. Marvin directs the novice actors particularly intensively. For example, he takes Cindy and Araceli to one side to work with them on simple miming techniques. Cindy is supposed to be cooking a fish soup and he meticulously guides her through the details of scooping the hot liquid, blowing in it before tasting it, adding spices and, while she goes through these motions, to continue a conversation about her grocery debts with Araceli, who plays her neighbour. Meanwhile, Jimmy shows Eduardo, who has never fished before, the exact position of the fingers for putting bait on a hook. They know they will be ridiculed by their audience composed of the fishing community if they do not get all these technical particulars right.

Wednesday afternoon: step five, the performance

Whereas normally they would have taken at least five or six Saturday afternoon sessions to consolidate scenes and mount their show, in this telescoped version of the process the Aguamarina actors barely use six hours. On Wednesday afternoon 16 July 1997 at 4.30 p.m., they perform their collective creation on a waterfront intersection in Barrio El Carmen, near the shelter where they had begun their research on Monday. Araceli is visibly nervous: she lives on the same block and feels embarrassed to perform before her mother, her friends, and neighbours. Some seventy people have come out of their houses to watch.

The actors, most of them in shorts and singlets, have no props to work with, but the water and the sky-diving pelicans behind them form an impressive backdrop. The play opens with Eduardo and Jimmy miming that they peddle their *panga* out of the harbour as their wives wave goodbye. Cindy, now more confident than in the rehearsals, then engages in a conversation with a still timid Araceli about her mounting debt at the neighbourhood grocery. From here, the dramatic focus shifts to the two fishermen at sea, first talking about soccer as they throw out their lines, but becoming more serious as the hours pass. Both actors are expressive and articulate improvisers: they are never lost for words and convincingly mime their actions, suggesting with their bodies that they are on a small, unstable boat out at sea. Jimmy, who is clearly fond of farce, reaps a lot of laughs by contorting his face and speaking with an accent, even though his character is the more tragic of the two. When Eduardo asks him why he has been so moody lately, Jimmy explains it has to do with his son whom, because of the domestic economic crisis, he had to take out of school and put to work. This is the moment where we see the flashback with Paulo playing Jimmy's son, who comes out of school enthusiastically announcing he has received a scholarship to study abroad.

Although they keep their distance, the spectators are obviously engaged by the play. Some fishermen, comfortable in their anonymity, yell out technical advice when Eduardo and Jimmy mime hauling in their lines and try to catch a hammerhead shark. Later, when they try to sell their catch on the wharf, another spectator shouts: 'Don't forget the sharkfin, mate!' Ivan plays a tough fishmonger and acting-wise now clearly holds his own against Jimmy and Eduardo, who exit to drown their sadness over the bad sale in gin at a nearby bar. The play ends with Ivan selling Jimmy and Eduardo's catch at a big profit to Marvin, who, in turn, by phone sells it again at double the price to a fish exporter in San José.

> *El Pescador* is over in less than half an hour. Aguamarina gets a timid applause. Marvin, who lives down the road, knows that despite their spontaneous remarks, people here are shy and would never respond in public to requests for comments immediately after the performance: 'Yet, it is a fundamental part of the process to give the material back to the community and invite their reactions. We did the same with the original fisherman's play in 1979, performing it first in la Chacarita and then here as well.'

Thursday: step six, feedback

The next day, Marvin and Eduardo return to the area to look for some of the people they had interviewed on Monday and who, they knew, had come to see the Wednesday afternoon performance as well. An older man, nicknamed 'Dollar' because of the golden dollar necklace he wears around his neck, is now more than willing to provide feedback in the comfort of his own home. He tells them he enjoyed the show and that Jimmy and Eduardo had portrayed most of the technical aspects of fishing at sea correctly, but that some of their terminology could be improved. 'Dollar' also explains that the Aguamarina play had not quite reflected how small fishermen can lose their boats to fish merchants if they have a succession of bad catches and then can no longer repay the loans they have had to take out to buy gasoline and bait. 'Dollar' also explains that they should have brought back more fish than they did and that the reason why someone in the audience shouted about the sharkfin was because he had noticed the actors did not know that the fin is by far the most valuable part of the shark. But, in general, 'Dollar' confirmed they had correctly dramatized how the small fishermen are at the mercy of the merchants, who can determine whatever price they like.

When we walk back to the Casa de la Cultura to store our equipment, Marvin explains that each Aguamarina performance is different, because it contains so much improvisation and continues to be updated with audience feedback:

The script is never written down until the last time we perform a play. That is when we audiotape it and finally transcribe it for our archives. Until that moment, we improvise within a known scene structure. We know the blocking and the narrative line and, although there is no precise script, everyone knows what they are going to talk about to the other. The exact words don't matter; it's more natural that way.

'All we do,' adds Eduardo, 'is agree on a particular word as a cue for the other actor to start speaking.' Marvin also emphasizes that there is more to Aguamarina's collective creations than the actors' contributions during the improvisations alone: 'In different plays we have worked with stilts, with fireworks, and with masks. All those things require research as well, to find ways of connecting them to the theme. They help to maintain the attention of the spectator because a well conceived image can convey so much more than words.' But despite the continuous artistic learning process, he admits that Aguamarina's responsibility to the community remains foremost:

> People in San José who have had professional theatre training join a company and try to make money. We make community theatre that simply realizes there is a problem and tries to express it in words and images that the people can relate to. And when you present something and people come and tell you, 'that was very good what you did, it precisely reflects our problem,' that is our recompense. Often we run into people in the street we don't know and they ask you, 'Look, how is the group?' Or someone else you don't know comes and ask you, 'Look, we have a problem in our community; I would like your group to come and do a play about it.' Those are the things that tell tell us we're on the right track and that community theatre is worthwhile. Unlike politicians who promise much and never deliver anything, we don't tell people that we'll help them. We tell them: 'We're with you and if you want to struggle to change things, we'll be behind you.'

Whether Aguamarina can continue to service disenfranchised communities in Puntarenas for another twenty-five years will depend largely on how successful the now middle-aged core members will be in passing on their transparent cumulative improvisational method to a new generation of socially conscious and collectively minded actors. But not just anyone can lead a group through a collective creation process. It takes vision, stamina, and advanced theatre-making skills that can only be acquired over time. Marvin Lara is convinced that letting the young actors undergo as many *creación colectiva* processes as possible provides the best training for them: 'sending them out to do their own research and to interview people will mark their lives more than me lecturing on an issue'. But Eduardo Martinez also has a good point when he argues that the young actors will never be able to hold their own in improvisations, if they are not taught basic acting techniques first. Either way, the main challenge for the Aguamarina veterans will be to increase the number of motivated and responsible members with people who, as Marvin says at the end of the video, can appreciate the priceless benefits of community theatre.

Notes

1 Oscar Fessler, who died in 1993, is a French drama teacher who had studied under Max Reinhart and was active in the popularization of French theatre after World War II. In the early 1950s, he was invited to Argentina by the José Martí theatre in Buenos Aires to direct a Brecht production. He was subsequently contracted by the Foro Nacional de los Artes, the most important arts training institute in the country. He set up workshops and was then asked to establish a regional theatre school in Santa Fe, which he directed for several years. Catania was one of his students there in the mid-1950s.

2 Personal interview with Alfredo Catania, San José, Costa Rica, 29 July 1997.

3 Salvador Solís mentions the existence of a National Institute of Dramatic Art in Costa Rica from 1961 until 1966 (1991–1992: 76). The Costa Rican Ministry of Culture, Youth, and Sport was the first of its kind in Central America (Cuevas Molina 1993: 127). After their victory in 1979, the Sandinistas established their own Ministry of Culture. Headed by priest-poet Ernesto Cardenal, it implemented an extensive progressive policy of popularizing cultural activities at the grass roots until it was disbanded in 1984. Since then its outreach tasks have been taken over by the Sandinista Association of Cultural Workers (ASTC) and, since 1990, by the Association of Cultural Promotors (APC) (Klünder 1997: 22–24).

4 Personal interview with Vladimir de la Cruz, San José, 29 July 1997.

5 Hans Ehrmann sketches a sober picture of Chilean theatre during the Allende years. He does, however, favourably mention the work of 'El Teatro del Angel' and refers to community theatre attempts by peasants, miners, and factory workers, but argues that their initiatives never got the chance to mature and that a genuine widespread leftist popular theatre movement never really got off the ground (see also Rojo 1985).

6 Boal's participatory Theatre of the Oppressed, although it also originated in the 1950s and is collectively oriented, follows a different trajectory and methodology than what is generally referred to as collective creation. Even so, Boal's Arena Theatre is routinely mentioned together with 'La Candalaria', TEC, 'El Galpón', 'Teatro Escambray' and other collective creation-minded *Nuevo Teatro Popular* companies (Weiss *et al.* 1993: 152).

7 Buenaventura (1970: 153) points to similarities between his work and the audience participation practised by the Living Theatre and Bread & Puppet in the United States.
8 Personal interview with Hector Aristizabel, Los Angeles, 1 June 1997.
9 TEC acknowledges that they borrowed elements from the Russian formalist Tomachevsky for this purpose (Garzón Céspedes 1978: 318).
10 Personal interview with Gerardo Bejerano, Puntarenas, 13 July 1979.
11 Personal interview with Danilo Montoya, Cocal (Puntarenas), 14 July 1997.
12 Personal interview with Marvin Lara, Cocal, 14 July 1997. Mazatlán, by the way, is the twin city of Puntarenas.
13 Personal interview with Samuel Rovinski, San José, 29 July 1997.
14 Personal interview with Rafael Cuevas Molina, Heredia, 30 July 1997.
15 Personal interview with Sonia Villalobos, Puntarenas, 24 July 1997.
16 Personal interview with Arabela Valverde Espinoza, Puntarenas, 17 July 1997.
17 Source: Arabela Valverde, 'La Ciudad de Puntarenas: Una aproximación a su historia económica y social, 1858–1930', unpublished MA thesis for the University of Costa Rica, July 1997.
18 Personal interview with Miguel Gomez, Puntarenas, 24 July 1997.
19 Personal interview with Gerardo Arias Elizondo, Puntarenas, 17 July 1997.
20 Personal interview with Jimmy Castro, Puntarenas, 14 July 1997.

Bibliography

Aguilar Bulgarelli, Oscar (1993) *Costa Rica y sus hechos políticos de 1948*, San José: Editorial Costa Rica.
Análisis situacional de salud (1997) San José: Caja Costarricense del Seguro Social y Ministerio de Salud.
Arcila, Gonzalo (1983) *Nuevo Teatro en Colombia: actividad creadora-política-cultural*, Bogotá: CEIS.
Arturo, Jorge (1992) 'Diquis Triquis: Teatro Danza para humanizar el arte', *Aportes* (July): 31–32.
Barzuna, Guillermo (1989) *Caseron de Teja: Ensayos sobre patrimonio y cultura popular en Costa Rica*, San José: Editorial Nueva Década.
Barzuna, Guillermo, Bolaños Ligia, García, Nelly and Valembois, Victor (1989) 'Noticia de una investigación sobre Sociedad y Teatro en Costa Rica entre 1968 y 1977', *Escena* 11 (22–23): 18–24.
Bayona Borrero, Alvaro (1984) '¿Cúal es el nuevo teatro colombiano?', *Magazin Dominical* 61 (27 May): 1819.
Bonilla, Maria (1992) 'Presente, futuro y teatro costarricense', *Latin American Theatre Review* (Spring): 59–66.
Bravo-Elizondo, Pedro (1991) 'Melvin Méndez: Una nueva dramaturgia costarricense', *Latin American Theatre Review* (Fall): 141–145.
Buenaventura, Enrique (1970) 'Theatre and Culture', *The Drama Review* 14, 2: 151–156.
——— (1984) 'Dramaturgia Nacional y Nuevo Teatro', *Magazin Dominical* 71 (12 August): 16–18.

Castro, Silvia (1993) 'De la enagua de manta a los "blue jeans": una visión del cambio cultural en Costa Rica', *Herencia* 5, 1: 137–145.

Catania, Alfredo (1980) '¿Hacia otro teatro en Costa Rica?', *Escena* 2, 3: 25–29.

Cuevas Molina, Rafael (1993) *Traspatio Florecido: Tendencias de la dinámica de la cultura en Centroamérica (1979–1990)*, Heredia: Editorial de la Universidad Nacional.

—— (ed.), *Suplemento Cultural*, published monthly by the Interdisciplinary Program on Cultural Identity, Arts and Technology (ICAT) of the Universidad Nacional since March 1994.

Ehrmann, Hans (1974) 'Chilean Theatre, 1971–1973', *Latin American Theatre Review*, (Spring): 39–43.

Fernández Saborío, Guido (1977) *Los Caminos del teatro en Costa Rica*, San José: EDUCA.

García, Santiago (1983) *Teoría y Práctica del Teatro*, Bogotá: Ediciones CEIS.

Garzón Céspedes, Francisco (1977) *El Teatro de Participación popular y el teatro de la comunidad: un teatro de sus protagonistas*, Havana: Unión de Escritores y Artistas de Cuba.

—— (ed.) (1978) *El Teatro Latinamericano de creación colectiva*, Havana: Casa de las Américas.

Gaudibert, Pierre (1977) *Action Culturelle:intégration et/ou subversion*, Paris: Casterman.

Gutiérrez, Sonia (ed.) (1979) *Teatro Popular y cambio social en América Latina*, San José: EDUCA.

Hall, Carolyn (1979) *Costa Rica: A Geographical Interpretation in Historical Perspective*, Boulder and London: Westview Press.

Halperín Donghi, Tulio (1993) *The Contemporary History of Latin America*, Durham, NC: Duke University Press.

Hernández, Gabriela (1987) 'Teatro: Palma de Oro', *Aportes* (October): 26.

Herzfeld, Anita and Cajiao Salas, Teresa (1971a) 'San José, Costa Rica – 1968, 1969, 1970 – Temporada Teatral', *Latin American Theatre Review* (Spring): 78–84.

—— (1971b) 'El Panorama teatral de Costa Rica en los últimos tres años', *Latin American Theatre Review* (Fall): 25–38.

—— (1973) *El Teatro de hoy en Costa Rica*, San José: Editorial Costa Rica.

Klünder, Michelle (1997) 'Actoren Acteren "Want Kennis is Macht": Nicaraguaans Volkstheater: Aan de basis van Verandering', unpublished thesis, Free University Amsterdam.

Luzuriaga, Gerardo (ed.) (1974) *Modern One Act Plays from Latin America*, Los Angeles: UCLA Center for Latin American Studies.

Márceles Daconte, Eduardo (1977) 'El Método de creación colectiva en el teatro colombiano', *Latin American Theatre Review* (Fall): 91–97.

Montoya, Danilo (1982) 'El Pescador', *Escena* 4, 8: 17–21.

Munck, Ronaldo with Ricardo Falcón and Bernardo Galitelli (1987) *Argentina: From Anarchism to Peronism. Workers, Unions and Politics, 1855–1985*, London: Zed Books.

Norden, Deborah L. (1996) *Military Rebellion in Argentina: Between Coups and Consolidation*, Lincoln and London: Nebraska University Press.

Ovares, Flora and Rojas, Margarita (1995) *Cien Años de literatura Costarricense*, San Pedro: Farben Grupo Editorial Norma.

Perri, Dennis (1975) 'The Costa Rican Stage: An Update', *Latin American Theatre Review* (Spring): 51–57.

Prado, Mimi (1979) 'De los Entremeses al teatro popular', *Escena* 1, 2: 12–13.

Quesada Soto, Alvaro (1990) 'Sobre la identidad nacional', *Herencia* 2, 1: 102–111.

Riszk, Beatriz J. (1989) 'The Colombian New Theatre and Bertolt Brecht: A Dialectical Approach', *Theatre Research International* 14, 2: 131–141.

Rojas, Mario A. (1990) '*Gulliver Dormido* de Samuel Rovinski: Una parodia del discurso del poder', *Latin American Theatre Review* (Fall): 51–63.

Rojo, Grinór (1985) *Muerte y Resurrección del teatro Chileno: 1973–1983*, Madrid: Meridión.

Röttger, Kati (1992) *Kollektives Theater als Spiegel Lateinamerikanischer Identität*, Frankfurt: Vervuert Verlag.

Rovinski, Samuel (1975a) *Un Modelo para Rosauro*, San José: Editorial Costa Rica.

—— (1975b) *Las Fisgonas de Paso Ancho*, San José: Editorial Costa Rica.

—— (1981) *Los Intereses compuestos*, San José: Compañia Nacional de Teatro.

—— (1985) *Gulliver Dormido*, San José: Compañia Nacional de Teatro.

—— (1994) *Tres Obras de teatro*, San José: Editorial Costa Rica.

Santana Méndez, León (1990) 'Reflexiones sobre cultura popular costarricense', *Herencia* 2, 2: 83–89.

Séjourné, Laurette (1977) *Teatro Escambray: una experiencia*, Havana: Editorial de Sciencias Sociales.

Solís Z., Salvador (1991–1992) 'El Movimiento Teatral Costarricense (1951–1971)', *Escena* 13–14, 28–29: 70–79.

Soto Larios, Ernesto (1998) 'El Texto Dramatico dentro del proceso de creación colectiva a partir de la experiencia del teatro popular Nicaraguënse', unpublished thesis, Utrecht School of the Arts.

Stone, Samuel (1975) *La Dinastia de los Conquistadores*, San José: EDUCA.

Taylor, Diana (1991) *Theatre of Crisis: Drama and Politics in Latin America*, Lexington, MA: University Press of Kentucky.

Thomas, Charles P. (1986) 'Chilean Theatre in Exile: The Teatro del Angel in Costa Rica, 1974–1984', *Latin American Theatre Review* (Spring): 97–101.

Tossatti, Alejandro (1989a) 'Festival de Teatro en el Caribe', *Aportes* (September): 28–30.

—— (1989b) 'Festivales de Teatro en America Latina', *Aportes* (October): 32–34.

—— (1994) 'La Fiesta de los Diablitos', *Aportes* (February): 33–35.

Vargas, José Angel and Vasquez, Magdalena (1988) 'Reseña del Drama en Costa Rica a partir de 1950', *Escena* 10, 19–20: 105–110.

Vega Carballo, José Luís (1980) *Hacía una Interpretación del desarrollo costarricense: ensayo sociológico*, San José: Porvenir.

Venegas, William (1991) 'La Máscara: Teatro, Proyectos y Amores de María Silva', *Aportes* (November): 36–37.

Vladich, Stoyan (1984) 'Aspectos del teatro popular en América Latina', *Escena* 5, 12: 32–36.

—— (1987) 'Notas Para una historia del teatro costarricense', *Escena* 9, 18: 36–41.

Weiss, Judith *et al.* (1993) *Latin American Popular Theatre: The First Five Centuries*, Albuquerque: University of New Mexico Press.

Zavala, Magda (1980) 'Entrevista a Santiago García', *Escena* 2, 4: 15–20.

Zuñiga, Alberto (1987) 'Teatro la Máscara: Experiencia de un grupo independiente', *Aportes* (November): 20–22.

Zúñiga, Rosita (1995–1996) 'Festival Internacional de las Artes', *Escena* 18–19, 36–37: 70–72.

Internet connections

Website of San José daily newspaper *La Nación*:
<http://www.nacion.co.cr>

Chapter 5

Community theatre in Kenya

Other than a few weeks in northern Morocco back in 1977 I had never set foot on the African continent until I arrived at Jomo Kenyatta International airport in the evening of 5 September 1997. Opiyo Mumma, a drama lecturer at the University of Nairobi, took us in his car to the YMCA, just behind the university campus. A few days later, accompanied by cameraman Julius Obala and soundman George Anang'a, we travelled three hours to the northeast to encounter a youth theatre group in rural Meru province, a theatre for development dance performance about alcoholism. We stayed with them for a week before journeying to western Kenya, where we would spent two and a half weeks with a women's theatre collective in Sigoti village.

Following the Berlin Conference of 1894, the British colonized Kenya in 1895 and ruled the country until independence was officially declared in 1963. Although this period of western imperialism seems relatively brief compared, for example, to the four centuries of foreign domination in the Philippines, the cultural scars it left are no less prominent. For one, British cultural influence remained strong during the first post-colonial decade, particularly through expatriates who continued working in high schools, universities, and urban cultural institutions. When Daniel arap Moi took over as the country's second president after Jomo Kenyatta's death in 1978, western influence became perhaps less exclusively British but no less dominant. And the image of Kenya in the western mind was being constructed by an increasing horde of European and North

American social scientists, as Angélique Haugerud, perhaps not quite self-consciously enough, acknowledges:

> Until the early 1990s Kenya was often portrayed in the West as a 'beacon of success' and an 'economic miracle'. Western observers praised the country as a showpiece of economic prosperity and political stability. It was an appealing 'success' to tourists in search of exotic animals and Indian Ocean beaches, to development economists impressed by high rates of post-independence economic growth and by sharp increases in marketed smallholders' production, and to Western nations pursuing the 'strategic' interests in superpower politics.
>
> In the early 1990s, however, this burnished image suddenly was overturned. Prominent Western media voices asserted that political and other violence threatened Kenya's vital tourism industry, 'corruption' threatened its economy, and government repression threatened its nascent 'democracy' movement. Post-cold-war geopolitics lessened the 'strategic' imperative of Western support of rulers such as Moi.
>
> (1995:3)

Haugerud then goes on to thoroughly analyse such popular political institutions as the *baraza*, community-level political gatherings that, provided one see through the superficial rhetoric which seemingly reinforce social harmony, offer a glimpse into the mechanisms of the hierarchical Kenyan political machine all the way from the Presidential office down to the smallest locality. The *baraza* reveals, Haugerud claims, a much more complex picture of the diverse undercurrent of conflicts within Kenyan society and culture than the rather monolithic, or at best bipolar, representations constructed by many of her western colleagues. In her effort to adopt a post-modern 'constantly shifting angle of vision: one that captures the interplay of local, national, and international forces', Haugerud also very briefly discusses the role of political songs and theatre. Unfortunately, her angles of vision do not really shift beyond a professional 1991 production by Nairobi's Phoenix Players of the Gilbert and Sullivan musical satire *The Mikado*, nor does it seem to be informed by Kenyan artists who have quite a different tale to tell about the pre- and post-independence theatre in their country. Ngũgĩ wa Thiong'o, for example, warns western experts of Kenyan culture that they will only be able to contribute to its development if they 'manage to free themselves from limiting angles of visions', adopt an anti-imperialist stance, and demonstrate genuine concern for their African counterparts that goes beyond the pages of their next publication (1993: 86). With such advice, then, it seems wisest to let Kenyans themselves assess the development of their community and school theatre.

Ngũgĩ wa Thiong'o (1938), the internationally famous novelist, essayist and playwright, is a Gikuyu by birth and has been living in exile since 1982. He is currently a professor of Comparative Literature at the prestigious New York University. Ideologically, his ideas bear a strong Marxist-Panafricanist stamp, which he formulates in elegant no-nonsense essays. His publications were once banned, not only because of their activist tone, but also for the grass-roots forces they represented. Since 1992, when under international and national pressure Moi allowed other political parties besides his own KANU to participate in the presidential elections, the authoritarian control of public life seems to have relaxed somewhat. Consequently, Ngũgĩ's books are now openly distributed by East African Educational Publishers in Nairobi and available in the better bookstores of the largest Kenyan cities.

Although Ngũgĩ understandably draws the majority of his examples from his native Gikuyuland, Kenyan social science research (Ngau 1993; Ogot and Ochieng 1996: 224, 230–231) confirms that he is a factually accurate commentator on Kenyan society and culture in the period after World War II up to his exile. Ngũgĩ's own direct involvement in theatre started in the 1950s, in school plays at the exclusive Alliance boarding high school. This was the time that the anti-colonial movement was gaining momentum, spearheaded by the short-lived but groundbreaking activities of the Mau-Mau guerrillas. The Mau-Mau, with one of Ngũgĩ's brothers in their ranks, enjoyed wide support in Gikuyuland and even developed their own anti-imperialist theatre (Ngũgĩ 1981b: 69).

In *Decolonizing the Mind*, Ngũgĩ particularly stresses the detrimental impact of the official British ban on traditional drama forms that were once 'part and parcel of the rhythm of daily and seasonal life' and the imposition of their own drama instead (1986: 37):

In Alliance High School which I attended, Shakespeare, like the Speech Day, was an annual event. Between 1955 and 1958 I saw *As You Like It*, *Henry IV Part One*, *King Lear* and *Midsummer Night's Dream* roughly in that order. In the fifties through the British Council and a government-appointed colony-wide drama and music officer, the school drama was systematized into an annual Schools Drama Festival. The many European-controlled theatre buildings erected in the major towns – Mombassa, Nairobi, Nakuru, Kisumu, Kitale, Eldoret – between 1948 and 1952 specialised in West End comedies and sugary musicals with occasional Shakespeare and

George Bernard Shaw. The two most famous were the Donovan Maule Theatre in Nairobi, a fully fledged professional theatre, and the Kenya National Theatre, a colonial government establishment projected as a future multi-racial cultural centre. Independence in 1963 did not change the theatre status quo

(ibid.: 38)

At least not for the first five years or so, while British expatriates continued to direct the National Theatre and, as teachers, determined the orientation of high school drama, which only occasionally included an original Kiswahili play. A major turnaround came about when, in the late 1960s and early 1970s, a new university-educated generation began to reclaim some of the cultural space. Playwright-directors John Ruganda from Uganda and Joe de Graft from Ghana had come to the University of Nairobi to teach in the English Department. They inspired the formation of student theatre companies and, partly through productions of scripts they themselves had written, stimulated a greater interest in African drama among graduates who would go on to become high school teachers of English.

In 1959, Ngũgĩ left Kenya to study English literature at one of the University of London's prestigious African extension colleges, Makarere University College in Kampala, Uganda. Studying mostly the canonized British authors, Ngũgĩ published his first short story in Makarere's student magazine *Penpoint* (1986: 70), of which he subsequently became editor. In 1962, the Makarere Students Dramatic Society produced his play *The Black Hermit* at the Uganda National Theatre to celebrate the country's independence. In the early 1960s, Ngũgĩ also completed the manuscript for the novel that Heinemann would later publish as *The River Between* (1965), although chronologically the first novel that he published was *Weep Not, Child* (1964), when he was working as a reporter for Nairobi's *Daily Nation*. Ngũgĩ's reputation as Kenya's most powerful novelist was confirmed by *A Grain of Wheat* (1967), which he had written while a graduate student at Leeds University. At Leeds, his lifelong project of 'moving the centre' began in the newly established Department of Commonwealth Literature. Ngũgĩ returned to work as a lecturer in the Nairobi University English Department in 1967, taking a brief leave of absence during 1969 as a Creative Writing Fellow at Makarere (1993: 8).

Throughout the 1960s, Ngũgĩ and others had been pondering the question of how to Africanize literature and literary studies (1986: 23–25). Their unequivocal answer exploded in what is now referred as 'The Great Nairobi Literature Debate', which rocked the University of Nairobi for a half decade starting in late 1968. It resulted in the establishment of an

African Studies Department and an Afrocentric Literature Department instead of the Eurocentric English department that existed before. In addition to prioritizing Kenyan, East African, African, and Third World literatures over western literature, this reoriented department, by 1973 almost fully staffed by Africans, would also emphasize the importance of indigenous cultural heritage through the study of oratory (1986: 94–95). These concerns subsequently started affecting high school curricula as well as Kenyan theatre.

Although the number of productions of Kenyan- or African-authored plays increased in the first half of the 1970s, the Kenyan National Theatre and Cultural Centre continued to cater to expatriates and the local middle class with predominantly western fare. Clearly, alternative performance spaces needed to be created because the establishment venues persisted in keeping their doors closed to locally created plays (Ngũgĩ 1993: 92–93). African lecturers thereupon successfully lobbied to get Education Theatre II, a large lecture hall with a stage on the University of Nairobi campus, converted into a performance venue for new Kenyan plays. And in 1974, drama professor John Ruganda founded the Free Travelling Theatre (FTT), fashioning it after a similar initiative at Makarere, which had been active since 1966. Opiyo Mumma, FTT's current director, was a student back in 1976, when Ngũgĩ wa Thiong'o was still head of the literature department. He explains that the notion of a free theatre had been prompted by the Film and Stages Act of 1963, which stipulated that a government licence was required for public performances that charged admission: 'This meant that you had to send in your scripts to be censored.'[1] Mumma also draws a direct link between the emphasis on oratory, FTT, and the re-emergence of community theatre:

> The brief of FTT was to create plays in different Kenyan national languages, tour them free of charge in people's own spaces: a village, a hall, a football field, or a market square. In the formative years, 1975 and 1976, FTT was trying to find its feet in terms of form and style through which it could express itself and could communicate with the people. The question of orality and written material was essential to its development. It is fair to say that because of FTT community theatre started being re-articulated. As an age-old African tradition, community theatre had never really died; it had just gone underground. Only at this time, people were able to communicate its concept much more intelligently. The community plays of the Ngũgĩs in the late 1970s built on FTT's earlier work in the communities and schools.

In 1976, preparations began for the Kenyan contributions to the FESTAC 77 African Arts Festival, a groundbreaking pan-African cultural event that was scheduled to be held in Lagos the following year (Ngûgî 1997: 14–18). FTT actors and others formed an ensemble they called the Kenya Festac 77 Drama Group. Guided by director Seth Adagala, they embarked on several collective creation processes that resulted in two overtly political plays. The first one, an anti-neocolonial work called *Betrayal in the City*, was scripted by the promising young playwright and Alliance High School alumnus Francis Imbuga (1947). The second, *The Trial of Dedan Mimathi*, tried to reconstruct the Mau Mau revolt and the trials and tribulations of their charismatic leader, Mimathi, from the perspective of the peasantry and working class. It was scripted by Ngûgî wa Thiong'o and Micere Githae Mûgo, another young lecturer at Nairobi who had just completed her doctoral dissertation.[2] These two plays, although they were still in English, had an enormous impact in Nigeria and, upon their return, were performed throughout Kenya, both indoors and outdoors. The next logical step was to implement creative processes actively involving rural community residents expressing themselves in their own local languages. The most thoroughly documented example of this approach was undoubtedly *Ngaahika Ndeenda* ('I Will Marry When I Want'), which assumed legendary status after Ngûgî wa Thiong'o's much publicized detention without trial from December 1977 through to December 1978. It was followed in 1981–1982 by *Maitû Njugîra* ('Mother, Sing for Me'), which provoked a violent response from the police and resulted in Ngûgî's self-exile and that of his Kamiriithu project partner, Ngûgî wa Mirii.[3]

Ngûgî himself labelled *Ngaahika Ndeenda* 'the first major modern play in one of Kenya's languages' (1981a: 47) and regarded it as a breakthrough in his own writing career, as from then on he resolved to only write in Gikuyu.[4] But although Ngûgî wa Thiong'o and Ngûgî wa Mirii are listed as the nominal authors on the cover of the published version, the play is arguably one of the first scripts generated through a genuine participatory community theatre process to become canonized as a major literary work.

The Kamiriithu saga confirms several crucial methodological elements of community theatre. First and foremost, Ngûgî and the other university-based facilitators were explicitly invited by members of the Kamiriithu community. Second, he intimately knew the local culture and language because he was a native of the area and still lived in nearby Limuru, daily commuting the thirty odd kilometres to his office at the University of Nairobi. Participants included rich, middle-class, poor, and landless farmers as well as seasonal labourers, who expressed their commitment to the enterprise by constructing their own outdoor stage from bamboo and other locally found materials. Thanks to the decision to work in Gikuyu, they were able to fully participate in all aspects of the theatrical process, contributing lively details about the way they lived and their working conditions on the land and in the factories, about their history, their involvement in the Mau Mau revolt, local transitions after independence, landgrabbing by western entrepreneurs through local strawmen, and traditional African performing arts. Songs and dances served as crucial vehicles for drawing out local stories, explains Ngûgî:

In *Ngaahika Ndeenda* we too tried to incorporate song and dance, as part of the structure and movement of the actors. The song arises from what has gone before and it leads to what follows. The song and the dance become a continuation of the conversation and of the action.

(1986: 45)

Ngûgî dedicates relatively many words on the growing awareness of the class struggle among the Kamiriithu community actors and relatively few on the actual method he and his team used to generate original material for their play. The basic plot outline of a peasant family's ill-fated interactions with that of a rich landlord through the romantic liaison between their respective daughter and son seems to have given rise to lots of extended debates about particulars of speech and class- and generation-determined behavioral patterns. These conversations were subsequently processed into a more or less fixed script authored by the two Ngûgîs. Actors were recruited through public audition and rehearsals took place in the open air, attracting large crowds. Sometimes, Ngûgî reports, rehearsals turned into impromptu Forum Theatre:

People could see how the actors evolved from the time they could hardly move their legs or say their lines to a time when they could talk and move about the stage as if they were born talking those lines or moving on that stage. Some people in fact were recruited into the acting team after they had intervened to show how such and such a character should be portrayed. The audience applauded them into continuing doing the part.

(1986: 57)

The *Ngaahika Ndeenda* cast always worked on their play – and on the simultaneous construction of their outdoor theatre – on Saturday and Sunday afternoons in order not to interfere with work or church. The entire process lasted from January through September 1977 and directly or indirectly affected the entire Kamiriithu community of 10,000. This figure seems high but really is not in a place with few other forms of entertainment and only sparsely available electronic media. The eventual performances in October and November drew capacity crowds on six consecutive Sunday afternoons, until the Kenyatta regime banned the play and closed the outdoor stage. On New Year's Eve, Vice-President Moi signed the warrant for Ngũgĩ wa Thiong'o's arrest.

While Ngũgĩ wa Thiong'o was in the Kamiti Maximum Security Prison until 12 December 1978 and continued to be harassed by the new Moi government after his release, the Kamiriithu spirit did not die.[5] Adult education classes and other developmental activities continued under the coordination of Ngũgĩ wa Mirii and in 1980 the published Gikuyu version of *Ngaahika Ndeenda* became a phenomenal popular success, selling out three printings within three months. The next year, 1981, saw the publication of Ngũgĩ's prison diary, *Detained*, and *Writers in Politics*, a collection of his most important essays from the 1970s. In November 1981, the two Ngũgĩs and some of the other university-based artists involved in *Ngaahika Ndeenda*, held auditions for a new Gikuyu political musical they had written for the Kamiriithu community. Under the title *Maitũ Njugĩra* ('Mother, Sing for Me'), the three-month process evolved into a multilingual multimedia performance that involved not only locals from Kamiriithu, but also peasants, workers, students and teachers from eight other nationalities. Set in the 1920s and 1930s,

Maitu Njugira depicted the heroic struggle of Kenyan workers against the early phase of imperialist capitalist 'primitive' accumulation with confiscation of land, forced labour on the same stolen land

and heavy taxation to finance its development into settler run plantations. Dance, mime, song were more dominant than words in telling this story of repression and resistance. The visual and the sound images carried the burden of the narrative and the analysis.

(1986: 58)

Maitû Njugîra was booked for a long run in Nairobi's National Theatre in the first half of 1982 when it was refused a performance licence. Subsequent public rehearsals of the play in the university's Education Theatre II were eventually also forbidden after ten massively attended sessions. This official repression of theatrical activity climaxed on 12 March 1982, 'when three truckloads of armed policemen were sent to Kamiriithu Community Education and Cultural centre and razed the open-air theatre to the ground' (ibid.: 59). But although the centre henceforth had to stop all activities, this exaggerated display of dictatorial control could not have better validated the power of community theatre.

The world-wide attention that Ngûgî drew to the Kamiriithu experience through his writings may create the impression that it was by far the most radical if not the only oppositional cultural initiative in Kenya at the time. However, other sources indicate that after Moi took office in 1978, general dissension rose steadily and climaxed in the middle of 1982 with the revelation of an alleged revolutionary plot at the University of Nairobi followed by a Kenya Air Force coup attempt in August (Ogot and Ochieng 1996: 198–199). Ngau reports a deeply rooted government apprehension of grass-roots development initiatives during this period (1993: 183). And even on the theatre front there were indications that more was happening than Kamiriithu alone. In *Decolonizing the Mind*, Ngûgî himself refers to other

people-based cultural festivals like the annual Vihiga Cultural Festival in western Kenya (which) were not a copy of Kamiriithu but were inspired by a similar felt need for a renaissance of Kenyan culture which would be achieved by going to the roots of its being in the lives and languages of these people.

(1986: 60–61)

And in *Drama and Theatre: Experiences in Western Kenya*, Opiyo Mumma points to other community theatre initiatives in his native Luoland.

Drama in schools and colleges

Following Professor Joe de Graft's plea to include tertiary colleges in the National Drama Festivals in order to increase the skills of primary and secondary school teachers, the first Colleges Drama Festival was held at the National Theatre in 1975. As Mumma points out, an influential artist who benefited from this move was Felix Osodo Osodo, who was teaching at Siriba Teachers College at the time. After doing American and British drama for a decade, he had begun to create original plays with students based on improvisations and local folklore. Through the new college drama festival, his example was disseminated to other parts of Kenya. In collaboration with visual artist Joseph Dianga, Osodo then set up the Esiapala Arts Centre in Maseno, West of Kisumu City, which, like Kamiriithu, had an outdoor theatre space and offered adult education classes. As a result of this and similar initiatives, including Ngũgĩ's, more and more plays participating in the National Drama Festivals began to be written in local Kenyan languages. This trend culminated in 1979 with the ministerial appointment of Wasambo Were as the country's first non-expatriate Festival coordinator. He immediately set up a parallel festival for primary schools as well, overtly promoting the use of Kenyan languages, folklore and traditional dance.

In the late 1970s, the Free Travelling Theatre continued to be active around the country. Opiyo Mumma, a member of the troupe until his graduation in 1980, recalls:

> After the restructuring of the literature department had been completed, students would be sent out to communities in the field to try and draw out oral material such as stories, riddles, proverbs, music, instruments. Back at the University of Nairobi, they would be translated from the languages in which they had been expressed into Kiswahili and English, using some material for research purposes and the rest to be developed for FTT's next touring production. That way we made a link between FTT and the oral research of the Literature Department. The student researchers would stay with the people for three or four months and then the FTT would return there with a performance, thus providing feedback and follow-up for the research. This link-up influenced the dance dramas you started seeing in the school and colleges drama in the early 1980s, and the widespread development of lyrical dance.

But just like any other grass-roots cultural activity in the early 1980s, the FTT work was beginning to arouse the suspicion of the authorities. Following the 1982 crackdown, many dissident artists left the country. Those who stayed were forced to adopt a low profile, as did the FTT, which in those years shifted its operations from the university campus and public spaces in rural communities to less conspicuous high school classrooms in outlying regions. Even the name FTT disappeared for a while from public view, although it was temporarily replaced by another performance group at the University of Nairobi that called itself 'People's Art' and which even managed to infiltrate national television.

After graduating from Nairobi in 1980, Opiyo Mumma became a high school teacher of literature and drama near Kericho, creating FTT-style plays with students drawing on local forms of cultural expression. In the same year, fifteen other graduates, all members of FTT, took teaching jobs in other parts of Kenya. Three times a year they touched base at the different National Drama Festivals. For secondary schools, preliminary rounds followed by regional and national finals were held from January to April; for primary schools from May to August; and for colleges from September to November. In 1983, these sixteen high school teachers decided to form a loose, unregistered Drama and Education Association to try and build some kind of national cultural movement on the basis of their drama work in schools.

As civil servants employed by Kenya's Ministry of Education and as regional drama officers, high school drama teachers obviously ran the risk of getting entangled in Moi's machinations. The National Schools Drama Festival clearly illustrated this danger. It is Kenya's most important annual cultural event, involving virtually all the schools in the nation. From its inception under British colonial rule in 1959, the final round of the festival had been held in the National Theatre with school groups travelling from all over the country to the capital. In 1981, however, resourceful Festival coordinator Wasambo Were opted to let Festival winners go on a government-sponsored tour through Kenya's regions, which made a big impact on rural and urban crowds that flocked to see the shows (Mumma and Levert 1995: 40). At this point, Moi cancelled the tour and for 1982 invited the best school ensembles to come perform for him at his residence, giving the winning teachers promotions. 'It was a clear attempt to regain control,' explains Mumma:

> As long as the Festival had been locked inside that National Theatre building it didn't present any threat, but as soon as it came outside and it was seen how people were expressing themselves in

different languages and making sense in different communities, that constituted an immediate danger. So no longer the technically and artistically best schools won, but those with the most palatable political content. This is what caused us to distance ourselves from the event and to start focusing more on theatre work in the communities.

Despite the overt attempt at cooptation, government authorities were unable to curb the decentralisation of the festivals. Starting in 1982 at Mukumu Girls High School in Western Kenya, an eight-day event attracting more than 5,000 participants, the Schools and Colleges Drama Festivals have been rotating around Kenya's eight provinces. Since then, the number of performances that contain dialogues in regional languages and traditional dance and music has been increasing steadily, an evolution accompanied by growing thematic interest in such issues as the hazards of road travel and sexually transmitted diseases (Mumma and Levert 1995: 41–45).

In 1984, the gap between the national government and high school drama teachers widened even further through a major overhaul of the educational system. It forced two formerly separate subjects, English and Literature, to be merged, causing the loss of valuable curriculum time for drama. Mumma and his colleagues saw this as yet another attempt to undermine high school theatre activities, 'because it was mostly the English and Literature teachers who used drama methods to teach their subjects. Probably half the year they spent on drama with only occasional references to language. As a result, quite a few of us resigned from our teaching jobs.' Several of these ex-high school teachers then became involved in Theatre for Development, a form of grass-roots intervention that was beginning to enjoy growing support in NGO circles.[6] Mumma himself left the country to pursue a theatre-in-education MA in Britain from 1985 to 1987. Upon his return, he worked for a year in a teachers' training college before he joined the staff of the Literature Department at the University of Nairobi and became faculty advisor of FTT, which had just come out into the open again after years of working only sporadically.

Funding

Two FTT projects from 1989 reveal the grass-roots potential of Kenyan community theatre as well as some problems it encountered in terms of North–South collaboration. Ever since a Swedish development worker falsely accused an FTT faculty advisor of misappropriating a small sum in the 1970s, Mumma claims the company has been wary of strings that western donors habitually attach to their subsidies:

> FTT performs free of charge unless there is a particular occasion and the audience has been informed well in advance that they will be asked to make a donation. But whenever we approach a donor organization we are constantly asked how we are going to sustain ourselves as soon as a particular project is over. They worry that we'll come back and ask for more money. They try to get us to sell our art so we can make some money and move on. But we can't make a commitment to sell our art for a particular project. The Licensing Act and other similar anti-theatre legislation has made it imperative for us that, if we are going to retain our autonomy, we perform free of charge. So we tell a donor very honestly, 'what we do is impossible to quantify, it is priceless, it is something that exists in our minds, as a dream, as something that you won't be able to link to money. We want to change attitudes and behaviour, which is impossible to measure. You can't say after a particular period of time: we have now changed people's attitude towards particular cultural forms, we have now established a theatre-going tradition, we have now changed behaviour pertaining to a particular disease.' Empowerment is so elusive.

As a specific example of the ever-looming conflict over funding and artistic policy, Mumma mentions FTT's three-month collaboration with English theatre-in-education company Big Wheel. After a series of improvisation workshops, asccording to Mumma, the Big Wheel director wanted to publicly perform a piece based on material generated in the workshops. The director wanted to set it in a *matatu*, an idea the Kenyan participants regarded as too stereotypical and conceived with an eye only to entertainment. Mumma recalls:

> We were doing this project in between teaching duties and one day we walk into a rehearsal from our other work and the mistake the English director then made was that he categorically demanded that FTT do this performance. When he did that the whole chemistry of the place changed. He said, 'I am paying you guys to do this.' Then we found out that they had made their own contracts with the people who had brought them to Kenya without involving us. So, as a compromise we agreed to do the piece but resolved not to work with them ever again. It was a clear example of a case where people first give you money and then determine policy, artistry, and contents.

Women and community theatre

Also in 1989, FTT had a more rewarding experience remounting and touring a women's play, *Aminata*, which playwright Francis Imbuga had originally scripted back in 1985 for the UN Women's Conference, which was held that year in Nairobi. Aminata, a young educated woman from a traditionally ruled fictional village called Membe, challenges male privilege with iconoclastic actions. She opposes widow inheritance and the exclusive male right to land inheritance, polygamy, dowry, and wife beating. The main conflict of the play centres around Aminata's determination to return to her native village to settle on her deceased father's plot of land because that was his dying wish. Although overall her plight is presented sympathetically, pros and cons (including an old, conservative woman who favours tradition) are given ample space. Even Aminata's final victory is overshadowed by a male suicide as a symbolic reminder that women's emancipation cannot be achieved without loss of both the valuable and the more oppressive dimensions of tradition (Imbuga 1988: 81). After a 280-stop tour, in 1990 FTT restructured the play, which deals with the tension between traditional village life and modernity, and between male-dominated tribal hierarchies and a new generation of educated women demanding a greater say. It addressed aspects of freedom that were in the air everywhere, as Kenya was gearing up its eventually successful pressure on Moi to abandon his one-party rule (Ogot and Ochieng 1996: 239–261). Throughout this turbulent period, FTT's restructured *Aminata* performances turned into Boalesque audience intervention pieces with Mumma and actress Mweni Luni acting as Jokers.

Although FTT's community theatre activities involve both genders and occasionally directly address women's concerns, the organization continues to be controlled by men. This may have to do with the limited access to tertiary education, particularly for rural women (Mbugua 1989: 109). The few available Kenyan women's studies publications, however, indicate that literally thousands of ideologically diverse grass-roots women's groups are active throughout the country. Many of these either started as cultural groups or, over the years, have incorporated cultural activities, varying from entertaining visiting male politicians (Kabira and Nzioki 1993: 57, 72) to more explicitly women-oriented community theatre. Asenath Bole Odaga, a theatre artist who runs the Kisumu-based Gender and Development Centre, mentions the existence of more than 30,000 women's groups, most of which function predominantly as economic cooperatives for poor and lowly educated rural and urban women.

But there are also groups with special missions that have been set up to create awareness on gender issues and to sensitize the women on basic matters related to their rights, while others – like the literature and drama ones – aim at promoting women dancers, singers, actors, writers, and storytellers: thus creating forums through which the grass roots women and women as a whole may freely share and express their views.

(Mumma and Levert 1995: 50)

Although the thematic and social limits of this alleged women's freedom of expression may vary from clan to clan and community to community, there seems no doubt that, as Bole Odaga claims, 'almost all women's groups in Western Kenya and the Republic as a whole, carry on some stage and drama activities and are involved in theatrical performances at one time or another' (Bole Odaga 1995: 49–56). Beyond the songs and dances with which they entertain at a Chief's *baraza* or contribute to a *harambee* communal fundraising event, theatre offers many Kenyan women an opportunity to publicly discuss gender relations that may still be taboo in their homes.

KDEA

It is difficult to assess to what degree women have been empowered within the Kenyan theatre world in general. Clearly, in the 1990s, the University of Nairobi's Literature Department and the Free Travelling Theatre continued to play a crucial role in the development of the country's schools, colleges, and community drama, including that created by women. According to Mumma, they tend to work as follows:

Between June and September we have a repertoire of twelve different plays in eight different languages. Two of these would be published plays, two collectively devised and authored, and the rest would be created by the group on their own. They perform these in all provinces and districts of the country over a three-month period. Then we try to start amateur groups in a school or in a community and leave those groups to find their own way of working. This is also inherent to limitations of time and our way of travelling, which causes FTT not to be able to stay in communities for more than a couple of days.

The FTT clones at Kenyatta, Moi, and Egerton Universities have adopted a similar approach, helping Kenya's community and school theatre movement to gain momentum. Their work was enhanced by momentous developments in 1991 and 1992. In addition to Moi's re-election, some drama teachers succeeded in officially registering the Kenyan Drama and Education Association (KDEA), benefiting from the support of the International Drama/Theatre and Education Association (IDEA), which had just been founded in Portugal and the relative democratic space that suddenly opened up, when 'on 10 December 1991, Parliament passed the constitutional amendment repealing Section 2A, thereby effectively ending KANU's legal monopoly of political power' (Ogot and Ochieng 1996: 245). But the formation of KDEA was not devoid of controversy, recalls Opiyo Mumma, who was pursuing a PhD degree at Manchester University at the time:

> We had been anti-registration; it is something that we had defied all along. But when I was in England, two other Kenyans who had joined me in Portugal went back and managed to get KDEA registered. That almost ripped us apart because from then on we had to work both within the system and against it. One of the main issues was how we would deal with the cultural legislature that we were against, like the Witchcraft Act of 1925, the Chiefs Act of 1937, the Public Order Act of 1950, and the Films and Stages Act of 1963. These four laws affect theatre work, public gatherings and culture. Also in 1992, Theatre Workshop moved out of the University of Nairobi to become an independent group.[7] The reason for this was that we wanted to spread out our work to different groups around the city. We also decided in 1992 to try and get the travelling theatre concept well-rooted in other universities, such as Egerton, Kenyatta, and Moi, and that meant that a lot of our members also spread out across the country and then started making an impact from within on the Kenyan Schools and Colleges Drama Festival movement. KDEA would become the centralizing body to coordinate all these initiatives. At the same time, being an officially registered body allowed us to have smaller branches all over the country and a lot of seeds were sown that way.

Since its foundation, KDEA has been lobbying on a national political level to change repressive cultural legislation and reintroduce drama as a legitimate curricular subject after its removal in 1984. At the grass roots, Mumma explains, KDEA preaches diversity:

> We don't interfere with the existing structures of groups in a community. If a local structure is functioning that is important to

respect; it's really up to them. Our focus at this particular time is really to get a movement going that defies individuals and time, and to set up structures that enable anybody to fit in. We obviously have to improve skills, train people who have never performed before. Then we have to work with and in educational institutions, because they are the singlemost widespread community institutions in the country.

The significance of this remark was emphatically illustrated when on 2 October 1997 the 240,000 members of the Kenyan National Union of Teachers (KNUT) went on strike over a wage dispute, affecting more than 7 million pupils in this nation of 25 million and thus indirectly virtually every Kenyan household.

It is hardly surprising, then, that schools, along with the communities to which they are so firmly connected, continue to provide a fertile playground for Kenya's expanding theatre movement. But if we are to believe George Odera Outa, the Schools and Colleges Drama Festival, in which KDEA is so intricately involved, is also a political minefield (1997: 223–224). KDEA's future success seems to depend, then, on how well it will manage to steer clear of regional, tribal, and personal rivalries that are more of a hindrance than Dr Mumma cares to admit. His promotion of the University of Nairobi's Free Travelling Theatre as KDEA's performance flagship has already caused irritation in some regions[8] and seems to contradict the association's professed aim not to impose aesthetic or organisational standards on others.

The FTT entrance in a remote village in Meru province on 12 September 1997 was overwhelming, to say the least. The actors had parked their university van near Chogoria, just off the main road to Meru City, and had danced and sung the entire 5 kilometres on the dust road to a field in front of a rural primary school, where they had arranged to meet the local Kairithu youth group for a cultural interaction. But rather than collaborating, the 20-strong FTT troupe, with all their youthful exuberance and undeniable performance skills, stole the show with some satirical educational skits and stage poetry interspersed with contageous rhythmic calls and responses. Their urban energy and confidence were received enthusiastically by the school kids and their teachers, but had the effect of intimidating rather than inspiring the quiet and unassuming rural Kairithu performers, who listlessly took to the stage after FTT's hard-to-follow act. Similar irritations could be detected at the chaotic Third IDEA World Congress, which KDEA hosted in Kisumu from 10 to 19 July, 1998. Peter Kimani, reviewing the event for the *Daily Nation* on 24 July, pointed to 'the advantageous position that the FTT enjoyed throughout the congress, to the chagrin of other groups'.

CASE STUDY: THE KAWUONDA WOMEN'S THEATRE OF SIGOTI

The text below is informed by a western anthropological (Berg-Schlosser 1984) and a western sociogeographical source (Sterkenburg 1982) and by many personal interviews with mostly male and some female Luo residents from the Greater Sigoti area. In reading it, it is important to understand that this was only my first thorough encounter with life in a western rural Kenyan setting where polygamy is still relatively widely practised, particularly among the older population. I had requested, but for what I was told were 'practical' reasons, did not get, a high-school-educated Sigoti woman to serve as interpreter. Consequently, all our interactions with the Kawuonda Women's Group, most of whom were poorly educated and spoke little or no English, were facilitated by at least three but often even more educated local males in their twenties and thirties. Frequently, some of the older men also observed our activities from a distance, intrigued it seemed by the filming process but nevertheless through their mere presence inhibiting the women from freely expressing themselves. I did, however, eventually correspond with a young Sigoti woman, Carolyne Odero, who was studying to become a teacher and who did facilitate my second, much more open-hearted exchange with the Kawuonda Women's Group in July 1998. All these diverse voices I have, I hope, reflected respectfully in the sentences that follow. Sigoti gender relations are what they are. It would be simplistic to judgmentally apply allegedly 'superior' western gender studies standards when both men and women in Sigoti responded so generously and honestly to my sometimes confrontational questions. Sigoti is in that respect a remarkable community in its openness to outsiders. Over the years, it has hosted many theatre artists from other parts of Kenya and from abroad. Its schools participate in the schools drama festivals. Some local teachers also work with youth outside school hours in someone's homestead on their own scripts. Even the Sigoti male elders sometimes perform in dramas of their own creation. Thus, in Sigoti, an open space near the ridge – the future site for the Sigoti Arts Centre – frequently becomes an arena where community theatre serves as the medium through which the young communicate their concerns to the old, the men to the clan at large, and the women can tell their husbands, sons, and daughters things they would not (yet) be free to say in their own private domains.

Profile of the Sigoti area

The Kawuonda Women's Group is an integral part of the Sigoti-Ramogi clan, a tightly knit community organized in a village of scattered dwellings and small agricultural plots on top of a steep escarpment over-looking the large Kano Plains, which, to the West, border on Lake Victoria. Uganda is vaguely visible in the distance, as is the Nandi table-land ridge to the North and the smoke rising from Kisumu City, sprawling inland from the lakeshore below. Down there, western culture and indeed the world beckon in the guise of buses, trains and planes to Entebbe and Nairobi, videos, music, fashion, and a genuine Internet café. But even though Kenya's third largest city is only 30 miles away as the crow flies, in Sigoti no one owns a car and only a few fortunate souls possess bicycles. The occasional automobile that reaches the village either belongs to a successful relative visiting from Nairobi, to the Location Chief, or to someone in Sondu, the nearest township on the main tarmac road from Kisumu to Kisii. From Sondu there are many *matatus* (collective taxis) and buses that can take you to the Kisumu bus station within the hour, but in order to get to Sondu, people from Sigoti first have to walk some 6 kilometres. Only with luck can they pick up a ride along the way from one of the rare *matatus* that ventures on the pot-holed, rock-infested dirt road connecting Sondu with Nyabondo, a larger village between Sigoti and Sondu and the headquarters of the Sub-Location Chief.

Sondu and Nyabondo are the nearest places where Sigoti residents can do more elaborate shopping, buy yesterday's newspaper, or make a phone call. Sigoti itself only has a small row of five small shops opposite the open-air marketplace. In these establishments, which effectively consti-tute the village's social and commercial hub, one can obtain soft drinks, batteries, cookies, or have small repairs done by the mechanic or tailor. Due north from the centre lies Sigoti's small clinic, a white brick con-truction right on the edge of the escarpment. Villagers can get medication here from a skeletal staff of nurses whenever they have a malaria attack; for more complicated treatment they have to travel to Kisumu, or, in life-threatening cases, to Nairobi. The clinic, the shops, not even all the schools and only very few houses have electricity, which came to Sigoti in 1990. The handful of old black-and-white television sets in the village have a bad picture and can only pick up the government channel KBC. Several people own battery-powered radios and cassette players. A large part of Nyakach District, to which Sigoti belongs, continues to be without electricity as well as running water. In the absence of street lamps and motorized traffic, Sigoti nights are pitch black and its silence is only broken by the all-too-frequent ominous drums of funeral wakes.

A narrow footpath leads from the Sigoti Clinic to a 'water point' halfway down the escarpment . It is usually the kids' task to fetch drinking water for their mothers in plastic jars once they get out of school. Beyond the spring, the path continues to another village, Sigoti-Kandaria, which lies on a lower plateau. From there, the escarpment drops abruptly all the way down to the level of Lake Victoria. Sigoti-Kandaria and the Kano Plains below it look a trifle greener and wetter than Sigoti-Ramogi, which lies more exposed to the elements, but on the other hand, because of the cooler and windier micro-climate higher up, it also has slightly fewer mosquitoes. Barring the odd Eucalyptus tree and brush, the brown volcanic soil looks barren with numerous goats roaming through it in search of grass. Most people earn a subsistence living by growing onions, cabbage, groundnuts, maize, millet, tomatoes, cassava, and potatoes on their relatively small plots of land. Whatever is not needed to feed their families is sold twice a week in the small local market in the village centre. But because of unusually long droughts, in 1996 and 1997 there was less to go around than usual.

Administratively, Sigoti is a rural community of approximately 500 inhabitants, all of whom are related in a clan through blood ties or marriage. Together with Sigoti-Kandaria and several other nearby villages, it forms a Location of some 15,000 inhabitants, which is administered by a Location Chief. Some 14 such locations form the Nyakach constituency, which has a total population of more than 150,000 and is subdivided into two administrative units – Lower Nyakach, where Sigoti-Kandaria is located, and Upper Nyakach, upon the escarpment. These are governed by two District Officers (DO), one based at Pap-Onditi and the other one at Ogoro.[9] The Location Chief in Nyabondo is one of six Chiefs in Upper Nyakach who report to the DO. The two DOs are responsible for public security and development in their respective areas, coordinating police, health, education (including more than 140 primary and at least 30 secondary schools), agriculture, and social services. They, in turn, are supervised by the District Commissioner (DC) in Kisumu City, whose immediate boss, the Provincial Commissioner, is directly answerable to the President.

Traditional social and ceremonial power in Sigoti-Ramogi is effectively in the hands of a council of male elders, although an officially registered cooperative of some 70 women in the age range of 20 to 80 has been slowly gaining ground since its establishment in 1967. These women will be the focus of this case study. Alcoholism, especially consumption of cheap locally brewed *chang'a*, appears to be a widespread problem, particularly among young and middle-aged males, of whom there are relatively few when compared to kids under 15 and elderly men over 55. Most male high school graduates tend to migrate to the cities in search of jobs or tertiary study. Employment opportunities in the villages, other than farming and teaching, are virtually non-existent and rural joblessness rates among out-of-school youth are consequently very high. Most Luos who migrate to the cities retain close ties with relatives who stay behind. They return home several times a year and, when the time comes, permanently, when men are buried on their ancestral land and women on their husband's.

Religion continues to be a significant binding force in Sigoti, although increasingly less so for the young. The Catholic Church of Nyabondo appears to be the most influential religious institution in the area. It runs a boarding school and is, generally, the driving force behind many development projects. The older people in Sigoti still speak fondly of Father Leo Bartels, a Dutch missionary who was a teacher and development worker in the area from 1936 until 1976. There are also several other smaller Protestant, charismatic, or African Independent Church congregations in the area, while traditional animistic Luo beliefs, rituals, and herbal medicine continue to be practised by some.

Mr Augustino Swa Odongo Mumma (b. 1933) was educated by Father Leo at Nyabondo Primary and Secondary School and went on to succeed him as headmaster before becoming a school inspector until his retirement in 1986. In his spare time, he served on several local and divisional development committees and school boards. Once, he even went on a long government-sponsored overseas trip with other community leaders from around Kenya to study development initiatives in Europe, the Middle East and the Caribbean. For all these reasons and because of his strong personality, he is regarded as one of the most influential elders in Sigoti. His uneducated father, Odongo Komollo, and his mother, Maria Okumu, lie buried behind the traditional thatch-roofed and mud-walled Luo dwelling that Mr Mumma has left standing behind the more modern brick house where he and his wife Emma now live. Their relatively large and neatly maintained compound also includes two other houses. According to

Luo custom, as one walks in, the house belonging to their first-born son, Opiyo, is located on the left, and that of their second son on the right. Seating arrangements in the main house are similarly codified: the male host sits at the head of the table left of the entrance, other clansmen sit to his left with their backs to the kitchen door, while guests are supposed to sit to his right with their backs to the entrance. Female relatives serve food and tend not to sit down to eat with the guests, who may, however, include women not living in Sigoti. Augustino Mumma explains that once a woman has married and has become a member of the husband's clan, the ties with her native com-munity are drastically reduced: 'So when my sister marries into another clan, she participates much less here. She cannot be given land here; only where she is married. When she comes here, she is a visitor.'

The Luo people are considered a 'Western Nilotic' tribe (Berg-Schlosser 1984), meaning that they migrated down the Nile from Sudan and ended up in Western Kenya via Uganda. Sigoti-Ramogi was settled in 1905, when Augustino Mumma's grandfather, Omollo, and his great uncle, Otula, discovered a pond, expanded it, and built the first dwellings around it. Their father was called Awuonda, who had other sons settling elsewhere in Nyakach. Augustino Mumma's great-grandfather, then, is the reason why the Sigoti women's cooperative calls itself the Kawuonda Women's Group, for female identities and names continue, at least nominally, to be determined by male lineage. All the women in the collective are married, polygamously or monog-amously, to a male descendant of either Omollo or Otula. Thus, Omollo had three sons, Opiyo, Otielo, and Odongo, the latter being Augustino's father.

European colonizers arrived in Nyanza around 1901, four years before the Kawuonda clan settled Sigoti. There was very little direct contact between Sigoti residents and the British, to whom the plateau was of no other interest than to supply cheap labour and soldiers. Possessing a strong oral culture, the old people in Sigoti still talk about the conscrip-tion of Augustino Mumma's uncle, Swa, who was sent to fight in World War II. But pseudo-forced labour under the euphemistic label 'employ-ment by agreement' had a more profound impact on the community, Mr Mumma recalls:

> There was no British police patrol as such, but if the planters wanted people to work for them they sent agents who conscripted people to work on sugar, coffee, and tea plantations. People had to

go for three or five years, depending on the 'agreement'. But people didn't know what they were getting into. By the time you realized what kind of hard labour was involved and you didn't want to be there anymore, you had signed already for all those years. Many people from Sigoti went for 'agreement' in this way. It broke the culture. Once a husband leaves for five years it is hard on the wife, who was not allowed to join him. Before these disruptive colonial practices, family culture was very different. People worked communally in a very tight way, also to protect each other against enemies. That's why Luo people always married many wives, so that they would have many sons to defend the community in tribal wars. But if someone was taken to work by agreement or to fight in a war, then he had no chance to marry many wives.

Under colonial rule, tribal culture was officially treated as primitive and tribal languages were banned from schools. The British also introduced modern marriage registration, whereas traditionally it was an informal agreement, sometimes prepared by a male intermediary visiting the father of the intended bride on behalf of the suitor, and always settled with a dowry, after which the new wife became an unalienable part of the bridegroom's community. Since independence was declared in 1963, rural clans have been making a conserted effort to revive their cultural heritage. Community theatre and school drama have contributed significantly to this revival, which, however, increasingly excludes oppressive gender relations. Particularly younger educated women are less and less interested in polygamous relationships and a village existence where they are expected to do the bulk of the agricultural labour in addition to the household and childcare.

The female nurses of the Sigoti clinic counsel many local women and detect increasing stress levels. They point to poverty, long working hours, multiple responsibilities, single motherhood, alcoholism, marital rape, and a growing number of widows who have lost their husband due to HIV/AIDS. They also regard polygamy as a source of stress, because of the competition and intrigues that sometimes occur between co-wives. From their city-educated perspective, the nurses do not think women are given the same opportunities as men. They recognize, however, that this is a problem that can only be effectively dealt with if men also become conscious of gender inequality.[10] Carolyne Odero, a 23-year-old Sigoti native, argues that not only men are responsible, but that many older women resist change as well:

A woman who wants to leave her house to carry out some business which is not family business is unheard of unless she is single. Even other women would feel something is wrong with her. I think that women themselves have developed a mentality that once they're married they should only move within the square of river, kitchen, market, and back to the compound. They fear men and the men, realizing this, tend to take advantage.[11]

Like Carolyne Odero, the head nurse of Sigoti clinic would not mind having an equal partner for a husband:

I would love for him to help me cook and he is also welcome to help me with the laundry and cleaning the house – particularly high dusting; he can then leave the bedding and mopping to me. Now that's cooperation. I am lucky that I can discuss such things at home with my husband, but even so, as a woman you must have a shock absorber – to antagonize is useless. You might be tempted to fight, but you're always fighting against the president.

She suggests that, instead of confrontation, women should resort to more creative strategies if they want to expand their space within the community.

Although he once believed polygamy was a good idea, Augustino Mumma has never practised it himself and now thinks it will soon disappear: 'If you marry too many wives, your chances of getting AIDS increase and people now also begin to see that if you have too many children, you cannot feed them.' And while he admits that women work harder and have more responsibilities than men, he is not yet ready to accept that all these changes should be translated into expanded political power for women. Moreover, he regrets that western cultural and educational influences have caused the Luo woman's connection to her community to erode.

The Kawuonda Women's Group

Carolyne Odero, who graduated from teacher's college in 1998, has been working with the Kawuonda Women's Group off and on for several years. She believes that as a young educated woman she is now more free to speak her mind than before, although she is grateful for the traditional culture her grandmother has passed on to her. One of the main reasons why the Kawuonda Women's Group started doing theatre was exactly because older women were noticing that their cultural influence was beginning to wane. Helida Molo Odongo, Kawuonda's treasurer, explains:

> We like doing drama because we find that today the young people forget their relatives, they forget our cultural practices and adapt to the new ways. A long time ago children used to sleep in the grand-parents' houses, but now they sleep in their own small rooms. When they used to sleep in the grandparents' houses, they would be told stories that educated them. Now we use drama to educate children about our grandmothers, grandfathers, and our ancestors plus our cultural practices. Secondly, it gives us strength and happiness to talk in front of people. Drama also teaches us how to dialogue with men. If a woman stays at home she may have more problems. When we come together, we can share our problems and give each other comfort. It gives women courage to talk in public. It enhances women's freedom.[12]

The Kawuonda Women's Group was informally established in 1967, when they were invited to sing and dance at Jomo Kenyatta's home, a rare honour that the older women still remember proudly. Originally, the collective was almost exclusively economically oriented, although even in those early years the women would tell each other stories and some-times sang and danced whenever they needed a break from work. They had learned these chants and dances from their mothers and grand-mothers, who had told them that the roots of these forms of expression went all the way back to Sudan. They did not start doing 'real' theatre, in the sense of consciously acted scenes based on their own stories, until the mid-1990s.

Susan Adhiambo Odongo, Kawuonda's current chair, is the wife of one of Otula's great-grandsons. On the video, she explains that the pond, where the Sigoti ancestors first settled, continues to be a power-ful spiritual symbol for the women. Quite practically, it is a place where they daily meet to do the laundry, to let their cattle drink, and scoop up water for irrigation and construction of mud walls. It is a literal source of life for Sigoti and for the women a natural location for telling each other stories.

It is unclear when exactly Kawuonda started creating and perform-ing contemporary dramas, although Sigoti native Opiyo Mumma, Augustino's son, must have had something to do with it. His mother, Emma, a retired school teacher and hence a respected woman in the community, is Kawuonda's secretary. After first performing in Sigoti with a high school group in 1973, Opiyo Mumma has frequently returned to his village with Nairobi's Free Travelling Theatre. Starting in the early 1990s, he has also facilitated several extended visits by European and North American drama teachers. A Dutch drama teacher, Joyce Colijn, helped found an educational theatre group composed of Sigoti Teachers in 1994, which later linked itself to KDEA (Mumma and Levert 1995: 88–98). In 1995, Opiyo Mumma, his father Augustino, and several other teachers from schools in the area organized the first Sigoti Arts Festival, which has since become an annual event. Some of these initiatives surely rubbed off on the Kawuonda Women's Group, who, in typical Kenyan community theatre fashion, subsequently experimented to develop their own rudimentary playmaking method.

The Kawuonda method of community playmaking

One of the women begins to tell a story during a natural break from work, after which they collectively decide to turn it into drama. They cast the parts by consensus but the narrator, as the story's owner, has a decisive voice and functions as a director. Blocking is done by arranging props in a makeshift set and positioning characters within it. Then they improvise scenes. Songs and dances serve as beginnings, endings, scene transitions, and throughout as a background soundtrack. The Kawuonda women improvise as many different versions as they think necessary, sometimes recasting or changing dialogues to try out alternative suggestions from a group member. The process can take anywhere from a few days to several weeks and, where possible, is integrated with economic activities. As Susan puts it: 'If the play takes us to a point where we should be tilling the land, then we actually go and till so that our drama coincides with the work.' The women perform their plays at public functions and sometimes use the same process for off-limits in-house improvisations on more delicate women's issues.

On Thursday morning, 18 September 1997, some thirty women gather by the pond to do their laundry. While some scrub and others carry water, Rose, who is in her mid-twenties, starts talking about the long absences of her husband. She is interested, she says, to learn from the older women how they used to deal with such situations. She then asks her mother-in-law, Clementina Onditi Swa, to tell the story of her husband, whom, she knows, was forcibly conscripted to become a soldier in World War II.[13] To help her along, Rose sketches the scene for Clementina by saying she remembers that the men had just started to drink in celebration of a good harvest and to gossip about some of their more troublesome wives, one of whom had apparently complained about her husband's beatings. Out of the blue, Rose goes on, a colonial recruiting agent then came storming in and ordered the Sigoti men to select one of them to fight for the colonial army. Rose, who as narrator now also assumes the role of director, invites Clementina to tell the other women what she felt when her young husband, Swa, was selected and forced to leave the community for an uncertain future on some foreign frontline. Clementina begins to improvise, lamenting about being left alone to work the land as well as looking after two children. Helida and another woman spontaneously get up to play Swa's brothers and offer to assist her. Rose stops them and asks the women to begin improvising from the top, starting with the drinking session. She will provide narrated transitions between the scenes.

The women visibly enjoy playing male roles, for it offers them an opportunity to satirize male behaviour and to speak foul language, which as women they would not normally be allowed to do in public. The older women tell the younger ones what the male and female seating arrangements were like in 1940 and what the usual procedure was for a harvest party. For example, they explain how the millet beer was brewed and how the men would drink through long straws from one and the same big pot standing in the middle. They play the scene all the way through to the moment when Swa is dragged away by two colonial agents.

During the next break from washing, the women act the story out again, but this time the storyline and the characters change substantially. Before Rose begins her prologue, the women all rhythmically move in a circle while they sing a song, in call and response fashion, about women for whom it is all right to sing, drink, and dance as long as they first complete their domestic chores. Some women then mime making beer and send Swa's young wife to invite the other men to come drink. The young woman seizes this opportunity to complain about Swa's beatings. When the men are alone, drinking, Swa, whose role is played by Susan, explains that he is sometimes forced to discipline his wife when she cooks bad food. One of Swa's brothers, played by Emma, responds that beating is not good but that he agrees that young women are less disciplined than before. Swa's young wife, who has also been drinking, then tells the men in the presence of her husband that she may one day leave him if he continues to abuse her. But her speech is rudely interrupted by the army recruiters, who take Swa away, while his wife, quickly forgetting her earlier complaints, begs them not to.

Another song, this one about the soil which needs to be stepped on hard because it has taken so many people away, provides the transition to the next scene that dramatizes the poverty of Swa's wife and children and the help they receive from the in-laws. A third song, about a proud crane bird whose movements resemble that of a human being, announces Swa's return from the war and the party that follows. The play, which seems to emerge from and then disappears back into the circular songs and dances, is finally swallowed up, as it were, in a song and dance about a hornbill, that, in Luo mythology, is a messenger of disaster to come.

Susan and Rose explain that they flesh out their improvisational scenes each time they rehearse. Today, they do a third version of the 'Swa play' after they finish the laundry. Rose re-assigns roles and insists that Clementina play herself. As the narrator, Rose reiterates that as a young wife in 1997 she has a problem similar to that of her mother-in-law in 1940, although she does not specify whether this concerns her husband's frequent absences, his abuse, or her possible contemplation to leave him. This time, the improvisations are interrupted more frequently by those women who are not cast in a particular scene giving technical or dramaturgical advice. Thus, one of them comments: 'Can you begin from the top. I don't even see the door. Where did she go through? And that beer pot over there is not placed the way it should be. It might fall and spill.' Someone else explains that the male elders should already be seated before the women bring in the beer pot and an older cast member remarks: 'I can't sit over there. I would love to but my husband died recently and I haven't remarried, so the cultural laws do not allow me to sit together with those people.' Rose, fearing an endless discussion, urges them to get on with it: 'You don't have to be so strict, it is only a play, not reality. Let things be the way they are, so that we can continue this play.' Thus, improvisations evolve with periodic interruptions from the women in the audience, suggesting, for example, to add a more appropriate drinking song, or to change intonations and gestures so that a particular woman acts more convincingly as a man. This time, they end the third run-through not with the pessimistic hornbill song but with a more upbeat one about an unorthodox mother who visits her daughter's village and joins in a dance, thereby shocking the parents of her daughter's husband. The caller calls out the actual names of Kawuonda women, who then each take turns stepping into the circle to represent the unorthodox mother, an obvious symbol of a liberated woman.

After they have finished working on the 'Swa play', Clementina says she hopes it teaches the children of Sigoti what these old drinking ceremonies were like, how young people were supposed to relate to their elders, and how a community should join forces to help each other:

'What you just saw is a true story. My husband was conscripted and I remained behind with the children. The fact that my husband was away for seven years was hard on me, but it helped me become a free woman. He left me with a child whom I educated. We worked the land, we made pots, wove baskets so that we could survive. And I had my brothers-in-law who loved and helped me.' And although Rose likes the story because it reminds her of how men and women lived fifty years ago, she claims that today, unlike in the old days, women are better off relying on other women than on brothers-in-law when their husbands are gone.

On Saturday evening, 20 September 1997, the Kawuonda women take time off from their bakery shift to dramatize Yunia Awiti Otula's story about her husband, who left her for three years to work as an industrial labourer in Nairobi back in the 1930s. He was legally compelled to go because of an insidious colonial taxing scheme that amounted to forced labour. Yunia and Rose first narrate a reconstructed version of the story. One day the cops came in and took Yunia's husband away. After his departure she managed to keep working the land and weave baskets with the help of her children and other women from the community, but her husband's brothers became envious of her rich crop and angry about her independent attitude and therefore schemed, unsuccessfully as it turned out, to take the woman's land away.

The women begin to sing and dance in a circle, which apparently gives them a sense of unity and strength and inspires their subsequent improvisations. The women who do not act create a soundtrack by continuing to sing and dance quietly in the background, while the others break out of the circle and perform their scenes in the middle. The main variations the women try out in the two versions they create this evening centre around the resolution of the conflict, which in version one is decided by a colonial administrator siding with the brothers-in-law and in the other by a male clan elder, who confirms Yunia's land rights but at the same time scolds her for her impertinent outbursts to men. With this play, Kawuonda seemed to express that, according to Luo traditional law, women as adoptive daughters of their husband's community have full rights to the land, but at the same time question the traditional prohibition of women to be publicly critical of men. Or as Yunia put it: 'I realized that if my husband had been there, there wouldn't have been any problems, because they respect men.' Community theatre, then, allows the women to say things they cannot yet say in non-performative situations and to process profound emotions, as Yunia's reaction indicates: 'When we re-enacted the story, the feelings came to me as if they were real and I felt very sad at one point. I was very bitter then. Very bitter.'

The forced labour and landgrabbing play is bracketed by two powerful songs. The opening song, 'Kawuonda Is Grinding', is a proudly performed composition in which the women collectively embrace the identity of the group and vouch to keep grinding meal even if the machine were to break down, thereby signifying their determination to stick together indefinitely. In the final song, the women collectively complain about mosquitoes and tse-tse flies biting their backs, while they throw both arms over the back of their shoulders to get rid of the harassing creatures. A year later, when I was able to speak to them through a female instead of a male interpreter, they explained that the mosquitoes and the tse-tse flies symbolize the abusive men in their lives.

On Tuesday, 23 September 1997, the women meet at the Sigoti market, a few hours before sunset. After spreading out their wares and asking friends to look after things, they form a circle in an open space and begin a public rehearsal of a play about the Kenyan fight for independence in the late 1950s and early 1960s. Reconstructing the history of Kenyatta's incarceration and release from a Luo women's point of view, Helida, who serves as narrator, emphasizes that in 1963 women as well as men gained their freedom, because women fought equally hard to get rid of the colonizer, yet they never received recognition for their efforts.

The rehearsal in the marketplace is somewhat chaotic, possibly because of the noise from the crowd attracted by our film crew. Some women, who were supposed to act as policemen arresting the unidentified independence activist, therefore miss their cue, causing the hero, also played by Helida, to break out of her role to prompt them on. Theatrically, the play is little more than a repetitive sequence of political rallies at which the independence leader first urges his audience to fight for freedom and get rid of the white people, and, after his release from prison, to practise *harambee*, which means pulling all available resources together and collectively work towards development. In terms of the creative process, however, Helida, who both plays the lead and directs, takes firm control of the process, recasting some of the roles and urging the actors to be more expressive. For example, she asks the woman playing the leader's wife to act more shocked when she hears of his arrest: 'When you have slapped yourself, you say he has been arrested for freedom politics, you understand? Then all of you should really act happy about the independence to which I led you. And then you, Jane, should start agitating for change. And I should return from jail very lean and tired.'

After the second run-through, Helida explains that she wanted to dramatize this particular story to inspire children who are growing up today to learn from their grandparents' fight for independence, but also to help them understand that for women this independence struggle is far from over yet:

> Women are still under men's yoke. This play educates them that they should work towards independence through dialogue, not by force. In Luo tradition, men's opinions are more powerful than women's. So, once a woman marries she has to adopt the ideas that prevail in her husband's community. This gives so many women problems and results in numerous separations. Therefore, the stories we tell today show ways of making things smoother and less forced. And dramas are performed in places where people come together. And wherever people are together they have conversations, so our dramas help the process of adopting new ways of doing things.

On Thursday morning, while a number of women are weaving baskets in Susan's compound, Rose tells a story about a waiter at the Egerton Hotel in Kisumu, who one day received a letter announcing that he has been awarded a grant to study overseas. His wife is quite happy that he will go away for a while, because it will give her freedom and, after her husband's return, an increased income. But after she has accompanied her husband to the airport, the story takes a tragic turn: the woman takes her small baby to a bar, where she flirts with a man and then sleeps with him. According to Luo belief this is a taboo and the next day, when she arrives back in her husband's community, her baby gets sick. Her parents-in-law advise her to go see a traditional healer but she prefers to consult a modern doctor, who, because of the taboo-related ailment, cannot diagnose any of the symptoms. Eventually the child dies and a few years pass before the husband returns with a second wife from another African country. The jealous first wife expresses her anger and the conflict that ensues is further aggravated when the husband finds out that she has caused his child to die.

Rose's story, which touches on social norms of behaviour for women and on the contrast between modern and traditional beliefs, provokes an animated discussion that reveals clear generational differences among the women, who continue to weave while speaking their minds. Susan suggests that both the husband and the first wife deserve criticism, while someone else objects to the husband's returning with another wife. An older woman claims that when she was young they would never have dared to behave the way the young woman did in the story. But Rose disagrees, insinuating that back then women frequently had promiscuous relationships with their brothers-in-law. Although the different generations thus continue to differ on what is morally acceptable behaviour for women, they all agree with Susan's claim that women are stronger than men: 'She has to work the land carrying the baby on her back, she has to look after the animals in the homestead, she has to milk the cows, and if she doesn't make the bed it will remain untidy the whole day. A woman works so hard and yet she is always very composed.'

The play the women subsequently create from the story about the man who went abroad becomes an elaborate drama. It contains extensive dialogues and many scenes, including a finale in which the 'husband' first kicks and then chases his promiscuous wife all around the compound, merrily fired on by all the other women, who behave more freely that morning because there are fewer men around than on earlier occasions.

In the afternoon, they meet at the Mumma homestead where they continue weaving and picking coffee beans in the small plantation behind the house, while dramatizing the story of a young woman, played by Rose, who returns from the city to become a member of the women's collective. It is the most explicitly political play they have done all week and encapsulates all the artistic, economic and social dimensions of Kawuonda's work. After distributing the roles, Rose begins to tell a story of a wife and husband who live and work in Nairobi. The man is active in anti-government politics in the period leading up to the introduction of a multi-party system before the presidential elections of 1992. Like many other Luos, Rose's fictional husband is arrested and she is sacked from her job. She returns to her husband's village, Sigoti, and since she is now jobless and needs to feed her kids, her mother-in-law advises her to ask Kawuonda if she can join them. She is received with open arms and to explain how they work, the Kawuondo women give Rose a guided tour of their farm, with different members taking turns to say something about Kawuonda's history.

In the video we can see how Mama Emma opens the narrative by telling the story of the first collectively purchased chicken and the calf, Aryana, the offspring of which is placed in the hands of another woman from the collective. She then leads the spectators, mostly women and a few children, from the animal shelter to the coffee plantation while the chorus sings a song. Once they reach the coffee bushes, everyone begins to pick the ripe beans, singing as they go and after about fifteen minutes of working this way Rose, in character, addresses the chairlady to thank her and the collective for welcoming her into their midst. Susan concludes the play with an uplifting epilogue about how young villagers who are lured to the bright lights of the city should never forget about the hard-working women who stay behind, because one day they may get fired too and will then come rushing back for help.

That following Sunday afternoon, the Sigoti branch of KDEA has organized a cultural festival on the shadeless edge of the escarpment. It is a four-hour event that attracts hundreds of locals and residents from nearby villages, especially children. Groups from primary schools perform songs and dances, some teachers perform a farce, a youth group from Sigoti performs an AIDS-awareness play written by a teacher, and traditional musicians in tribal goat skin attire play music on drums and trumpets made of antelope antlers. As is usual on such occasions, the Sub-Location Chief, looking authoritative in his khaki uniform and military beret, also makes an appearance. Around 4.30 p.m., it is the turn of the Kawuonda women. They first create a circular space by singing and dancing to 'Kawuonda Is Grinding,' after which they perform a shortened version of Helida's play about the struggle for independence. This time, Susan plays the lead, dressed in her husband's Sunday best suit. The actresses playing the cops are clearly more concentrated than during the Tuesday rehearsals at the market, entering on cue to arrest the political leader, whom they drag off somewhat more forcefully than intended, causing the crowd as well as the performers to crack up. Instead of playing the scene where the leader gets released from jail, they therefore decide to finish their performance at this unanticipated climax with the 'mosquitoes' song. In terms of acting and sheer energy their play was far superior to the shows that preceded theirs.

> The community theatre of the Kawuonda Women's Group is, then, first and foremost a sanctuary where the women can nurture their creativity, express their frustrations and jubilations, and explore strategies of domestic survival and communal development. And as public performance, their community theatre functions as a cultural binding force. It takes over the grandmother's traditional storytelling role by replaying scenes from the past lest the children forget. But at the same time, the Kawuonda plays also build bridges to those men who care to listen and watch.

The Kawuonda women's collective, which is led by a rotating committee of nine, draws a great deal of strength from its theatre activities. As Susan explains in the video, their simple but effective improvisational method is all about turning ideas and stories into dramatic action, which is the same principle the women apply in their economic activities. But most of all, she emphasizes, 'our theatre has brought us closer together'. Through it, the women express that they appreciate genuinely disinterested male support, but abhor being trampled on by men who, like irritating mosquitoes and tse-tse flies, sit on their backs while they let women do all the work. Kawuonda's plays demonstrate that, if need be, the women can make it very well on their own, drawing strength, affection, and creativity from their collective bond as clan sisters. As they literally put their foot down with each dance step, Sigoti residents – young or old, male or female – stop and listen to Kawuonda, and if the spirit grabs them, respond with a play of their own. Through their community theatre, then, Sigoti is revitalizing a cultural practice that, according to Ngũgĩ, once was 'part and parcel of the rhythm of daily and seasonal life of the community. It was an activity among other activities, often drawing its energy from those other activities. It was also entertainment in the sense of involved enjoyment; it was moral instruction; and it was also a strict matter of life and death and communal survival' (1986: 37).

Notes

1 Personal interview with Opiyo Mumma, Nairobi, 3 October 1997.
2 She obtained her degree, through correspondence, from the University of New Brunswick (Canada) in 1973. Her dissertation, a Marxist comparison of

Chinua Achebe, Margaret Laurence, Elspeth Huxley, and Ngũgĩ wa Thiong'o, was published in 1978 by the Kenya Literature Bureau under the title *Visions of Africa*.

3 Ngũgĩ wa Mirii, a graduate of the University of Nairobi Institute for Development Studies, fled to Zimbabwe, where he first became the theatre coordinator for the Zimbabwe Foundation for Education with production (ZIMFEP), which he helped found in 1982. He is currently director of the Zimbabwe Association for Community Theatre (ZACT), which was founded in 1986. Kimani Gekau, Kamiriithu's artistic director, joined wa Mirii at ZIMFEP; later, he took a job in the English Department of the University of Zimbabwe.

4 B.A. Ogot relativizes the ideological purity of this stance, arguing that, 'Ngũgĩ ignores the fact that, as an established writer, whatever he has written in Gikuyu has immediately been translated into English for wider distribution' (Ogot and Ochieng 1996: 224).

5 In *Detained*, Ngugi reports death threats to himself and his immediate family as well as being sacked from his position as Associate Professor at the University of Nairobi. The day of his release, 12 December, coincided with Uhuru ('Independence') Day, the national holiday on which amnesty is often granted.

6 The TFD methodology as described by Mumma (Mumma and Levert 1995: 14–25) draws quite strongly on the ideas of Freire and Boal (see also Epskamp and Boeren 1992, and van Erven 1991).

7 This disconnection of Theatre Workshop, which Mumma describes here as a peaceful initiative to spread theatre beyond the university confines, according to George Odera Outa was caused by a much more sinister repressive measure from above (1997: 221–222). In 1991, when Theatre Workshop was still operating under the aegis of the University of Nairobi, its productions of Dario Fo's *Can't Pay, Won't Pay* and a devised original piece entitled *Drum Beats of Kerenyaga* were banned by the government censor. Fearing repercussions, the University of Nairobi expelled Theatre Workshop and its artistic director, Oby Obyerodhiambo. In his essay, Odera Outa cites several other examples of government censorship and repressive infiltration in the Kenyan theatre throughout the 1990s, including the ever popular Schools and Colleges Drama Festival, of which he is considerably more suspicious than Opiyo Mumma.

8 The Luo dominance of KDEA, which tends to monopolize the image of contemporary Kenyan theatre abroad through its involvement in IDEA, is of concern to many non-Luos.

9 Personal interview with Augustino Mumma, Sigoti-Ramogi, 28 September 1997.

10 Personal interview with the head nurse of Sigoti clinic, 17 September 1997.

11 Personal letter, 20 October 1997.

12 Personal interview, on video tape (3: 23:34), 22 September 1997.

13 According to Berg-Schlosser, some 75,000 Kenyans fought for the allied forces in the Middle East, the Orient, and in Ethiopia and Madagascar.

Bibliography

Adhiambo Mbeo, Mary (1989) Women and Law in Kenya: Perspectives and Emerging Issues, Nairobi: Public Law Institute.

Aseka, Eric (1992) Jomo Kenyatta, Nairobi: East African Educational Publishers.

Bates, Robert H. (1989) Beyond the Miracle of the Market: The Political Economy of Agrarian Development in Kenya, Cambridge: Cambridge University Press.

Berg-Schlosser, Dirk (1984) Tradition and Change in Kenya, Paderborn: Schoeningh.

Björkmann, Inge (1989) 'Mother, Sing For Me': People's Theatre in Kenya, London: Zed Books.

Bole Odaga, Asenath (1995) 'Theatre and Women's Groups', in Opiyo Mumma and Loukie Levert (eds) Drama and Theatre: Experiences in Western Kenya, Nairobi: KDEA.

Desai, Gaurav (1990) 'Theater as Praxis: Discursive Strategies in African Popular Theater', African Studies Review 33, 1: 65–92.

Epskamp, Kees and Boeren, Ad (ed.) (1992) The Empowerment of Culture: Development Communication and Popular Media, The Hague: CESO.

Erven, Eugene van (1991) 'Freedom, Revolution, and Theater of Liberation', Research in African Literatures 22, 3: 11–27.

Haugerud, Angélique (1995) The Culture of Politics in Modern Kenya, Cambridge: Cambridge University Press.

Imbuga, Francis (1972) The Fourth Trial, Nairobi: East African Literature Bureau.

—— (1988) Aminata, Nairobi: East African Educational Publishers.

—— (1989) The Burning of Rags, Nairobi: East African Educational Publishers.

Kabira, Wanjiku, Karega, Muthoni and Nzioki, Elizabeth (1990) Our Secret Lives: An Anthology of Poems and Short Stories by Kenyan Women Writers, Nairobi: Phoenix Publishers.

Kabira, Wanjiku and Akinyi Nzioki, Elizabeth (1993) Celebrating Women's Resistance, Nairobi: African Women's Perspective.

Kanogo, Tabitha (1992) Dedan Kimathi, Nairobi: East African Educational Publishers.

Kidd, Ross (1983) 'Popular Theatre and Popular Struggle in Kenya', Race and Class 24, 3: 286–304.

Mbugua, Wariara (1989) 'Women's Employment Patterns: Emerging Aspects of Economic Marginalization', in Mary Adhiambo Mbeo and Oki Ooko-Ombaka (eds), Women and Law in Kenya, Nairobi: Public Law Institute.

Micere Githae-Mûgo (1978) Visions of Africa, Nairobi: Kenya Literature Bureau.

Mouhtadi, Abdelhak (1993) 'A New Challenge to the African Writer in Search of Social Perspective', unpublished thesis, Utrecht University, the Netherlands.

Mumma, Opiyo and Levert, Loukie (eds) (1995) Drama and Theatre: Experiences in Western Kenya, Nairobi: KDEA.

Ndumbe Eyoh, H. (1991) Beyond the Theatre, Bonn: DSE.

Ngau, Peter (1993) 'Political restructuring and the development process in

Kenya', in Edward G. Goetz and Susan E. Clarke (eds) *The New Localism: Comparative Urban Politics in a Global Era*, London: Sage.

Ochieng, William R. (1974) *An Outline History of Nyanza Up To 1914*, Nairobi: Kenya Literature Bureau.

—— (1984) *The Third Word: More Essays on Kenyan History*, Nairobi: Kenya Literature Bureau.

Odera Outa, George (1997) 'African Politics and the Struggle for the Artist's Freedom: Viewpoints From Kenya', *Research in Drama Education* 2, 2: 219–225.

Ogolla, Lenin (1997) *Towards Behaviour Change: Participatory Theatre in Education and Development*, Nairobi: PETAD.

Ogot, B.A. and Ochieng. William R. (1996) *Decolonization and Independence in Kenya, 1940–93*, Nairobi: East African Educational Publishers.

Okombo, Okoth and Nandwa, Jane (eds) (1992) *Reflections On Theories and Methods in Oral Literature*, Nairobi: Kenya Oral Literature Association.

Ominde, Simeon H. (1952) *The Luo Girl: From Infancy to Marriage*, Nairobi: Kenya Literature Bureau.

Onyango-Ogutu, B. and Roscoe, A.A. (1974) *Keep My Words: Luo Oral Literature*, Nairobi: East African Educational Publishers.

Osundare, Niyi (1993) *African Literature and the Crisis of Post-Structuralist Theorising*, Ibadan, Nigeria: Option Book and Information Service

Oucho, J.O. (1996) *Urban Migrants and Rural Development in Kenya*, Nairobi: Nairobi University Press.

Ruganda, John (1987) *Black Mamba (and Covenant With Death)*, Nairobi: Heinemann.

Sterkenburg, Johan (1982) *Rural Housing Conditions in Kisumu District, Kenya*, Utrecht: Department of Geography of Developing Countries, Utrecht University.

Thiong'o, Ngũgĩ wa (1964) *Weep Not, Child*, Nairobi: East African Educational Publishers.

—— (1965) *The River Between*, Nairobi: Heinemann.

—— (1967) *A Grain of Wheat*, Nairobi: Heinemann.

—— (1968) *The Black Hermit*, Nairobi: East African Educational Publishers.

—— (1970) *This Time Tomorrow: Three Plays*, Nairobi: Kenya Literature Bureau.

—— (1972) *Homecoming Essays On African and Caribbean Literature*, London: Heinemann.

—— (1977) *Petals of Blood*, Nairobi: East African Educational Publishers.

—— (1981a) *Detained: A Writer's Prison Diary*, Nairobi: East African Educational Publishers.

—— (1981b) *Writers In Politics*, Nairobi: East African Educational Publishers.

—— (1982) *Devil On the Cross*, Oxford: Heinemann.

—— (1986) *Decolonizing the Mind: The Politics of Language In African Literature*, Nairobi: East African Educational Publishers.

—— (1987) *Matigari*, Nairobi: East African Educational Publishers.

—— (1993) *Moving the Centre: The Struggle for Cultural Freedoms*, Nairobi: East African Educational Publishers.

Thiong'o, Ngũgĩ wa (1997) 'Enactments of Power: The Politics of Performance Space', *The Drama Review* 41, 3 (Fall): 11–30.

—— and Githae Mûgo, Micere (1976) *The Trial of Dedan Kimathi*, Nairobi: East African Educational Publishers.

—— and wa Mirii, Ngũgĩ (1982) *I Will Marry When I Want*, Nairobi: East African Educational Publishers.

Chapter 6

Community theatre in Australia

I arrived at Sydney's Kingsford Smith International Airport for my fourth visit to Australia on a sunny Friday morning, 24 October 1997. Gordon Beattie, Senior Lecturer in the University of Western Sydney's theatre department, picked me up and drove me to his home in Penrith, all the way to the edge of the western suburbs at the foot of the Blue Mountains. As the crow flies, it is a distance of 60 kilometres, but virtually impossible to bridge by public transportation and even by car a slow two-hour trip, first through the congested suburbs south of downtown and then on the M4, a tollroad currently being widened for the 2000 Olympics and hence prone to long delays. My aim was to document the work in progress of what was reputed to be one of Australia's most exciting community theatre organizations, Death Defying Theatre (DDT), which in April 1997 had renamed itself Urban Theatre Projects (UTP). I had selected this company on the recommendation of Monica Barone, a community and youth theatre artist I had worked with in Holland in 1996. Barone's inside view of DDT, for which she had directed productions in the past, was confirmed by other friends, theatre artists, and scholars. And the 'Trackwork' project itself sounded fascinating: a funky show created and performed on regular trains by residents of western Sydney, supposedly the most troubled area of this 'sprawling' metropolis.

Australia and Sydney's western suburbs

At the end of October 1997, Australian headlines were dominated by the Asian stock market crash and by John Howard's conservative federal government's struggle to nullify the rights of Aboriginal access to pastoral lands. Oversimplifying grossly, one could say that the left feared that the gap between rich and poor would only further widen under the new Liberal–National coalition, which had come to power in March 1996 after thirteeen years of uninterrupted labour government under Hawke and Keating. On the far right, independent Queensland MP Pauline Hanson attracted media attention with unsubstantiated allegations that Aboriginals, unabating hordes of Asian immigrants, and Australia's multiculturalism advocates were wreaking havoc on the country's sociocultural fabric. But at the same time, Peter Murphy and Sophie Watson coolly parried Hanson's racist attacks in their *Surface City*, countering that

> recent arguments that immigration should be curtailed because of high rates of urban unemployment are simplistic and verge, at worst, on blaming immigrants (usually those from non-English-speaking background groups) for labour market problems. Such arguments also distract attention away from the complex combinations of global, national and local forces which cause unemployment in the work force at large.
>
> (1997: 115)

Danielle Tuwai and Ebony Williams, respectively a Fijian-Tongan and an Aboriginal hip-hop artist from the inner city, put it more bluntly in the rap they created and performed during *Trackwork*'s finale at Granville station, simply shouting: 'Pauline Hanson sucks.'

An impressive list of recent Australian publications in the fields of urban and cultural studies urge the interested outsider to look beyond such conveniently intriguing symbolic dichotomies as expanding city suburbs infringing on an unyielding natural wilderness, a conflict that is annually re-enacted in the form of heroically reported summertime battles between firefighters and wild bushfires. Coming as I do from one of the world's most densely populated and wettest countries, Australia's hot and rugged outback has obvious attractions, as do epic battles between man and nature. But *Trackwork* brought me to a more familiar urban setting in Sydney, with a population of almost four million easily Australia's largest city, and, with its dazzling Darling Harbour, its beaches, its parks, bays and Harbour Bridge, one of the world's most attractive. 'But,' as Murphy and Watson warn, 'beneath the complacent and cheerful surface of successful Sydney there are cracks and fissures which are too easy to ignore from the 6-metre catamarans sliding on the harbour past the gleaming sails of the Opera House' (1997: 165).

According to the 1991 Census, a quarter of the Australian population was born overseas (Murphy and Watson 1997: 14; Smith 1992: 17). Most of these immigrants live concentrated in the urban areas on Australia's southeastern seaboard. Some 40 per cent of Sydney's population is of first- or second generation non-English-speaking background (NESB) and 43.9 per cent of these live in the less affluent western suburbs (Grace et al. 1997: 6). Since World War II, West Sydney has been stygmatized in the local and national media as the city's arsehole: unsophisticated, architecturally unattractive, and socially depressed. Being called a 'Westie' was (and is) regarded as an insult, although some Westies have now begun to proudly embrace the rich cultural identity the label also signifies. To be sure, the under-resourced western suburbs, an area comprising fourteen municipalities, have to deal with relatively high rates of crime and unemployment. Murphy and Watson detect a clear split between western suburbs and the rest of Sydney in terms of rich and poor, employed and unemployed, a divide they claim has been growing steadily since the mid-1970s (1997: 97). But they challenge the biased way the media resort to western Sydney as the prime example of Australia's immigration-related urban problems (ibid.: 24),[1] a prejudice also tackled in Diane Powell's Out West: Perceptions of Sydney's Western Suburbs (1993) and in the collectively authored home/world: space, community and marginality in sydney's west (Grace et al. 1997).[2]

Large flows of immigrants started coming into western Sydney after World War II as the industrial development that was to form the backbone of Australia's economic boom during the subsequent decades required a mass immigration programme to supply the necessary labour force (Powell 1993: 53). A disproportionately large number of these migrants moved from temporary housing camps and migrant hostels such as Villawood in Fairfield to often self-constructed homes on the rapidly expanding western edges of the city, where in the 1950s the New South Wales Housing Commission was making available cheap land for this purpose (Grace et al. 1997: 60). But out west there were no sufficient shops, schools, hospitals, sewage, and public transport, even though most 'Westies' were employed in the inner city (Powell 1993: 76).

A closer look at the origins of all these migrants reveals an interesting shift in federal policies, if not always in attitude from the Anglo majority.

In the period immediately after World War II, most immigrants were fair-complexioned and first came from northern and then from southern Europe, because it was felt they would be able to assimilate more easily. The first cracks in this 'White Australia Policy' became visible in the mid- to late 1960s, when Lebanese and Turkish immigrants were suddenly allowed into the country (Murphy and Watson 1997: 14). This change was consolidated in an official multiculturalism policy formulated by Whitlam's Labor government (1973–1975).[3] Yet, the Lebanese-Australian anthropologist Ghassan Hage is quick to relativize the long-term impact of this policy shift on daily life: 'The negative Anglo gaze has not totally disappeared; even today, as a number of interviewees indicated, children at some schools are still taunted about their "ethnic lunches"' (Grace et al. 1997: 113).

Benefiting from easier available arts and welfare money for grass-roots cultural initiatives in multicultural working-class communities since the Whitlam government, Death Defying Theatre, the main focus of this chapter, carried out a number of projects in newly constructed housing areas of western Sydney throughout the 1980s. In 1991, the group decided to permanently settle there. Tracing the reasons for this relocation and the development of Death Defying Theatre before and after the move, requires a closer look into the recent history of community theatre in Australia at large, not in the least because some of the company's key players also have had significant community arts experiences in other states, worked for short spells as arts policy-makers and government consultants, or were once major figures in the country's experimental theatre scene.

Australian community theatre

Richard Fotheringham and David Watt, two of Australia's leading scholars of community theatre, locate its roots in Britain's popular theatre movement of the late 1960s and 1970s (Fotheringham 1992; Capelin 1996; Watt 1992). Their research indicates that artists who started doing community theatre in Brisbane and Melbourne in the early 1980s, had gained their first experience in a groundbreaking extended community arts project in Scotland in the late 1970s. A complex of additional factors, including examples of popular or 'poor' theatre activities in the United States and Europe that reached Australia via academic channels, experiments with home-made documentary drama by the legendary Australian Performing Group in Melbourne and the Nimrod Street Theatre in Sydney, and a radical change in government arts funding under Whitlam, led to the prolific community theatre movement of the 1980s. Death Defying Theatre was among a number of significant companies that emerged from this unique set of circumstances.

Tracing the development of Death Defying Theatre from its foundation in 1981 constitutes only one among many possible itineraries through the multi-faceted Australian community theatre landscape, which, in turn, could be considered a subdivision of Australian theatre as a whole. John Baylis, the company's current artistic director, used to work for three years as theatre programme officer for the Australia Council, the country's main federal arts funding body,[4] and before that, from 1986 until 1992, with The Sydney Front, a leading contemporary performance collective. He is therefore well situated to provide an overview of Australian theatre. First of all, he dismisses the state theatre companies, which to his mind offer little more than a standard fare of polished Shakespeare, contemporary western classics, or poor Australian imitations thereof: 'It is all polish and training and there is no heart to it. It caters for a usually over-40s upper middle-class audience, is expensive, and the foyer you have to go through is an obstacle to anyone who is not of that social class.'[5] He thinks that major independent companies such as Company B at Sydney's Belvoir Street and Playbox in Melbourne provide better quality theatre, producing contemporary plays by foreign and Australian writers, or interesting reinterpretations of classic texts. 'But although they do work which is more intelligent, it still never steps outside the basic structure of writer-director-actor, four to six weeks rehearsal,' he comments. 'None of them have an ensemble, so it is always off the shelf actors per production.'

Further out on the fringe, Baylis places a set of smaller companies with an interest in developing new Australian plays and circus-type troupes which have been emerging since the mid- to late 1980s, developing theatrical performances on top of physical skills.[6] In this category he also includes groups such as Sidetrack and Open City in Sydney, who have a contemporary performance profile similar to that of The Sydney Front, but with the provision that Sidetrack has come to avant-garde theatre from a more explicitly political popular theatre background in the 1980s (Watt 1992: 11–12; Burvill 1986, 1998). Australia also has quite a few professional theatre-in-education companies, like Freewheels in Newcastle, which operate between avant garde and community theatre. So do youth theatre companies, which Baylis regards as one of the more vibrant theatre practices in Australia today. There are only two full-time contemporary Aboriginal theatre companies: Ke im Biji Dara Indigenous Arts in Brisbane and Yirra Yaakin in Perth, in addition to the

Aboriginal and Islander Dance Company in Sydney and professional troupes catering to the Queensland tourist market.

A handful of fully funded community theatre organizations are operational in Australia in the late 1990s. These include Mainstreet Theatre Company, which operates in a small country town in South Australia (Watt 1991); the Italian-Australian group Doppio Teatro in Adelaide; the Melbourne Workers Theatre; and Death Defying Theatre in Sydney, which was renamed Urban Theatre Projects in April 1997. In addition, there a number of production houses, such as StreetArts (now calling itself 'Arterial') in Brisbane, Brown's Mart in Darwin, and Footscray in Melbourne which, for example, supports the Women's Circus. But, according to Baylis, most community work in Australia happens in the shadows of these permanent companies and institutions, through the work of individual artists with *ad hoc* project funding they obtain through youth centres, community organizations, and local governments.

DDT's history

Death Defying Theatre was founded as a street theatre collective in 1981 by Paul Brown, Alice Spizzo, Christine Sammers, and Kim Spinks, all coming out of the University of New South Wales.[7] Writing in 1987, Kim Spinks described DDT's brief as drawing 'upon the traditions of popular theatre to devise comic works which critically examine the institutions of Australian society' (Fotheringham 1992: 154). The company's name refers to Peter Brook's *Empty Space*, in which he calls escapist theatre 'deadly'. Calling itself Australia's only exclusively outdoor theatre company, the company of eight even used to rehearse outside in Centennial Park, near their office in the Paddington Village Community Centre. Apart from devising issue-driven shows which were taken on tour, starting in 1983 DDT also began to offer free community theatre workshops financed by local councils or the Housing Department. These were intended to bring some cultural life into newly constructed and under-resourced housing estates in Sydney's outer west. DDT used to go to these areas to teach children simple circus skills, for example, typically concluding their interventions with low-key outdoor shows after eight-week residencies.

DDT's approach was obviously inspired by the popular theatre tradition that had developed in Europe and North America in the 1970s, generating audiences by conspicuously announcing its presence in a particular community. Stylistically, it structured its collectively devised performances into small self-contained, energetically performed, and visually striking units that were underscored by live music. Shows were often followed by informal discussions with the audience, because, as Spinks put it, 'This is a process-oriented theatre in which the community and the occasion can and should radically affect the work' (Fotheringham 1992: 157). The most famous project that DDT's first generation created was *Coal Town* (1985) and took place in Collinsville, North Queensland (Brown). It was the outcome of an 'Art and Working Life' project with a striking mining community, which subsequently toured other mining areas.[8] A film documentary was made of the project and the Community Arts Board, a special division that had been established within the Australia Council in 1975, subsequently promoted *Coal Town* as the best thing Australian community theatre had to offer.

By the end of the decade, DDT's first generation began to run out of steam and founding member Paul Brown therefore started exploring ways to change from a performance-oriented company catering to community audiences to a production house for participatory community theatre projects created and performed by amateurs under the guidance of professional artists (Watt 1992: 10). In 1990, Brown appointed Fiona Winning, an experienced community theatre facilitator from Queensland, as DDT's new artistic coordinator.

Fiona Winning

Fiona Winning had discovered theatre while devising shows with a student drama group in Brisbane. After finishing her BA, in 1982 she acted in several productions of Popular Theatre Troupe (PTT), one of Australia's leading political theatre companies at the time (Capelin 1996: 82–83). After the PTT tour of *The State We're In* was banned by the Queensland government, Winning decided to stay on in northern Queensland, finding part-time jobs in a women's shelter and in an adult education institute. While preparing a group of adult Torres Strait Islanders and Aborigines for further education, she thought of assigning them poems and songs: 'Sort of by fluke I made shows with them. They had a range of performance skills they had brought from their communities. It was fantastic and my first experience as a community theatre worker. Because I don't consider the stuff we did at Popular Theatre Troupe as community theatre; that was political theatre speaking *at* an audience.'[9]

After this eye-opener, Winning accepted a position as Community Arts Officer in Brisbane in 1985, initiating projects in the local women's prison and in outlying suburbs. In 1986, she was appointed general coordinator for StreetArts, a community theatre company that had been founded in 1983 and operated mostly in the inner city's West End area, then a rundown place populated by working-class migrants and Aborigines. StreetArts had a small ensemble of four performers and engaged in a range of community projects.[10] Winning ended up staying with StreetArts for two years, after which she joined theatre makers Ruby Red and Libby Sara in *Women in the West*, a groundbreaking community theatre enterprise that took them to sixteen small country towns in western Queensland in 1988 and 1989:

> We would do a two-day theatre performance workshop in each town, spending the third day writing up and documenting all the stuff that had come out of the workshops and talking to the women about creating a small performance piece of their own for when we would come back. So in each of those towns we had a short but very intense time. After doing sixteen towns, I wrote a script, Libby composed music, and Ruby directed the resulting show. We then went back to all these towns. The local women's groups hosted our performance, publicized it, got an audience, did the catering, and performed in a local section that opened the night. And then we got on and did the professional hour-long show that was based on their lives. It was just fantastic. By chance Libby then became the Community Arts Officer in Queensland after that project. She now had contacts in all these towns as a spin-off from *Women in the West* and a whole lot of pilot projects started happening there as a result.

Reorganizing DDT's funding and company structure

Feeling the need for a change from the cliquish Brisbane arts scene, Winning moved down to Sydney and, after a brief spell as a consultant for the Australia Council, took over as coordinator of Death Defying Theatre at the end of 1990. Over the next five years, she would revamp the floundering ensemble into a soundly financed, solidly organized, and creatively innovative community theatre production company firmly rooted in the western suburbs. When Winning began, on average DDT was producing three new shows per year, touring thirty weeks on an annual budget of A$ 120,000, from which salaries as well as production expenses had to be paid. By 1997, Urban Theatre Projects was working with an annual budget of A$ 320,000, coming mostly from the Australia Council's Theatre Fund and from the New South Wales Ministry of the

Arts, with additional money from special project grants and area assistance schemes for western Sydney. In 1998, the company qualified as one of only ten professional Australian theatre organizations for a triannual grant.[11]

During her first year, Winning directed a school show on children's consumer rights she had inherited from her predecessors. She also oversaw the move of the company office from Bondi in the east to Auburn in the west and overhauled the company's board, which continued to be dominated by former DDT actors. Winning argues that an active board with substantial and culturally diverse community participation is essential to the effectiveness and longevity of any community theatre organization. The challenge, she knows, is always to get local people involved with passion for the work: 'But the problem with those kinds of community-minded people is that they already have huge commitment levels to all sorts of other things. Or else you go the other way, like this young Arabic hiphopper who was involved in some of our projects, joined the board but had no interest in talking about funding. He got bored and stopped coming to our meetings.'

> **Winning's reshuffle of the DDT board revealed a fundamental dilemma for the company that has not really been resolved to this day. How does one channel community input in creative projects and daily operations? Do you want your board members to be representative of different community sectors and thus provide the company with the necessary moral legitimacy, or do you want them to possess sophisticated managerial skills, in which case most candidates tend to be Anglo, middle class, and tertiary educated? DDT has resorted to alternative mechanisms for community involvement, such as a community liaison figure – usually a paid staff member or trainee – and *ad hoc* community steering committees for each new participatory project.**

Winning had an opportunity to test the effectiveness of DDT's reorganization in her first major production, *Café Hakawati*, for which she engaged Paul Brown as script writer. DDT had just moved into its new office in Auburn, an area with a large population of immigrants from the Middle East, when the Gulf War broke out. The impact of this

international conflict on Auburn's Arab community was quickly identified as an obvious theme for a new DDT production. Eliza Chidiac, an
Auburn youth worker, was hired as community liaison and together with
DDT's young Lebanese administrative trainee, Mona Zaylaa, recruited an
active steering committee for the project.

Café Hakawati, basically a storytelling performance interspersed with
Arab songs, was performed bilingually in an Auburn community hall
that, for the occasion, was converted into an Arab coffee house. The play
opened half a year after the start of Operation 'Desert Storm', in which
the Australian navy also participated. It didn't try to sugarcoat the conflicting sympathies among the Palestinians, Jordanians, Syrians and other
Arabs residing in Auburn. Says Winning: 'We didn't edit these things
out, but we were also really careful in the way we presented them in the
show, so that non-Arab spectators wouldn't necessarily even get what
those challenges were within the Arab communities, who were already
feeling very vulnerable and didn't want to air their dirty washing.'

A *hakawati* is a traditional storyteller and in DDT's storytelling café,
the audience was seated at tables while around them community actors,
representing several generations of Arab-Australians, told traditional
stories from the old country, related migration experiences, or dramatized
the uneasy identification of the adolescents with either Arab or Anglo
culture. The first half of the play focuses on the story of café-owner Layla
Zenoubia, a single woman in her thirties, whose family has been living
and working in Australia since the 1920s. She talks about how her uncle
Fouad, who came from Syria in 1948 to open a tailor's shop in the inner
city, married a young Arab girl who had come to work for him. After the
intermission, the play explicitly tackles the Gulf War as a variety of café
patrons recollect the anger, the fear, and the confused sympathies they
felt on 17 January 1991. Subsequent scenes depict the wartime ostraciz-
ing of Arab girls in high schools and Anglos, who suddenly start looking
at their next-door neighbours as terrorists. An Anglo journalist visiting
the café serves as a catalyst for most of these anti-Arab harassments and
eventually provokes a strong protest, in Arabic, from café co-owner
Layla: 'He sees us only as victims, or as villains. He should let Arab
women speak for themselves'.[12] The play ends where it began, with the
young waiter's story of two men fighting over a cheese. This time, however, a *hakawati* settles the dispute, not by stealing the cheese to keep it
for himself as in the first version of the story, but by dividing it into equal
slices and sharing it with as many people as possible.

Café Hakawati generated a lot of goodwill for Auburn's Arab-
Australians, but the predominantly Anglo male municipal council was

less impressed with DDT's problematizing of Arab–Western loyalties. Over the next two years, the fragile relationship between the local politicians and the theatre company would only deteriorate further.

In the season following *Café Hakawati*, DDT's main community participatory production was *Blood Orange*, a play that inter-culturally explored feminine issues of body, health, and sexuality through storytelling and song. With support from the Health Department in addition to regular arts funding, Winning had workshopped the material for the show with twenty Pacific Islander, Turkish, and Spanish women from the area. After performing their play in Auburn, playwright Noëlle Janaczeska, a talented artist who was beginning to gain a national reputation, rewrote the script for three professional actresses. Containing additional material dealing with eating disorders and HIV/AIDS, this second version of *Blood Orange* was subsequently taken on a school tour. Besides obvious educational benefits, such tours, which DDT continued to produce annually until 1997, were regarded as welcome extended employment opportunities for performers from non-English-speaking backgrounds.

In 1994, the dormant tension between the Auburn municipal council and DDT finally erupted after a new theatre project about the Olympic Games, which the IOC had just awarded to Sydney. The athlete's village and the main stadium were going to be constructed in nearby Homebush Bay, which falls under Auburn jurisdiction. The original idea for the play, which would later be entitled *Site – The Homebush Bay Story*, had come from a public meeting called by an environmental group, which pointed out that the 2000 Olympics would generate appalling effects on the local environment. Fiona Winning did initial research, looked up relevant publications, and interviewed local people. With this material in hand, she put together a conceptual framework that she presented to local residents in a next round of community comnsultations. After this, she recruited participants, held improvisational workshops, and hired a professional writer and composer to script and score the play, which was eventually performed in October and November of 1994.

Site itself hardly warranted the ire of the Auburn council, although it did contain references to politically loaded issues, such as the contaminated land on which the sports facilities for the Olympics (loudly promoted as the 'Green Games') would be constructed: the former locations of the biggest slaughterhouse in the southern hemisphere and an armaments depot. In twenty-eight scenes, the show traced the fictional career of Auburn resident Suzie Bektas, the first Turkish-Australian on the Australian Olympic swimming squad, from her debut as a 13-year-old talent in 1987 until a few seconds before the 200 metre breaststroke final at Sydney 2000. Interwoven with the Bektas saga were scenes depicting a satirical history of world politics intersecting with the modern Olympics movement, starting with Athens 1896 and on to London 1908, Paris 1924, Berlin 1936, Melbourne 1956, Mexico 1968, and Munich 1972. In addition, there were songs, extended monologues based on the authentic stories of a local meatworker and a drag racer, and several scenes in which Auburn and Homebush residents express their concerns about a new zoning code that many feared might lead to evictions and real estate speculations.

DDT became the first victim of the pre-Olympic evictions it predicted in *Site*: after the production, the company was unceremoniously kicked out of their office in the Auburn town hall. Harley Stumm, DDT's new publicist and future manager, led the search for a new office, which he found in the middle of 1995 at the Casula Powerhouse Arts Centre, a facility run by the Liverpool municipality.

Despite the move, 1995 turned out to be a remarkably productive year. In May, Fiona Winning directed *Yungaburra Road*, a touring show about violence for upper-level highschool students. It was the second DDT script from Noëlle Janaczeska, who in the meantime had become a respected poetic playwright with an interest in multicultural, postmodern and feminist theory. This collaboration was indicative of DDT's growing openness to working with experimental theatre artists. While still fundamentally based on authentic stories Winning and Janaczeska had gathered in December 1994 through interviews with high school students, Bosnian and Timorese refugees, and volunteers from a lesbian and gay anti-violence project, the resulting play was a sophisticated non-linear choreopoem. In it, Rita da Costa, the fado-singing owner of a Portuguese-Australian establishment appropriately called 'Café Mundo', weaves together the fragmented dramatizations of violence from different cultural contexts. Her own husband, an uninsured factory labourer, is no longer able to work after an industrial accident caused by his inability to read the English instructions on newly installed Japanese equipment. Political violence is movingly evoked in the memories of a young Timorese man and a Bosnian woman, whose experiences temporarily blend with West Sydney suburban sounds, in which those who care to hear can detect the lamentations of an Italian-Australian lesbian molested by a gang of queer bashers: 'And the screams of the woman, / Pierced like a pin-board shopping list, merge with the television voices / Shrieking and wailing / Through their fictional fights, / Through their nightly punch-ups / Beat-ups, set-ups./ And somewhere nearby a young woman / Raw from a war-split land / Shuts her eyes and ears / To screams too close to home.'[13]

The mixture of rhythms, music, and lyrics packaged in a stylized theatrical format were further exploited in that year's community participation project, *Hip Hopera*, with which DDT wanted to baptise their new space in the converted Casula Powerhouse. And to let the rest of Sydney know that young 'Westies' had considerably more to offer than drugs and violence. The project was inspired by the success of the 1994 experimental school touring show *Eye of the Law*, researched and developed by Canberra-based director Monica Barone, which had also used hip-hop as a soundtrack for dramatizing authentic experiences of people in legal trouble of one kind or another. *Hip Hopera*'s eighty participants spanned the multicultural spectrum of the western suburbs and were recruited through youth and community centres. From August to October, under professional guidance they developed raps, funk-, break- and capoeira dances, grafitti, and video footage in five different workshop locations (including the Minda juvenile detention facility). In a final rehearsal period at the Casula Powerhouse, director Morgan Lewis had united all these disparate elements into a potent multimedia spectacle that attracted the attention of all the major media in Sydney and two capacity crowds, one in Casula and one at Pier 4 downtown. The widespread existence of a self-conscious gender-balanced 'Westie' hip-hop culture must have been an eye-opener to many in a society where, as Mark Davis claims, the Anglo baby-boomer elite enjoy their materially comfortable midlife at the expense of particularly the non-Anglo youth (Davis 1997: 232–254).

In addition to firmly establishing DDT's presence in the Liverpool-Casula area, *Hip Hopera* also convinced the company of the enormous potential in cross-fertilizing community theatre with suburban youth culture. Since then, the personal contacts of company administrator Mona Zaylaa, who lives in Auburn, and Harley Stumm's earlier experience as a producer of community and youth radio for the ABC, have guaranteed the recurring presence of hip-hop in DDT's work. In 1996, DDT produced a school-touring sequel to *Hip Hopera* called *Danger*. Directed by Gail Kelly, it featured young Aborginal, Polynesian, Lebanese and Croatian rappers from the preceding event, who were attracted to work once more with such well-known hip-hop artists as Khalid Sabsabi and Sharline Bezzina. Containing raps about different aspects of danger for young people living out west and choreographed by a National School of Drama student, the raw physical performance helped spread DDT's name around more than forty area schools. The community participation show in the second half of 1996, Going Home, also contained raps, as did the main project in 1997, Trackwork, which finished with a 20-minute hip-hop concert at Granville Station. In the process, DDT/UTP also became a booking agent for some of the hip-hop artists involved in their shows, helping them to get professional gigs in community centres and other such venues.

Going Home, DDT's first theatrical collaboration ever with different generations of the sizeable Maori and Islander communities in western Sydney, proved an overwhelming popular and critical success. Effectively exploiting the large main space of the converted power station at Casula, Going Home featured almost fifty performers, including a live band that provided the backing for both contemporary rap songs and traditional Maori and Islander *waiatas* and *hakas*. These musical elements formed the transition between short scenes about migration, unemployment, the significance of traditional cultural practices for teenagers living in a sub-urban world full of hip-hop and hanging out in malls, and about lost roots for the older generation that has been living in Australia for thirty years or more.

Community theatre meets contemporary performance

Despite the popular success of Going Home and, to a lesser degree, of the experimental show Noroc, in DDT's Artistic report for 1996 Harley Stumm indicated that the new artistic committee construction the company had set up earlier that year to relieve Fiona Winning was putting too much stress on the remaining staff. Now only assisted part-time by a committee of three artists – Monica Barone, Gail Kelly and Winning – Stumm and Mona Zaylaa had had to organize 85 performances, which attracted 13,600 spectators, and 58 workshops for 115 participants. Recognizing the seriousness of Stumm's complaint, the DDT board decided to advertise for a full-time artistic coordinator. Harley Stumm faxed the ad to John Baylis, Theatre Programme Officer of the Australia Council, asking him to put the word around. But, suprisingly, Baylis applied himself:

> I said, 'This might be exactly the job I want.' I knew how organiza-
> tionally good the company was; I knew how sound its funding was,
> I knew what its artistic history was, and even though it had its ups
> and downs it had always survived them because of its strong philos-
> ophy. I knew that it wasn't going to fall over tomorrow. During

Fiona's time there the company had moved towards looking at more contemporary performance methods. She had started the move away from whatever traditional community arts' practice had been. There was now a two to three-year history of looking at new ways of doing community-based work. So I thought, 'as long as they understand totally what my background is then maybe this will work.'

Baylis was convinced that the kinds of techniques he had developed with The Sydney Front could be adapted to a community context; they were simply other strategies for making performance. While he believed that The Sydney Front had always made experimental theatre that was accessible, he found that DDT's flirtations with contemporary performance had been half-hearted because they were separated from the company's community practice. Baylis singled out *Crop Circles* (1997) as an example of an experimental DDT production that lacked such a communal soul: 'I didn't see any point in bringing that production to the Performance Space, trying to appeal to a downtown audience looking for a particular aesthetic thing in theatre. No, I wanted the Performance Space audience to get on the train and come to see our work here, along with western Sydney people.' Which is exactly what UTP set out to do with *Trackwork*.

CASE STUDY: URBAN THEATRE PROJECT'S *TRACKWORK*

The original idea for *Trackwork* had been conceived in January 1996 by Monica Barone, then one of the three members of DDT's Artistic Directors Committee. Barone's aim had been to create a large-scale moveable theatre performance that would offer a more balanced view of the west than the negative stories about minority youth gangs that usually made the pages of *The Sydney Morning Herald* and prime time television current affairs shows:

> A big part of Australia lives in Sydney's western suburbs and there are a lot of lovely aspects about how they live and also a lot of problems. Forty-two per cent of kids out there live in families whose income is so low that they're entitled to some kind of government benefit. The layers of migration, the ways in which people have come and gone to areas like Cabramatta, where there once were lots of former Yugoslavians and now there are lots of Vietnamese. There

are all kinds of interesting stories, so I thought, well wouldn't it be interesting to hear them? The train happened to be the major transportation line. When you put in a railway station, people build homes and lives around it. So that was an interesting place to start.[14]

Due to a new job as cultural planner for the Warringah municipal council in North Sydney, Barone was unable to continue working on *Trackwork*. Harley Stumm then developed her draft concept into three more detailed grant applications, which were sent out mid-1996.

The grant proposals included the idea of performances off and on trains and suggested specific site and performance possibilities, such as a gospel choir singing at the abandoned Rockwood cemetery station, where once funeral trains used to stop. Already at this early stage, Harley Stumm realized that 'curating' or acquiring new or already existing artistic components to be inserted in the large geographical area UTP wanted to cover, was the only way to manage the scope of the event. Collectively creating all the material with community participants from scratch would be practically impossible and his grant proposals therefore specifically mentioned the PACT[15] and Powerhouse youth theatres as project partners. Only after John and Fiona had finalized the performance locations in October 1997, did they assign Auburn to Powerhouse and Berala to PACT, whom they also asked to create invisible theatre elements for performance on trains.

Before he submitted the grant applications, Harley had unsuccessfully tried to secure City Rail's cooperation. Had he pushed harder, he later realized, it would have prevented an unpleasant situation when, due to the Christmas Holidays, the rail corporation found out even before DDT itself that the Casino Community Benefit Fund (CCBF) had awarded A$16,000 for the train project. After fending off an angry phone call in January, Stumm did not contact City Rail again until April, when the management flatly told him they were not interested in *Trackwork*. But quick mediation from the New South Wales Arts and Transportation ministries resulted in verbal permission for performances on trains and platforms. Further negotiations with City Rail were left until September, when the theatre company would have a clearer idea of what the performances would entail.

The *Trackwork* budget

Besides the A$16,000 UTP received from CCBF, a further A$50,000 was subsequently awarded to *Trackwork* by the Community Cultural Development Fund of the Australia Council. A$10,000 from the Western Sydney Regional Arts Fund (a subdivision of the New South Wales Ministry for the Arts) and A$5,000 from ticket sales completed the project budget of A$81,000. From this money, all production expenses and *ad hoc* staff wages (Winning, Vela, Babicci, Peacock) were paid. Permanent staff wages (Baylis, Stumm, Zaylaa) and office overhead came out of UTP's core funding, which for 1997 included an A$130,000 grant from the Australia Council's Theatre Fund, a grant of A$72,836 from the New South Wales Ministry for the Arts, A$20,000 from box office, workshop fees and merchandising, and a special grant for developing a website and PR materials to facilitate the company's name change (A$18,000). Including the A$81,000 for *Trackwork*, then, in 1997 UTP had a total budget of A$321,836 to work with.

When John Baylis started working for DDT in March, he and Harley first looked into the possibility of performing on a specially chartered train. But they realized that, not to interfere with the regular timetable of the very busy western lines, such a train would have to keep circulating on freight lines and a few spare tracks, where the industrial landscape was not visually interesting enough to make that option worthwhile. Besides, a special train would make the experience too close to controlled conventional theatre in a hermetically sealed space, looking through a frame at the 'other'. On the other hand, doing the show on the regular services would entail difficult negotiations with City Rail, figuring out safety measures and the complicated logistics of timetables, and, finally, thinking through the ethics of mixing paying spectators with unprepared regular passengers, who had not freely chosen to be confronted with a performance.

Recruiting participants

Unlike ethnospecific projects such as *Going Home*, where participants were found through organizations catering to Maoris and Pacific Islanders, the recruitment process for *Trackwork* was more arbitrary. Fluorescent orange flyers, offering 'free workshops with professional theatre artists', were distributed all over the west through community networks. DDT, which on John Baylis' advice had changed its name in April '97 to Urban Theatre Projects (UTP) to better reflect the company's project-based way of working, also placed ads in local door-to-door papers. The average age of those who came to the first workshops was early twenties. The cultural background of these working, studying, and unemployed youth was more diverse: Cambodian, Greek, Turkish-Cypriot, Italian, Croatian, Uruguyan, Chinese, Samoan, and Anglo. The group also included three recovering mental patients.

The workshop process

John, conscious of his inexperience in community group dynamics, had convinced the UTP board to contract Fiona Winning as his co-director for *Trackwork*. The two of them began their community workshops on 8 September. Because of the geographical spread of the area they wanted to cover and to reduce transportation problems for potential participants, they had set up three separate workshop locations: one in Bankstown, one in Fairfield, and one in Auburn. Even so, attendance fluctuated quite strongly during the first few weeks and by the end of the month John and Fiona felt they only really had fifteen reliable people to work with. Thanks to a rapid telephone recruitment campaign they managed to expand their core group to twenty-two, including the aforementioned three ex-mental patients. But until the end of October, when we began documenting the UTP process on video, the directors had never been able to work with the same group of people in any of the rehearsals. The turnout in Bankstown continued to be so poor that UTP decided to cancel that venue altogether. And at the first Auburn workshop many of the rappers from *Hip Hopera*, *Danger*, and *Going Home* showed up, but their interests were so specifically musical that the directors decided to develop a special component for them, separate from the core group workshops, thus further strengthening the idea of 'curating' a number of the *Trackwork* acts.

John had hired composer Richard Vella as the show's musical director and visual artist Anthony Babicci to coordinate the design. Vella, a versatile composer who also runs the music division of the Currency Press and a contemporary opera company called Calculated Risks, facilitated several of the core workshops. He had planned to create a 'commuter orchestra' of performers seated among the passengers, producing a soundscape coming from all over the train. But when he discovered the participants were more interest in theatre than in music, he concentrated on having them perform simple ethnic folk songs instead. He would curate the rest of the *Trackwork* music with ready-made acts he hoped to find along the way, such as brass and ethnic bands, an Italian choir, and Chinese nightclub singer Terry Woo. Anthony Babicci was similarly forced to engage other visual artists when he found out the core participants were not really interested in helping him create design elements.

Weeks one to seven

All that the participants were told at the beginning was that *Trackwork* would be a theatre performance on a moving train, the original material for which they would create themselves in workshops. Fiona and John had brought some exercises to break the ice and to give the participants a quick sense of how it feels to perform for an audience in small enclosed spaces. For one of these exercises, the two facilitators sat on chairs while each of the participants took turns just standing in front of them for a couple of minutes. Afterwards, John and Fiona talked about strategies the participants inevitably would have to draw on to survive two minutes of thus being stared at. John drew on his Sydney Front experience to explain the possibilities of exploring the space between audience and performer. Richard Vella, who participated in most workshops, offered an exercise in which people were asked to make a sound in a particular space, such as singing a note as if in front of an audience of 2,000 and delivering it as if that were the greatest moment of their life.

After the initial inhibition-reducing and trust-building activities, in October John and Fiona began to develop themes and characters associated with trains. They invented an improvisation, in which everyone was given a turn to act as a tour guide, taking the group on a short journey to a nearby place. They also set one up with fake airline stewards working on trains. And Fiona made the participants draw maps of important features in their lives and neighbourhoods, asking them subsequently to talk about the major landmarks on these maps to the group. It effectively evolved into a process lasting several weeks, with participants taking photographs of their western Sydney neighbourhoods and concocting stories around these pictures that they ended up telling to the audience. Similarly, the tour guides and train stewards would also become major elements in the performance.

In addition to Monday night workshops in Fairfield and Thursday night and Saturday afternoon workshops in Auburn, John and Fiona spent the rest of the week brainstorming, coordinating with the youth theatre partners, and checking out other potential theatrical acts for the event. By the time we began documenting their work, they had just decided to perform on regular instead of specially chartered trains, selecting stations they found most interesting in terms of architecture and atmosphere. A timetable that would include as many of these stations as possible and not extend the show beyond three hours would determine the main structure for the *Trackwork* event. Meanwhile, Richard was looking for musicians and sorting out audiotechnical requirements, while Anthony was designing costumes, painting a huge canvas banner representing a City Rail train ticket, tracking down small brightly coloured suitcases that would distinguish the audience from regular passengers, and looking for visual artists interested in doing installations in some of the stations. Mona Zaylaa, in addition to doing the day-to-day administration, was busy liaising with community organizations and shop owners in her neighbourhood, Auburn, as well as with the participating hiphop artists. Harley coordinated all production-related elements, until production manager Janine Peacock, an expert in technically demanding site specific performances, started her contract on 3 November and relieved him of some of his responsibilities. Throughout, he remained responsible for the publicity campaign, the increasingly difficult negotiations with City Rail, and the project's finances.

Week eight (27 October–1 November 1997)

On Monday 27 October, the two-hour rehearsal begins with a full body and voice warm-up, which concludes with Rubena teaching the ten people who have shown up that night a simple Maori song. Divided into pairs, the group then writes scripts for their steward characters. Anything goes at this stage; Fiona only warns the participants against exaggeration. The stewards' acts should be like the uniforms that Anthony is designing, she explains, just a touch surreal to make the audience wonder what is going on. She and John also coach the participants to be prepared for silly remarks from regular train passengers, the ethics of which they do not consider any more problematic than for street theatre: as a performer you prepare for any eventualities and as a spectator you either stay and watch or move on. The directors worry more about lack of time and, in order to speed up the process, they announce that they themselves will put together a draft script from all the steward improvisations they have seen so far, promising they will have it ready for next week's rehearsals. John would later admit that they wrote those scripts themselves in a bit of a panic: 'We said to each other, "Okay, we're going to do that steward scene, it's going to be twenty minutes long, oh my God, we only have five rehearsals left."' [16]

Every Thursday at 11 a.m. all the professional artists, including the youth theatre partners, come together for a weekly production meeting. Because there are so many subprojects unfolding in different places, it is important for all those involved to keep track of what is going on. Each coordinating artist therefore takes a turn to report on the latest developments. Every production meeting inevitably brings new cancellations and additions that have budgetary and sometimes complicated technical consequences for the outdoor event; fun to deal with at first but increasingly annoying as the first performance dates now rapidly approach and the realization sinks in that there will be different line ups for each performance weekend and that a full dress and tech rehearsal with all the participating artists will be impossible. Publicity is the least problem: posters, postcards and flyers are ready three weeks before the first show; western Sydney door-to-door papers have promised to run articles, as has *The Sydney Morning Herald* and the *Sunday Herald*. The main expense will be a daily ad in the *Morning Herald*'s theatre directory. Anything more would be overkill as *Trackwork* can only accommodate 160 paying spectators in each of the four shows.

Richard Vella is in charge of the first half of the Thursday evening session. At this point, he still has not given up on the idea of a soundscape and, therefore, has brought a collection of funny toys such as squeaky dogs, bells, bubbly wrap and rattlers, with which he wants the participants to create a texture of audio effects capable of filling a railway carriage. He experiments with all kinds of time delays, echoes, and movements, but the results remain unsatisfactory. Besides, Fiona is concerned that a soundscape will be too inward-looking, whereas she also wants the audience to look outside, at greeneries, backyards, and industrial complexes. Before everyone goes home, she hands out sets of disposable cameras with instructions to take pictures of their houses and neighbourhoods and invent stories, which the participants should be prepared to tell to small groups of spectators while sticking the pictures to the train window. The cameras should be returned no later than the following Saturday, so that there will be enough time left for film processing and rehearsing with the photographs.

On Saturday afternoon, while the actors work on their steward roles, John, Richard and Fiona discuss the soundscape problem and conclude that it is not going to work. They opt for ethnic songs instead. During the last hour of the workshop, the stewards try out their new scripts, which John and Fiona have completed. They play in front of the directors and the rest of the group seated on chairs arranged as if in a train carriage. John and Fiona time these acts and give feedback on gestures and delivery of lines. Although the stewards' scripts seem to work theatrically, the actors clearly require additional rehearsals to improve their space awareness and interactions with the audience, which are the key to their effectiveness.

Fiona and John now have a more concrete notion of what the different elements should look like. They have decided to work on four separate acts for the stewards: a slightly surrealistic welcome on the Redfern to Auburn leg, a guided tour of Berala station, ethnic songs on board the Berala to Cabramatta stretch, and photo stories on the leg from Cabramatta to Granville. Each station will have a different theme: an urban street look at Redfern, a Felliniesque streetscape at Auburn, elderly people at Lidcombe, a surreal scene at Berala, Vietnamese folk theatre at Cabramatta, and hip-hop culture at

Granville. John accepts the inevitable danger of superficiality, which is most evident in the Berala tour guide segment: 'None of the participants come from there and so they'll be fantasizing, imposing their own fictional space. But having said that, it's impossible anyway to get deeply into the geographical community in a space that extends over 50 kilometres and encompasses 2.5 million people. All we can really do is having westerners create a mobile representation of West Sydney.'

Week nine (3–8 November 1997)

Starting on Monday night, John and Fiona direct the steward teams much more strictly than before, conscious that they only have four or five rehearsals left with each of their groups. The next morning, Fiona and Powerhouse Youth Theatre director Michael MacLaughlin spent several hours exploring possibilities for the PYT performance in the busy shopping street opposite Auburn station. They talk about the project to shop owners and obtain permission from an upstairs billiard hall to use a small room for dressing and storage.

Thursday's production meeting is dominated by freshly developing problems with City Rail. Harley's contact person now blatantly refuses to return phone calls and has failed to notify station masters. As Anthony Babicci reports, this has already caused hassles for visual artist José Da Silva, who is designing an installation for the Granville station waiting room but has been chased off the platform. Anthony is all the more worried because he is also planning to have live grafitti spray painting during the hip-hop finale. He and the others advise Harley to be patient one more week before taking firmer action.

Musically and theatrically, there have been some further mutations: Fiona has found some ballroom dancers to replace the elderly Chinese who had dropped out the week before. Richard reports that instead of three there is now only one brass band remaining, which, moreover, is only available for the first weekend. But he has confirmed the participation of an Iranian singer, an Italian women's choir from Haberfield, and a Turkish high school band. All of Richard's new additions have technical and budgetary consequences, however, because in terms of sound engineering outdoor concerts on station platforms are difficult to produce and, to avoid potentially dangerous cables, require expensive wireless connections and radio mikes. But in due time, Richard manages to talk one of Sydney's top sound engineers into coordinating *Trackwork*'s audiotechnical aspects and sound mix during the actual shows for a mere A\$600. As an additional bonus, this person will be able to get cheaper deals from audio rental firms than UTP can, so that this unanticipated expense will be more than compensated by the discounts.

That afternoon, Fiona and John run extra steward rehearsals at the Casula Powerhouse. The evening workshop at Auburn is dedicated to the ethnic songs that each of the participants is now planning to perform on the train. Pembe has prepared a Turkish children's song, Erin a Greek, and Clarissa an Italian tune. Richard's plan is to have the stewards walk through the carriage, identify a spectator by means of the colourful suit-case, introduce the song with a little story, and then try to teach it to whoever is interested: a song in search of an audience.

On Saturday, Mona Zaylaa has gathered fifteen hip-hop artists in one of the Casula Powerhouse studios at noon, so that Richard, who is rela-tively unfamiliar with rap music, can hear and see what they are capable of. Some artists have brought new compositions for the occasion as well as a few unannounced musical friends. After they have each performed a rap, Richard asks them all to return for another rehearsal on 22 November, so that he can make a definitive line-up. Later that after-noon, John and Fiona work with the actors on tour guide improvisations for Berala station, where the audience will have to wait for the next train to Cabramatta. Most participants have actually gone to explore Berala station and have come to today's rehearsal with texts they have written at home. As with the stewards, Fiona and John will subsequently edit these down to workable scripts. In order to get the actors used to moving around with a group and to exaggeratedly projecting their voices out-doors, they rehearse in the backyard of the Auburn workshop venue, which is in fact a former fire station now in use as a youth centre. John and Fiona's role is to encourage the participants' fantasies, while keeping track of what is practically do-able and theatrically effective. At the end of the session, they collect the disposable cameras and everyone leaves with a few *Trackwork* posters to be put up in their neighbourhoods. After the rehearsal, as we can see in the video, John meets production manager Janine Peacock at Auburn station to travel the actual performance jour-ney according to the Saturday train schedule and figure out logistical bottlenecks. Surveying the trajectory as if they were on military recon-naissance, they note delays, number of passengers, and length and types of trains, well aware that the modern trains are less noisy than the older doubledeckers.

Week ten (10–16 November 1997)

The Monday evening rehearsal is largely lost because the photographer for *The Sydney Morning Herald* shows up an hour late. To make up for lost time, the directors schedule an extra session for some of the steward teams that following afternoon at Casula. On Tuesday, Harley also scores a long-awaited breakthrough in his negotiations with the railroad, where he has discovered a more reliable partner in the public relations department. That afternoon, he and Janine visit all the station masters, assuring them that *Trackwork* is going to be much more low key and much less chaotic than they feared it was going to be.

Even more than indoor theatre, the potentially much more hazardous and unpredictable outdoor performances require meticulous blocking. In what position on what platform does a particular act begin and how do the performers move before they finish? This needs to be calculated in minute detail for each station and each train trajectory. And if a station has more than one platform, on which platforms should the performance and the audience be? Where will the mixing table be in relation to the performers and how far will the electronic gear then be from power points? Other problems to tackle concern the times that fast trains pass through stations and how long local trains stop, thus possibly blocking a performance. And no matter how carefully one plans, there are always unforeseen elements. There is not enough time to thoroughly verify how good some of the curated acts actually are, or how well, for that matter, ex-mental patients Colin and Davey will remember their lines under performance pressure or whether, indeed, they will even show up at all. Most scarily of all, the directors will not know what the show will look like in its entirety until the performance day itself. One week before the dress rehearsal, John and Fiona still have not had a chance to see anything of what PACT and PYT have come up with.

Fiona and John begin the Thursday night rehearsal by giving a detailed description of all the acts that have now been confirmed, in the order that they will appear. It makes the participants aware that there is very little time left and the rest of the evening they work with great concentration, first on their songs and then on the steward scripts and photo stories. 'Candy' and 'Barbie', two characters created by Michelle and Tania during an improvisation a couple of weeks earlier, are beginning to take definitive shape. Richard coaches some of the others on how to sing directly at a spectator. To prepare for any eventualities, they even try singing their folk songs before others in the group, who have been instructed to act as irritated passengers. Richard advises the performers to just walk away in such situations. The photos are also back from the lab now and after selecting the best ones, Fiona and John help the actors to weave a story around them and tell it effectively.

The work continues over the weekend. On Friday night, Richard, Fiona and John visit the Italian women's choir at their annual Christmas meal in Haberfield. At the Saturday rehearsal, the actors continue polishing their photo stories, steward acts, and guided tours. On Sunday morning, John attends a rehearsal of the Vietnamese youth theatre 'City Moon', whom he has asked to fill a 24-minute slot outside Cabramatta station, ostensibly to demonstrate that Vietnamese youngsters from western Sydney are capable of doing more constructive things than dealing drugs. Its artistic directors, exiled playwright Ta Duy Binh from Hanoi and Australian Bruce Keller, are preparing a traditional legend of a conflict between a river god and a mountain god, who fight over the daughter of Vietnam's first king. After an indoor run-through at their rehearsal venue in Bankstown, John travels with the ensemble to block the show in the designated outdoor performance space in Cabramatta, a shopping plaza where junkies hang out. The visit makes some of the middle-class, Bankstown-based City Mooners, who visit the area for the first time, visibly nervous.

Week eleven (17–23 November 1997)

The week before the dress rehearsal, a major crisis develops. On Monday afternoon, Harley calls his new contact person at City Rail to discuss logistics and, to his surprise, hears that the company's general manager has suddenly cancelled the earlier permission for on-train performances. Harley quickly regains his composure and sits down with Fiona, Janine, John and Mona to discuss possible alternatives. Harley suggests to hire buses, just as City Rail does when there is real track maintenance. That evening, John and Fiona openly share the bad news with the participants at the Fairfield rehearsal, promising them in the same breath that they are confident to find a solution. All the participants express their unconditional loyalty and energetically continue rehearsing for the show as if nothing has happened. Over the next few days, Harley, Janine and Mona work out the logistical and budgetary consequences of doing parts of the show on specially chartered buses to transport the audience between stations. But they cannot afford to give up on the original plan either, so on Tuesday morning Harley faxes an urgent letter to the railroad management with copies to the State's Transport and Arts Ministers, reminding them that UTP had been awarded state and federal funding on the explicit basis of performances on trains, for which, moreover, they had already received verbal approval back in September. In the letter, Harley also hints at possible damage to City Rail's already tarnished public image if UTP has to resort to performing on buses. The letter works: Harley's City Rail contact person rings back the following morning to announce that the general manager has given the green light and that an official letter to this effect is already in the mail. But another major problem surfaces. On Thursday, right before the production meeting, the City Rail contact rings once again to inform that a major track maintenance operation is scheduled for UTP's first performance weekend. However, after carefully studying the weekend time table, Harley and John conclude that, barring a few unavoidable delays, the damage can be contained. The main problem will be to expand the performance on the Redfern to Auburn stretch, which will now be diverted over a freight line, thus adding at least ten minutes to the journey. From Lidcombe on, trains will run pretty much according to the original timetable again.

Thursday evening, the stewards practise their folk songs and try to work out a way to theatrically support Karen Cummings, a Berala-born professional opera singer whom Richard has pulled out of his hat to sing Burt Bacharach repertoire on the journey from Berala to Cabramatta. However, the idea to have the stewards do Tamla-Motown-style dance steps and back-up vocals to support her is dropped after a few hilarious but messy attempts. There is simply not enough time to polish this act in the few remaining rehearsals.

Saturday at noon Richard does a final run-through with the definitive line-up for the Granville hip-hop finale. At 2 p.m., John and Fiona take the stewards to Berala station to try and perform their tour guides in the actual outdoor setting on the platform. The actors quietly speak their text after a train pulls in and bemused passengers alight. Fiona keeps time, fixes the blocking, and then takes the tour guides back to Sydney Central. There, at 4.44 p.m. all the stewards board the Penrith train and walk through the performance according to the actual *Trackwork* scenario. Some muster enough courage to practise their lines or sing their song. Woodhy, a Cambodian refugee, thus reaps his first applause, while Marika exclaims: 'I can't believe we're actually doing this.' Then, on Sunday afternoon, an improvised dress rehearsal takes place. The stewards now try out their complete acts on and off the trains. Anthony has brought them their caps to practise with. PACT, Terry Woo, the hip hop artists, and the production crew rehearse with the actual sound equipment in Auburn, Lidcombe and Granville, and City Moon performs their entire Vietnamese legend at Cabramatta. Most of the things seem to work according to plan.

In the week leading up to the first performance, the rehearsals are used to solve practical problems encountered during the Sunday dress rehearsal, like which steward team should cover the upstairs and which the downstairs of double-decker trains. In a special design meeting on Tuesday, Anthony tries to take care of any remaining last-minute requests. For example, PYT needs more costumes and oversize props to visually enlarge their act, which is played relatively far away from the audience on the shopping street below Auburn's elevated station platform. Anthony also still needs to design a makeshift theatre box office at Redfern and sign posting for the audience. In the the production meeting of Thursday 26 November, the project staff work their way through the production scenario one last time, from the moment the sound systems are set up to the point where the audience suitcases are reloaded into a hire truck for the next day's show. They also agree that John and Fiona will have to announce their imminent arrival to the crews at upcoming stations via mobile phone.

The performance

By 3 p.m. Saturday, 29 November, the stewards all gather to dress in the Travellers Aid Room at Sydney Central. At 4 p.m. they walk out to a quiet platform to stretch and warm up their voices. At ten past the hour, performances start on Redfern station: Pat Ryan's 'Spastic Mental Staircase Musical Circus Band' improvises funky music and girls from a nearby high school dance to an American pop tune playing through a ghetto blaster. Back at Central, the stewards take in their positions on the departure platform. They will each board different levels and carriages of the 4.24 train bound for Redfern. Arriving there three minutes later, the automatic doors open and they welcome their audience, whom they can recognize by the colourful little suitcases they have been given with their tickets. The show has begun.

On the Redfern to Auburn leg, things turn sour for Tania and Michelle,[17] whose 'carriage activities coordinator' act is rudely disturbed by a stressed-out middle-aged Anglo couple that is obviously not in the mood for a wacky theatre show on the train. Tania holds her own against the nasty remarks, but Michelle is visibly affected. Luckily the paying spectators take their side and, in a heated debate lasting several minutes, manage to shut the couple up. And after a good cry and a hug from Fiona at the next station, Michelle courageously continues.

At Auburn, the PYT show on the shopping street below still is too small, both in terms of sound and size, to make much impact and is cut short because the changed timetable requires the stewards to usher the audience to the other side of the station in time to catch the train to Lidcombe. The next stop is a winner: the audience is festively welcomed by Bill Belcher's Blacktown Brass Band, after which Terry Woo makes his grand entrance. Dressed in glittery rhinestone, he strides down the stairs as a Las Vegas superstar while singing 'Begin the Beguine' to a backing tape that can be heard through the entire station.[18] At Berala, the tour guides are a bit upstaged by another hit: female and male brides, performed by PACT actors, are tossed out of a wedding limousine, which comes to a screeching halt several times in a row on the street corner below. The dumped brides sob their hearts out and desperately try to climb the fence as the train pulls out on its way to Cabramatta. The ethnic folk songs that the stewards sing on this leg work like a charm, too, partly because they deliver them with a big smile to those spectators most obviously in a party mood. The Italian women's choir and Karen Cummings' Bacharach concert receive similar appreciation. At Cabramatta, a lone junkie tries to intimidate a few spectators but is quickly forced to move on when the City Moon performance begins. The photo stories on the last leg are lovely and invite personal exchanges between small groups of spectators and the stewards, who drop their dramatic personas as they talk about their real families and the streets they live in. The show concludes in an upbeat celebration of western Sydney youth culture with spray-painting grafitti artists, a visual arts installation in the waiting room, an odd movement improvisation with bedsheets by Gravity Feed, and PACT's voguing poses up and down the platform to the beat of 25 minutes of live hip-hop music.

Fiona and John are visibly delighted with the first performance and everyone seems considerably more relaxed before the second, except for Tania and Michelle, who are still flustered from Saturday's ordeal. But no problems occur on Sunday. After a day's rest, on Tuesday morning the project staff comes together for a debriefing and for planning the second

weekend, when they effectively have a new show with different performers and an altered timetable. Everyone agrees that the first weekend
had gone remarkably well, given the event's complexity. Richard reveals,
however, that at Granville there had been some friction between the
improvisation band and the rappers, because, he thinks, they never had
time to get to know each other properly. Fiona has to sort out a problem
with Colin, who still does not know his lines and thus destroys the act of
his two partners. She resolves to schedule an extra rehearsal with him
and Davey, who also has a history of mental trouble and freaked out on
Saturday, failing to return to do his poetry performance at Berala station
for the Sunday show. The project team then meticulously works its way
through the scenario for the second weekend, pointing out alterations in
line-up and timetable and the logistical and technical adjustments these
require.

Evaluation

On the second weekend, the performances work much better than on
the first. Even the conservative Granville station master, who had threatened to cut the power if Ebony and Danielle sang their
anti-Pauline-Hanson rap again, remained calm. In the end, all four performances were sold out and most spectators had enjoyed the shows.
Two inner city youngsters on their way to Stanmore for a barbecue ended
up following *Trackwork* all the way to Granville: 'We weren't imagining
to find anything out West, but we discovered it was really good to get out
here.' Another young couple waiting at Granville to go downtown inten-
tionally missed four trains because they decided to stay and watch the
whole show: 'It shows the West as a vibrant area with lots of community
stuff that you wouldn't know existed.' Most paying spectators particularly
appreciated the photo stories and the Granville finale, while many also
singled out the bride dumping as another highlight.

The participants themselves were also generally positive about the
experience. Hip-hop artist Danielle Tuwai liked the random audience
idea because it exposes normal commuters to art and performances they
would not otherwise get to see or hear about. Cambodian steward
Woodhy Chamron felt he had really developed his talents as a performer
and was glad with the way *Trackwork* had presented a positive image of
Asian people living in the Cabramatta area. Pembe Mentesh, who had
heard about the project through her work as a traffic safety officer in
Auburn, felt proud about her part in the show. She thought that it had
succeeded in demonstrating that western Sydney has many diverse

talents and that culture does not only happen in the inner city. She also claims she gained strength from the other participants, a feeling shared by Tania Gutierrez and Michelle Boukheris, who said that 'it was really good to meet so many interesting personalities interested in investing in their own communities'.[19]

Designer Anthony Babicci felt a bit disappointed that not more community participants had been involved in creating the visuals. But he had enjoyed working with the grafitti artists: 'It is an art form that is often confused with anti-social vandalism – whereas I have come to regard it as an emerging new art form and a new language for young people. Giving them a space within a real art work is a form of recognition for them. They're used to working in the dark in dangerous places and now their work is displayed in the public domain.'[20] And Richard Vella, although frustrated at times by the hip-hoppers' lack of punctuality, had similarly learned to appreciate their music: 'I had never worked with rappers before. I used to hate rap. Now I understand much better its political implications in the western suburbs. Most of the stuff you usually hear is from New York, but when you hear someone like Janaya sing about Bankstown or Ebony about Pauline Hanson it is fantastic.'[21] Our Filipino-Australian cameraman Ronnie Morelos, himself an experienced community and youth theatre artist, had found *Trackwork* a brave undertaking:

> Insisting on working on regular trains rather than on special services, was great. It's been highly successful in bringing to the foreground the faces that people would prefer to remain invisible. It was also good because it showed that community theatre can be done in different aesthetic modes, just as street theatre is no less theatre than black box theatre. That was central to that aggressive reaction from those people who criticized Michelle and Tania for having 'no polish'. They were imposing imperial Anglo standards on the performance, the yardstick of theatre practised in the 'real' cultural capitals of the world, not Bali but Broadway and West End.[22]

John and Fiona felt that *Trackwork* had achieved its objective of exposing the audience to the cultural diversity of western Sydney, but they expressed suprise at how much the participants had felt ownership of the project. Looking back on the process, Fiona believed that she and John wasted valuable time in creating the stewards' acts: 'Because of my lack of experience in site-specific work, it took me too long to get my head around what was going to happen on the trains, which is why we didn't have enough time to make the stewards wittier than they ended up being.' John, in turn, realized that in community theatre he needs to accelerate the pace of the creative process: 'I have always worked through improvisations, giving the performers an idea, taking notes from that, pushing it a bit further and letting it develop that way. What I have learned is that you can't really expect community participants to give me that much back. I was expecting them to do more with an idea. In the end they did very well, but they did what I asked and rarely took it further.'

Trackwork was less about giving a voice to a specific community through personal stories and more about demonstrating to the rest of Sydney that the West is not just some amorphous 'other', as Fiona put it, but composed of many communities and diverse cultures. Because they opted for that breadth, UTP ran the risk of being criticized for superficiality. 'Unavoidable,' John claims, 'We had to cram so much in, trying to give the audience the feeling of the diversity of the place, where a lot of things happen. Having chosen for that I don't think there was any way we could have gone for additional depth. But perhaps we should have added another scene like the photo story.' Which is exactly what Monica Barone, who had created the original concept for *Trackwork*, had been yearning to see:

> When that old Chinese singer came down the stairs, that implicitly told me a story. He didn't have to come and tell me his life story, I could tell from his accent, from his face and from what he was doing. I guess I had expected more brilliant theatrical moments like that and a few more stories as the Cambodian guy told me about the building of his Buddhist temple and what that had meant to him. So my criticism was, get rid of all the other stuff and just focus on the stories that tell me about where I am and who lives in these places. That's why I found the Berala tour guides a lost opportunity because to me it felt they put Berala down. I would rather have heard from the President of the local RSL what he regards as the high points of his area.

But Harley did not agree with Barone's critique, arguing that it reflects too limited a notion of what community theatre can and should be. In contrast to the Pacific Islander project, he explained, the *Trackwork* process had been open to everyone, which made it impossible to be seen as the organized expression of a specific community and therefore should not be assessed as one:

It demonstrated that community theatre can also be be funny and surreal. It doesn't have to be people saying, 'well, this is my suburb and this is why I love it.' You can throw that in next to people saying 'this is a big dump.' It is almost assumed that if you're going to see a community production or community exhibition, or any product of this kind of community cultural development initiative, that it always has to be about identity and pride. There was an element of that in *Trackwork*, of course, but irony is not just the preserve of clever inner city people or full-time artists. And don't underestimate the scale of the whole thing – the performance had to be over two hours long; you can't travel all over western Sydney and get a sense of the place in less time than that. So it needed to be big and have a lot of performance, because that is the only way to keep it interesting.[23]

Aftermath

Despite its many obstacles, or perhaps because of it, *Trackwork* is a good example of how to professionally produce large-scale moveable community theatre events. Particularly the work that John, Fiona, and Richard Vella did in the workshops is comparable to the improvisation-based approaches in other parts of the world. The complexities of, excuse the pun, keeping track of many simultaneously evolving creative processes, handling technical requirements, and supervising a two-and-a-half hour show that moves across fifty kilometres of railroad, should only be tackled if one has access to substantial funds and stress-free artists and production managers used to thinking big and working outdoors. Despite the headaches, *Trackwork* has certainly given the UTP staff a taste for more. In the first half of 1998 they worked on a performance with Aborigines in Campbelltown, home of the largest Aboriginal population in the state, and in September on a performance for and with the Vietnamese community. In the third community participation project of that year, UTP worked with Kurdish, Timorese, and Bosnian residents of Speed Street in Liverpool, creating a multimedia event with them in private homes and out on the street.

Notes

1 See, for example, *The Sydney Morning Herald* (Tuesday, 28 October 1997), p. 8.

2 The authors of *home/world* try dispel the west's negative image coming not so much from an enlightened enthnography inspired by postcolonial theory, but from a postmodern urban studies interest in 'the spatialisation of social relations' (Grace *et al*. 1997: 24). With the exception of Ghassan Hage's essay, however, they add little to Powell.

3 On 11 November 1975, the Governor General sacked Whitlam for incompetence after what many progressive commentators now regard as a *de facto* right-wing coup. Whitlam had come to power after twenty-three years of uninterrupted conservative government. Bringing Australian troops home from Vietnam, introducing a controversial divorce law, and other progressive measures may have been too much too quickly for Australia's right-wing elite.

4 The Australia Council was founded in 1973. Its Funding Division is subdivided into a Literature Fund, a Visual Arts and Crafts Fund, an Aboriginal and Torres Straight Islander Arts Fund, a Community Cultural Development Fund, a Music Fund, a Dance Fund, and a Theatre Fund. Theatre grants are awarded by a committee of artists who are appointed for three-year terms and who meet twice yearly. The Theatre Programme Officer advises grant applicants and provides background information to committee members.

5 Personal interview with John Baylis, Sydney, 5 December 1997.

6 This group includes Circus Oz and the Flying Fruitfly Circus. The internationally renowned stilt-theatre group Stalker, which relocated from New Zealand to Sydney in the late 1980s, would also fit into this category, although its artistic director, Rachel Swain, claims they were more influenced by LeCoq than by the circus tradition.

7 In 1997, Kim Spinks was working for the New South Wales Ministry for the Arts. Alice Spizzo is a lawyer working for the New South Wales government. Christine Sammers first worked for the Community Cultural Development Fund before becoming the Australia's Council's overall coordinator for arts funding. Paul Brown currently earns a living as a Geology lecturer at the University of New South Wales and continues to write. In 1989, he wrote *Aftershocks*, a play about the Newcastle earthquake, and in 1992 he wrote the script for the DDT production *Café Hakawati*.

8 'Art and Working Life' was a programme of the Australia Council's Community Cultural Development Fund aimed at channelling arts resources to working-class audiences, via trade unions. According to Fiona Winning, the union art officers who held the purse strings often required artists applying for grants to first demonstrate their new project's effectivenesss for recruiting new union members: 'That became a trap and ultimately dissatisfying for artists. The quality of the art wasn't great a lot of the time and I think that many artists who continued with "Art and Working Life" stuff were old-style unionists in lots of ways. They grasped too late that the working class had changed. Mind you, there is nothing wrong with a banner or a choir project, but a lot more could happen. The Australia Council eventually pulled the plug around 1993. This doesn't mean that union art cannot be funded – it can on a per project basis – but there is no longer any special programme called "Art and Working Life."'

9 Personal interview with Fiona Winning, Sydney, 2 December 1997.

10 SteetArts best-known community outreach took place in Inala, an under-

240   Community Theatre

serviced district of Brisbane. In 1983 it ran a series of circus skills workshops in a local elementary school and an ongoing cabaret workshop for adults in the evenings. In 1984 it created a huge outdoor show called *Once Upon Inala*, featuring 150 community participants. In 1985 it did a small women's project that resulted in the establishment of a separate community theatre company called 'Icy Tea' (I.C.T., meaning 'Inala Community Theatre') (Capelin 1996: 24).

11 The other nine include smaller mainstream companies such as Company B at Belvoir Street. The state theatre companies and national cultural flagships such as Opera Australia and the Australian Ballet receive direct funding (A$ 1.5 million and up) from the federal Minister for Communications and the Arts, not through the Australia Council.

12 Paul Brown, *Café Hakawati*, unpublished typescript, p. 36.

13 Noëlle Janaczewska, *Yungaburra Road*, unpublished typescript, pp. 19–20.

14 Personal interview with Monica Barone, Sydney, 4 January 1998.

15 PACT stands for 'Performers, Artists, Composers, Technicians.' Located in Newtown in the inner city, it used to be a theatre co-op in the 1960s. Nowadays, it is mainly a youth theatre run by professional artists, who also hire out their performance space.

16 Baylis interview, Sydney, 5 December 1997.

17 This was not their first community theatre experience: Michelle had participated in *Site* to overcome her shyness and Tania was in the community participation version of *Blood Orange*. Fiona invited them to participate in *Trackwork*.

18 Although he is virtually unknown to the general public, Terry Woo is a professional variety artist who came from China in 1950 and has managed to make a living for decades with gigs in Returned Servicemen League (RSL) clubs. In many smaller towns in Australia, these RSL clubs, along with union-coordinated Workers Clubs, are the main venues for cultural activities. Fiona worked with him earlier in 1997 on a community show for elderly Chinese, Arabs and Bosnians in Auburn called *Riples*.

19 Personal interview with Pembe Mentesh, Casula, 22 November, 1997.

20 Personal interview with Anthony Babicci, Casula, 22 November, 1997.

21 Personal interview with Richard Vella, Casula, 22 November 1997.

22 Personal interview with Ronaldo Morelos, Wombarra, 7 December, 1997.

23 Personal interview with Harley Stumm, Casula, 9 December 1997.

Bibliography

Anon. (1991) *The Arts: Some Australian Data*, Redfern, NSW: Australia Council.

Binns, V. (1991) *Community and the Arts: History, Theory and Practice*, Annandale, NSW: Pluto Press.

Brown, Paul (1987) 'Making Coal Town', *Meanjin* 46, 4: 477–486.

Burvill, Tom (1984) 'Sidetrack: Theatre and Community', *The Bulletin of the Australasian Drama Studies Association* 3, 1 (Autumn).

—— (1986) 'Sidetrack: Discovering the Theatricality of Community', *New Theatre Quarterly* 11, 5: 80–89.

(1998) 'Playing the Fault Lines: Two Political Theater Interventions in the Australian Bicentenary Year 1988', in Jeanne Colleran and Jenny S. Spencer (eds) *Staging Resistance: Essays on Political Theater*, Ann Arbor, MI: The University of Michigan Press: 229–246.

Capelin, Steve (ed.) (1996) *Challenging the Centre: Two Decades of Political Theatre*, Brisbane: Playlab Press.

Castles, Ian (1991) *Music and Performing Arts Australia 1991*, Canberra: Australian Bureau of Statistics.

Castles, Stephen (1992) *Mistaken Identity: Multiculturalism and the Demise of Nationalism in Australia*, Leichardt: Pluto Press.

Davis, Jack, Johnson, Eva, Walley, Richard and Maza, Bob (1989) *Plays From Black Australia*, Sydney: Currency Press.

Davis, Mark (1997) *Gangland: Cultural Elites and the New Generationalism*, St Leonards, NSW: Allen & Unwin.

Evans, Christine (ed.) (1998) Double Issue: Performance Anxiety. *W/Edge* 4–5 (June).

Fotheringham, Richard (ed.) (1992) *Community Theatre in Australia*, Sydney: Currency Press.

Frow, John and Morris, Meaghan (eds) (1993) *Australian Cultural Studies: A Reader*, St Leonards, NSW: Allen & Unwin.

Grace, Helen, *et al.* (1997) *home/world: space, community and marginality in sydney's west*, Annandale, NSW: Pluto Press.

Greenwood, T. (1983) 'Is Community Action an Essential Ingredient of Community Arts?', *Meanjin* 42, 3 (September): 309–313.

Headon, David, Hooton, Joy and Horne, Donald (eds) (1994) *The Abundant Culture: Meaning and Significance in Everyday Australia*, St Leonards, NSW: Allen & Unwin.

Holloway, Peter (1987) *Contemporary Australian Drama*, Sydney: Currency.

Kelly, Boris (1997) 'Urban Projections', *Real Time* 20 (August–September): 14–18; 37.

Mackay, Hugh (1993) *Reinventing Australia: The Mind and Mood of Australia in the 90s*, Sydney: Angus & Robertson.

Mudrooroo (1997) *The Indigeneos Literature of Australia: Milli Milli Wangka*, South Melbourne: Hyland House.

Murphy, Peter and Watson, Sophie (1997) *Surface City: Sydney at the Millennium*, Annandale, NSW: Pluto Press.

O'Neill, E. (1984) 'The Popular Theatre Troupe: Freedom of Expression and Community Theatre', *Meanjin* 43, 1 (March): 86–93.

Powell, Diane (1993) *Out West: Perceptions of Sydney's Western Suburbs*, Sydney: Allen & Unwin.

Radic, Leonard (1991) *The State of Play: The Revolution in the Australian Theatre Since the 1960s*, Ringwood, Vic: Penguin Books.

Reid, Mary Ann (1997) *Not a Puppet: Stories From the Frontier of Community Cultural Development*, Sydney: Australia Council.

Smith, Robin E. (ed.) (1992) *Australia*, Canberra: Australian Government

Publishing Services.

Tait, Peta (1994) *Converging Realities: Feminism in Australian Theatre*, Sydney: Currency.

Watt, David (1990) '"Art and Working Life": Australian Trade Unions and the Theatre', *New Theatre Quarterly* 22: 162–173.

—— (1991) 'Mainstreet: Making Theatre in the Country', *Meanjin* 50, 2–3: 219–230.

—— (1992) 'Community Theatre: A Progress Report', *Australasian Drama Studies* 20 (April), 3–15.

—— and Jenny Lee (1991) 'Decentring the Theatre: An Interview with Don Mamouney', *Meanjin* 50, 2–3: 230–240.

Internet connections

Artists Union Australia:
<http://www.alliance.aust.com/>

Arts Law Centre of Australia:
<http://www.ozemail.com.au/~artslaw>

Australia Council:
<http://www.ozco.gov.au/>

Australian Theatre Guide:
<http://www.dot.net.au/~ssands/athg.htm>

Urban Theatre Projects:
<urbantp@ozemail.com.au>

Urban Theatre Projects Web Page:
<http://www.ozemail.com.au/~urbantp>

Chapter 7

Conclusion

On Friday 10 July 1998, together with Gerardo Arias Elizondo of Aguamarina, Sally Gordon of Teatro de la Realidad, and Jos Bours and Marlies Hautvast of Stut Theatre, I flew to Kisumu, Kenya, where the next day we met up with UTP's Harley Stumm, PETA's Beng Santos-Cabangon and Bong Billones, and Emma Mumma and Susan Adhiambo of Kawuonda, with Carolyne Odero serving as Luo-English interpreter and myself for Spanish-English. The occasion was the International Drama/Theatre and Education Association (IDEA) world congress at Kisumu's Tom Mboya Labour College. IDEA had sponsored Gerardo's airfare and had provided facilities for us to meet. For four consecutive mornings we watched excerpts from the video documentary and commented on each other's way of working, together with between ten and twenty observers. On Saturday afternoon, 18 July, we screened the complete video for some 500 delegates, after which fifteen Kawuonda women performed their 'Mosquito' song in the round, with Marlies, Jos, Harley, Beng, Bong, Gerardo, Sally and myself joining in. Our exchange had come full circle.

All over the world, scholars, politicians, policy-makers and even the very practitioners themselves find it difficult to pigeon-hole community theatre, because, as we have seen, its creative methods are so diverse and the plays, which represent many styles, are usually performed beyond the reach of metropolitan limelights. The composition of the community groups is equally varied, as are the theatre vocabularies and techniques of the artists who work with them. Still, the above case studies show that on all six continents, the artists who practise community theatre also share significant methodological elements, organizational strategies, and complex concerns, such as the effectiveness of their work, the ethics of middle-class artists working with peripheral groups, and the aesthetics and status of community theatre as a distinct art form.

I believe all the groups discussed in this book would agree that the most important benefits for the participants in community theatre are improved self-esteem and cross-cultural understanding through collective art processes. But to achieve this common goal, each new community theatre project, no matter where it takes place, has to make its own unique journey that can never be fully predicted or simply duplicated elsewhere. Flexibility, the ability to adapt pre-planned structures and schedules to unforeseen developments, cross-cultural sensitivity, and the skill to generate original performances through improvisation seem, however, to be valuable assets for would-be community theatre artists all over the world. Community support is equally vital, regardless of whether this already exists naturally through long-term membership in amateur theatre collectives, or, in the case of professional organizations, through a formal board, liaison figures, neighbourhood networks, or *ad hoc* steering committees (O'Toole, 1992: 23). Self-reliant community-based groups, such as Kawuonda and Aguamarina, democratically determine their own themes and, generally, can get started right away. Projects involving outside professionals, however, require considerably more preparation and specialized skills, including fund raising, community liaison, recruiting participants, planning and conducting rehearsals, and coordinating the theatre production.

The most common obstacle everywhere seems to be domestic pressure on the community actors. In Sigoti, Susan Adhiambo explained, many other women would like to join in Kawuonda's theatre activities but do not get permission from their husbands. At the Kisumu conference, she was suprised to learn that in Utrecht, Los Angeles, and Puntarenas similar problems exist, each with their own cultural specifics.

In terms of their creative process, the Kawuonda women, who have worked and lived in the same tightly knit community for many years, move straight from informal storytelling to improvisational drama without elaborate warm-ups, although it could be argued that their songs and dances serve a similar purpose because they signal to them a mental transition from manual labour to playful creativity. However, when working with people from different neighbourhoods or from diverse cultural backgrounds, extensive get-to-know-you periods are indispensable for building the necessary trust that allows relative strangers to open up to each other and to comfortably embark together on sometimes delicate creative processes.

In Costa Rica and the Philippines rather than personal stories, field trip interviews provided the raw material for subsequent improvisations, for which the actors first mentally prepared themselves by means of elaborate discussions or by exploring the theme emotionally through other art forms, such as music, dance, and visual arts. In both these countries, it should be stressed, the sociocultural gap between the actors and the community residents they interviewed was minimal and the collective ownership of those involved in the actual playmaking process substantial. This process of extracting community stories from others and returning it to them is a valid way of strengthening the social fabric of one's community and nourish the practice of locally inspired art. But the Dutch, the Californian, the Kenyan, and to a lesser degree the Australian cases illustrate that an equally potent source for material is constituted by the lives of the community actors themselves, which, most commonly, are creatively processed through several rounds of improvisations into scenarios and, finally, more or less fully mounted performances.

None of the countries possesses its own undiluted community theatre method, although the Philippine BITAW and the Latin American *creación colectiva* seem more formalized self-conscious drama pedagogies than the more experimental or instinctive approaches of Marlies Hautvast, Sally Gordon, John Baylis and Fiona Winning, and the Kawuonda women. Every single one of the groups, including Aguamarina and Kawuonda, directly or indirectly borrows from others, whether it is Spolin, Heathcote, Boal, Barker, Alexander, Bolt, Garcia, Ngũgĩ, or Buenaventura.

The aesthetic influence of the facilitating artist was conspicuous in all the cases, but nowhere more so than in Utrecht, where a professional playwright was involved, and in Sydney, where a professional team composed of four artistic directors, a composer, a visual artist, a production manager, an overall coordinator, and a community liaison guided the project. But even in these well-funded productions, questions of group ownership and respect for authenticity were a continuous concern.

Community theatre everywhere works at bridging difference. The Kawuonda women, for example, use it externally to communicate things to the men in their community they could not publicly or privately express in any other way. In the relative safety of their bakery, they use theatre as a vehicle for negotiating difference between three generations of women. With Aguamarina, as in Kawuonda, the internal differences are less ethnic or cultural and more generational or ideological. Its collective creation process serves to process different interpretations of some social or cultural issue in the larger Puntarenas community. Both Urban Theatre Projects and Stut alternate 'mono-cultural' projects with 'cross-cultural' ones, having learned that people prefer dealing with their own culturally specific theme first before they are willing to engage with another culture. But as a Kenyan teacher at the Kisumu conference pointed out, this strategy would not work so simply in bridging African tribal differences. And when middle-class westernized urban artists from Manila enter tribal communities that effectively constitute oppressed cultural minorities whose heritage is threatened by extinction, the challenge to keep the existing indigenous cultural forms intact while trying to respectfully inject them with new issues, new meanings, and new interpretations, seems formidable indeed.

The people directly involved in the creative process are always much more deeply affected by community theatre than the spectators, although as Stut's periodic audience surveys suggest, the impact on audiences may well be profound and long-lasting, too. Sally Gordon claims that community theatre does much more than providing temporary relief for her participants: 'They get strength out of the art, out of writing a poem, out of making a beautiful mask. They realize they are artists and that they have creativity and imagination; that they are more than just a woman cleaning a house.' Yet, she and community theatre artists in other countries would also like to see their art recognized as a very demanding form of theatre that deserves, finally, to be taken seriously.

One would think that because of its widespread presence in the developing world and the increasingly cross-cultural and migratory dimensions in its western manifestations, community theatre should be of interest to post-colonial criticism and inter-cultural performance studies. Many of the authors active in these rapidly expanding fields implicitly speak for oppressed cultural minorities – indigenous or migratory – in a variety of places and from a dazzling array of subject positions. Still, not more than a handful demonstrate familiarity with community theatre and if they do, discuss it with a bird's eye view, the way L. Dale Byam does, for example, with the Zimbabwe Association of Community Theatre (ZACT) in Jan Cohen-Cruz' essay compilation, *Radical Street Performance* (1998: 230–237). The driving forces behind post-colonial (cultural) studies prefer to build their arguments on the works of internationally recognized artists, who have either direct or indirect roots in the former colonial world, but few of whom – with the obvious exceptions of Australia, New

Zealand and South Africa – still live there or can lay claim to genuine subaltern[1] experiences, either at home or as migrants or exiles in the diaspora. Edward Said, one of the more sensible post-colonial critics, seems to realize the internal contradictions of his perspective, when he acknowledges that 'It would be the rankest Panglossian dishonesty to say that the bravura performances of the intellectual exile and the miseries of the displaced person or refugee are the same.' Yet, he still believes it possible, 'to regard the intellectual as first distilling then articulating the predicaments that disfigure modernity – mass deportation, imprisonment, population transfer, collective dispossession, and forced immigrations' (1993: 403). This curious jump, which denies the displaced person and the refugee the capability of speaking for themselves through community arts, allows Said to illustrate his theories with the works of such towering artists as Salman Rushdie, Carlos Fuentes, Gabriel García Márquez, Milan Kundera, George Padmore, Kwame Nkrumah, C.L.R. James, Aimé Césaire, Christophe Senghor, Claude MacKay, Langston Hughes, Frantz Fanon, Amilcar Cabral, Walter Rodney, Chinua Achebe, Ngũgĩ wa Thiong'o, Wole Soyinka, Faiz Ahmad Faiz, Derek Walcott, and Toni Morrison. But Ariel Dorfmann, himself a post-colonial literary superstar, flatly denies that, as one of Said's expatriate intellectuals, he is capable of 'distilling then articulating' the experiences of the marginalized: 'I was an uprooted Argentinian boy, an American who tried to be a Chilean with all his might. That is, of course, very different from being a Chilean peasant' (Zoon 1998: 29).

The sub-fields of post-colonial *drama* studies and its close kin, intercultural performance studies, are similarly oblivious to community theatre. The promisingly named *Post-Colonial Drama: Theory, Practice, Politics*, for example, jointly authored by Helen Gilbert and Joanne Tompkins, deals with drama that aims to 'dismantle the hegemonic boundaries and the determinants that create unequal relations of power based on binary oppositions such as "us and them", "first world and third world", "white and black", "colonist and colonised"' (1996: 3) but instead of anti-hegemonic grass roots theatre they gather their evidence from internationally recognized Commonwealth playwrights such as Walcott, Soyinka, Morgan, Davis, Baxter, Lovelace, Tomson Highway, Fugard, Ngũgĩ and Utpal Dutt. Published play scripts and productions in major cities, after all, lend themselves more conveniently to analysis than community shows in out-of-the-way places. While Gilbert and Tompkins do acknowledge the existence of community theatre in, for example, Papua New Guinea, Jamaica, Nigeria, and Bangladesh, they refer to it in the same general terms as L. Dale Byam did with ZACT, or otherwise as performance text (ibid.: 186–187).

The field of inter-cultural performance theory is an equally mixed bag of philosophically or anthropologically oriented discourse on theatrical encounters between cultures, ranging from Artaud in Mexico, Genet in the Arab world, Laurie Anderson in Rio de Janeiro and Japanese Bhuto dance in New York, to Grotowski, Barba, Brooke, Wilson, Sellars, Schechner and Mnouchkine – with or without the assistance of non-western performers – in Europe, Asia, Africa, or Latin America. Barring the odd reference to grass-roots theatre, inter-cultural performance studies tends to concentrate on the meta-cultural abstract productions of an international avant-garde operating in prestigeous metropolitan venues and the world's grand festival axis running from Avignon via Edinburgh to Adelaide and Los Angeles. In an animated discussion with Bonnie Marranca, Marc Robinson, and Una Chaudhuri – three leading US inter-cultural performance theorists – Edward Said once warned them against the dangers, for inter-cultural performance artists and theorists alike, of getting lost in this abstract transnational world of insiders (Marranca and Dasgupta 1991: 56). But Said's own work, as I am sure does this book, circulates almost exclusively within that very same hermetically sealed off intellectual domain he (and I) would like so much to open up (Said 1982: 152, 158). This concern is shared by the Calcutta-based dramaturge and cultural critic Rustom Bharucha, who fears that most post-colonial and inter-cultural performance studies is being 'manufactured in first world academia by the erstwhile proponents of the third world in the global diaspora'. Bharucha holds these intellectual exiles responsible for a veritable overproduction of post-colonial anti-orientalist publications that are obsessed with cultural identity and 'feed on each other with an incestuous, parasitic intensity' (Bharucha 1997a: 1458; see also Bharucha 1996: 117). Philosophically and linguistically they are so intensely subtle and abstract, I might add, that community theatre artists and participants would well be justified in asking what on earth it all has to do with their work. High time, therefore, to return to their more immediate concerns.

The artistic status of community theatre

The relative invisibility of community theatre in post-colonial and inter-cultural performance studies is a function, I suspect, of its marginal position within the international artistic and intellectual hierarchy. Community theatre performances are seldom reviewed by national media and, because they frequently occur outside 'legitimate' arts milieux in the major cities, they have consequently tended to escape the attention of cultural theorists and theatre scholars. Having said that, in the Philippines, community theatre enjoys a relatively higher status than in most other places. This is probably because of the dual careers that many artist-teachers associated with the Philippines Educational Theater Associations maintain. Some are well-known professional writers, directors, and performers active in Manila's avant-garde, which caters to the urban middle class. Others alternate jobs in television and film with community theatre workshops or performances in the urban and rural grass roots. Therefore, the country's leading theatre scholars, notably Nicanor Tiongson, Doreen Fernandez and Joi Barrios (Cohen-Cruz 1998: 255–261), demonstrate a thorough awareness of and respect for community theatre, while influential arts administrators like Nanding Josef have a background in cultural resistance. In contrast, the recognition for Dutch community theatre has been a long time coming. For at least a decade after the much publicized demise of the admittedly heavy-handed socialist theatre-in-education movement of the 1970s, Stut theatre struggled against a general media and scholarly aversion against any kind of working-class theatre. Only now that Dutch working-class neighbourhoods are becoming increasingly multi-ethnic in composition and some of the more open-minded local politicians and journalists have seen the effectiveness *and* aesthetic quality of inter-cultural productions, the respect for community theatre is slowly growing. But not from colleagues in mainstream and avant-garde theatre or, for that matter, from theatre scholars. According to Marlies Hautvast: 'In Holland community theatre is at best regarded as a minor form of art, if it is regarded as an art form at all. In addition, the way society is structured, and the way access to culture is stratified, working-class people don't usually get the chance to explore theatre as an art form. Yet, in their way of being, in the way they normally express themselves, they have a lot of possibilities in their bodies; they are clearly spontaneous enough to work with theatre.'[2] She and her partner Jos Bours believe that the difficulties they have experienced in recruiting 'minority' directors for their projects is also related to the questionable status of community theatre. Directors of non-Dutch-speaking-background, they found, want to be recognized as artists in the mainstream and avant-garde; not as ethnically defined cultural workers.

In the United States, community theatre is fighting its own uphill battle for recognition, although academically speaking post-colonial studies and theatre for social change are rapidly growing subfields in the humanities. In practice, only such high-profile professional companies as

John Malpede's Los Angeles Poverty Department (LAPD) and Cornerstone manage to generate substantial funds and media interest for their projects. Others have to make do with shoestring budgets patched together from local sources or, like Sally Gordon, work uneasily within welfare-oriented institutions that frequently demonstrate little sensitivity to the specific needs of art and artists. The editors of *From the Ground Up: Grassroots Theater in Historical and Contemporary Perspective*, the proceedings of a national community theatre conference held at Cornell University in 1993, therefore appropriately warn that, 'though the acknowledgement of the value of grassroots theater is long overdue on a national level, such acceptance may only be the first step towards its greater imperilment, especially as the already scarce resources for this kind of work would get shared with organizations that have no grassroots history and only a professed commitment to it' (Cocke *et al.*, 1993: 11). They continue:

> There are indications that 'community' and 'community-based' will become in the 1990s what 'multiculturalism' and 'cultural diversity' were in the '80s, a set of ideas which most theaters lay claim to but which few practice in earnest. In fact, whether inadvertently or by design, multiculturalism has become a means by which the groups that dominated the national cultural discourse could continue their dominance. The lessons of the last decade are clear in this regard. Despite modest changes, most of the resources devoted to theater at the beginnings of the 1990s are going to the same theaters that received them at the beginning of the 1980s or the 1970s or even the 1960s (ibid.: 14).

After initially receiving considerable support from central and provincial governments, Costa Rican community theatre is currently in somewhat of a slump. But led by Teatro Aguamarina from Puntarenas and Teatro Cariari from Limón, the art is far from dead *and* is recognized by a handful of leading theatre artists and scholars in the capital region as an important cultural phenomenon. Yet, the national government and media pay little attention to it, a situation which has only further deteriorated since the neoliberal election victory in 1998. Alfredo Catania, the former Artistic Director of the National Theatre and a promoter of community theatre of the first hour, has a 'purist' take on the artistic legitimacy of community theatre. Echoing the crux of a crisis that almost destroyed Stut Theatre in the early 1990s, he points to the danger of community theatre being misappropriated to serve the mainstream aspirations of ambitious local artists, who in their hearts do not much care for the community and only see it as a convenient way to launch into 'real art': 'the community should always come first, but sometimes you see these people's egos beginning to take centre stage and before you know it they only want to do their own thing. They suggest a production of an Ionesco script or an adaptation of Marquéz, and then things start getting confused. It is a journey that eventually leads to elitism and only massaging one's own vanity.'[3]

In Kenya, few people outside the immediate Sigoti region would have heard of the Kawuonda Women's Group, but nationally speaking community theatre is a legitimate and widely practised art that is fully integrated in rural communal life, schools, and university drama departments. The Kenyan Drama/Theatre and Education Association actively promotes community theatre, which is celebrated in countless festivals all over the country and, furthermore, possesses influential advocates in the art and essays of internationally renowned writers such as Ngũgĩ wa Thiong'o and Francis Imbuga.

Although Australian community theatre artists complain about their own marginal status in the national arts hierarchy, compared to the other countries mentioned here, their position is enviable. In Australia, community theatre has been consistently funded through governmental arts budgets since 1973. Although here, too, the mainstream ignores or at times appropriates it, the Australian avant-garde theatre has been occasionally known to collaborate with community theatre and, generally speaking, treats it with considerable respect. In addition, such well-known Australian cultural studies scholars as Gay Hawkins and Sneja Gunew have instigated a sophisticated theoretical discourse relevant to community theatre, which through their work is beginning to be intellectually and politically recognized as a distinct, socially and culturally significant art form.

The aesthetics debate

In *From Nimbin to Mardi Gras: Constructing Community Arts* (1993), Gay Hawkins distinguishes several phases in the evolution of offical Australian government policy towards community arts. In the first period, from 1973 until 1980, it used to patronizingly stimulate social integration by providing arts instruction to amateur practitioners in the more backward constituencies so they could learn to better appreciate the superior forms of western high culture (1993: 37). In the 1980s, this approach gradually gave way to the contrary notion that community arts should nourish cultural diversity (ibid.: 72). From 1980 onwards, the federal government began to promote the professional artist-in-residence, whose art could be revitalised by exposure to community life. By the mid-1980s, this idea was replaced by a more collaborative alternative. Participatory community arts thus evolved from top-down emancipation for the culturally deprived via individual artists looking for new inspiration, to 'a resource for the affirmation of different social groups and the expression of various issues. Community arts practice was now a method for aligning the skills of artists with unrepresented groups in the struggle for cultural self-determination' (ibid.: 117).

The question of aesthetics is often left begging in emphasizing the seemingly more easily identifiable social benefits of community theatre, a problem that has also been raised in the related fields of drama and education (O'Toole, 1992: 21–22) and theatre-in-education (Jackson, 1993: 31–37). Hawkins proposes a way out by arguing that 'the meaning and value of all texts is socially anchored' and that one should therefore 'insist on the diversity of different cultural values and tastes and their social origins' (1993: 76–77). She draws on Bennett (who, in turn, inevitably invokes Bourdieu) to point out that the status of all legitimate art and high culture is confirmed by a bourgeois elite that promotes its own socially and culturally determined taste as naturally superior and relegates community art to a decidedly lower category of cultural expression (ibid.: 12). To redress this situation Hawkins argues that community arts, just as any other cultural practice, operates according to its own aesthetics and should not be evaluated according to standards that are actually alien to it (ibid.: 131–132; 136).

Hawkins introduces the problematic concepts of 'affirmation' and 'authenticity' as alternative criteria for validating community art, which, she laments, tends to be limited to documentary realism as its preferential form (1993: 164). While this may be true for the predominantly visually oriented Australian community arts projects she looked at, the six cases I documented amply illustrate that the stylistic and formal options available to community theatre are considerably broader than documentary realism alone. They include melodrama, naturalism, comedy, verse drama, parody, surrealism, musical theatre, movement, masks, stilts, fireworks, and women playing men. In Hawkins' usage, 'affirmation' refers to what she regards as the typical community arts tendency to produce positive images of people who are 'underrepresented or negatively represented in public culture' (ibid.: 137), affirmative cultural action as it were. But 'positive', of course, does not necessarily imply 'uncritical', 'monolithic', or 'without internal contradiction'. And as UTP's Harley Stumm argued, there is no reason either to restrict community theatre's stylistic register to the preordained forms of uplifting social realism that should, by definition, always be based on the authentic personal stories of community residents.

The term 'authenticity' itself merits closer scrutiny. At first sight, it seems a self-evident ingredient of community theatre, which, despite UTP's formal experiments and Sally Gordon's interest in the surreal, draws much of its performative power from community residents pre-senting their (often autobiographical) stories in their own voices, with genuine emotions and their identities barely masked. But as Marlies Hautvast points out in the Tears in the Rain case study, 'you can't say of people that they are being purely themselves 100 times in a row in the same way'. Theatre theoretician Mark Fortier makes a similar point when, in reference to Anna Deveare Smith's documentary performance art, he remarks that there is indeed 'always a gap between theatre and reality', because 'the very acts of selecting, combining and theatricalizing dissolve the terms of the real and put them into the terms of the imagi-nary' (Fortier 1997:124–125). This, it seems to me, is no less true for a professional performer like Deveare Smith, who composes her scripts from verbatim interview material, than it is for Teatro Balangaw building scenes from material gathered in an exposure trip to riverside hamlets affected by a mining disaster, or for Aguamarina creating a show based on interviews with Puntarenas fishermen. In El Pescador, Aguamarina went to great pains to ensure that their rendition of the fishermen's experience was 'authentic', but several rounds of improvisation, aesthetically guided by a director, resulted unavoidably in a mediatiated, composite repre-sentation framed within a fictional narrative structure. Similarly, PETA's Beng Santos-Cabangon explained in Kisumu that in a collective writing and mounting proces, 'the facilitators have to be alert that the partici-pants don't move too far away from authenticity and that the perspectives of the villagers are respected. In Marinduque, Dessa and Ernie were present during the exposure as well, so they try to make sure that the performance they create with the participants more or less approximates what they saw there.'[4] The storyteller-turned-director in the Kawuonda process is no less a mediator when she guides the drama-tization process of women's stories about local gender relations. And while Stut and La Realidad stay close to the actual real-life persons, the plots and theatrical forms these are cast in are considerably influenced by the artistic choices of the professional artists leading the process. As safeguards against inauthenticity, Sally Gordon and Stut record impro-visations on video or audio tape and playwright Jos Bours includes verbatim phrases and expressions in his script, which is then handed back to the participants for final approval. Jos Bours sees the recordings, which also include valuable material from thematic discussions, as a means to check himself and to stay in touch with the participants, whose words, phrases, and intonations he wants to be 'singing around' in his head while he writes. Director Marlies Hautvast, in addition, also makes a point of including non-verbal body language material to add authenticity and depth to the speeches of the community actors.

The question of mediation is complex, particularly when the 'mediator' is a relative outsider or when professional designers and musicians are engaged to elevate the aesthetics of the community play. As Hawkins argues, the chief mediators in community arts are often middle-class artists who design the project, raise the necessary funds, recruit the community participants, aesthetically shape the resulting artistic product, and determine its distribution (1993: 151). As long as the mediating artist does not pursue individual fame and is willing to jointly establish *ad hoc* standards together with community participants rather than imposing his or her own (Hawkins 1993: 127; see also Conquergood 1985 and Salverson 1996), this does not need to be a huge problem. But as the example of the middle-class led Jamaican working-class women's collective 'Sistren' illustrates, the danger of resentment towards the outsider-artist (in their case compounded by racism) is constantly lurking in the shadows (Ford-Smith 1997).

Funding and dependency

The question of community theatre's status within the national and international arts hierarchy is closely related to funding and identity politics. Community participants and their facilitators argue that community theatre deserves to be recognized as a legitimate art form operating in a different sociocultural context and hence with different (but by no means inferior) aesthetics than mainstream and avant-garde art. Be that as it may, the reality is that when it attracts funding at all, community theatre is usually only validated according to social development instead of aesthetic criteria, both in the north and in the south. Although she specifically refers to Australia, Sneja Gunew's explanation may well apply to other situations: 'Too often, the implicitly less-than-excellent is funded as a form of community development or welfare and thus is hardly art. From the point of view of excellence-as-individual creativity, these types of art are produced by groups of people, not artists' (Gunew and Rizvi 1994: 19). Judging community theatre by social welfare criteria alone, moreover, makes it susceptible to control by the institutional obsession for immediately measurable 'results' or the politician's desire to quickly 'score', thereby more often than not blatantly ignoring the artistic merits. In the developing world, Honor Ford-Smith concludes with thinly veiled irony:

> as far as most development agencies are concerned, the place of theater and the arts is a non-issue. The arts are unproductive frivolities that can be justified only if they can be proven to be useful in the crudest forms, as in education. 'Development' apparently does not include pleasure, even the pursuit of pleasurable opportunities for reflection or the creation of cultural products that mirror collective consciousness.
>
> (1997: 229)

As a way around the aesthetics impasse, Gunew somewhat utopianly proposes a periodically rotating, ethnically diversified staff reshuffle in arts funding bodies, galleries, theatres, and publishing houses to thus pave the way for a redefinition 'of "excellence" as something more than form, something that also entails cultural content, social relevance, of being at the cultural cutting edge, of asking the aesthetic questions of our time in new and invigorating ways' (Gunew and Rizvi 1994: 32). Only if we allow for the possibility of multiple instead of uniform universal standards of artistic excellence, then, will we be able to accept that great art can indeed also be created in African villages or migrant enclaves in western cities. To do so, we must equally leave behind romantic, essentialized ideas about 'community', a category which is all too often, as Gunew puts it, 'bracketed as an homogenised entity and frozen outside history and contemporary interactive relations. Such notions of community also precipitate the anxiety-provoking shadow of the ghetto which always lurks just behind invocations of ethnic' (1994: 6).

Community and ethnicity

All of the community theatre projects discussed in this book, I suspect, would subscribe to the central aim of providing the members of socially, culturally, ethnically, economically, sexually, culturally, or otherwise peripheral 'communities' with the artistic means to collectively and democratically express their concerns and passions in their own, albeit aesthetically mediated, voices. An equivalent, simultaneous aim, to speak with John O'Toole, may be to simply create a good piece of theatrical art in, for, and with the 'community' (1992: 21). But 'community' is a slippery concept in which geographic signifiers uneasily compete with shifting social and ethnic markers (Hawkins 1993: 160).

Anthony Cohen's *The Symbolic Construction of Community* (1989) is still regarded, north and south, as one of the better attempts at universally theorizing 'community'. In Cohen's definition, 'Community is that entity to which one belongs, greater than kinship but more immediately than the abstraction we call 'society'. It is the arena in which people acquire their most fundamental and most substantial experience of social life outside the confines of the home.' (1989: 15). Rather than with material boundaries or objectifiable institutions, Cohen is concerned with the way people imagine or psycho-culturally experience and interpret their community, which, he argues, has never been free of all sorts of internal divisions, even in its pre-modern manifestation (1989: 25; see also Smith 1996: 250), which is often invoked as some Paradise Lost-type wholesome state that community theatre would be capable of restoring to the alienated, disenfranchised, post-modern urbanite (Hawkins 1993: 20). But as Philippine sociologist Fernando Zialcita usuefully reminds us, even the tiniest non-western rural communities, where these blissful forms of social life supposedly occur, are far from monolithic, conflict-free units. His research reveals, for example, that huge solidarity differences have been detected between *barangays* and *barrios* in one and the same 100-square-mile region at marginally different levels of geophysical elevation, let alone between the country's Muslim south and tribal north (1996: 33).

One's religious affiliation, susceptibility to nationalist or nativist imaginings, economic status, class fraction, upward mobility, sexual orientation, gender awareness, age group, civil status, profession, and level of education, are only some of the multiple, constantly changing factors that figure in the construction of one's sense of 'community'. And once 'ethnicity', 'race', and 'migration' – in themselves evolving sociocultural constructs (Gilroy 1987; Hall *et al.* 1992) – are thrown in, the monolith quickly fractures before one's very eyes. To simply refer to a community as 'working class' or 'peasant' – even leaving aside that these categories may mean substantially different things in Sigoti, Benares (Bharucha 1993: 37), northeast Los Angeles or Huehuetenango – is, then, to ignore that it is constructed from all kinds of elements, including locality, race formation, class fraction, caste, faith, gender, generation, and nation, which each in different combinations can give rise to all kinds of subcultures (Gilroy 1987: 232). While it can never restore pre-modern communal harmony, which probably never existed in the first place, community theatre can be an effective medium to negotiate internal differences and represent these in artistic forms, in the creation of which local cohesion is enhanced and respect for 'otherness' increased. In other words, it can serve as a confidence-boosting medium that enables the 'subaltern' (or 'other'; or 'marginalised'; or 'migrant'; or 'excluded'; or 'disempowered') to speak for themselves as artists performing in the here and now, regardless of whether you call their ever-shifting speaking position 'trialectic' (Soja 1996: 140), the 'liminal' or 'in-between' where cultural hybridity is bred (Bhabha 1994: 39), 'borderlands' (Anzáldua 1987), or the 'hyphenated realm' (Trinh 1992: 157). As the participants in the projects covered in this study amply illustrate, community theatre's speaking subjects, furthermore, are far from traumatized victims of capitalism, racism, sexism or any other 'ism'. Granted, sometimes the stories they tell are painful, but shaping them into art is pleasurable, and performing them exhilarating. And a good community show can only come about through a democratic, mutually tolerant joint effort in which the inevitably multiple differences that exist in any group will have to be sensitively negotiated.

Notes

1 Spivak defines 'subaltern' as 'men and women among the illiterate peasantry, the tribals, the lowest strata of the urban subproletariat living in the margins or "the silent, silenced center"' (Ashcroft et al. 1995: 24).
2 All quotations from the Kisumu Encounter were recorded at the 'Swapping Stories' seminar, which took place on four consecutive mornings from 14 through 17 July 1998 at the Tom Mboya Labour College in Kisumu, Kenya as part of the IDEA World Congress.
3 Personal interview with Alfredo Catania, San José, 29 July 1997.
4 'If the situation allows,' Beng Santos-Cabangon explained further, 'we also interview opponents. But sometimes it is not possible to have access to the other side. In those cases, we side with those most affected by the situation' (Kisumu Encounter).

Bibliography

Anderson, Benedict (1993) *Imagined Communities: Reflections on the Origins and Spread of Nationalism*, London: Verso.

Anzaldúa, Gloria (1987) *Borderlands/La Frontera*, San Francisco: Spinsters/Aunt Lutte.

Ashcroft, Bill, *et al.* (eds) (1995) *The Postcolonial Studies Reader*, London: Routledge.

Bell, John and Newby, Howard (1971) *Community Studies: An Introduction to the Sociology of the Local Community*, London: Allen & Unwin.

Bennett, Tony (1980) 'Popular Culture: A "Teaching Object"', *Screen Education* 34 (Spring): 17–29.
—— (1985) 'Really Useless "Knowledge": A Political Critique of Aesthetics', *Thesis Eleven* 12: 28–52.
Bhabha, Homi (ed.) (1990) *Nation and Narration*, London: Routledge.
—— (1994) *The Location of Culture*, London: Routledge.
Bharucha, Rustom (1992) *Theatre of the World: Performance and the Politics of Culture*. New Delhi: Manohar.
—— (1993) *The Question of Faith: Tracts For the Times*, New Delhi: Oriental Longman.
—— (1995) 'Dismantling Men: Crisis of Male Identity in Father, Son and Holy War', *Economic and Political Weekly* 30, 26 (1 July): 1610–1616.
—— (1996) 'Under the Sign of the Onion: Intracultural Negotiations in Theatre', *New Theatre Quarterly* 12, 46 (June): 116–130.
—— (1997a) 'When "Eternal India" Meets the YPO: Fifty Years of Dependence', *Economic and Political Weekly* 32, 25 (21 June): 1458–1464.
—— (1997b) 'Axioms in Search of Independence', *Communalism Combat* (August): 18–19.
—— (1998) 'The Shifting Sites of Secularism: Cultural Politics and Activism in India Today', *Economic and Political Weekly* 32, 4 (24 January): 167–180.
Boal, Augusto (1998) *Legislative Theatre*, London: Routledge
Bristol, M.D. (1989) *Carnival and Theater*, London: Routledge.
Cocke, Dudley, Newman, Harry and Salmons-Rue, Janet (eds) (1993) *From the Ground Up: Grassroots Theater in Historical and Contemporary Perspective*, Ithaca, NY: Community Based Arts Project at Cornell University.
Cohen, Anthony (1989) *The Symbolic Construction of Community*, London: Routledge.
Cohen-Cruz, Jan (ed.) (1998) *Radical Street Performance: an International Anthology*, London: Routledge.
Conquergood, Dwight (1985) 'Performing as a Moral Act: Ethical Dimensions of the Ethnography of Performance', in *Text and Performance Quarterly*, 5: 1–13.
Craig, Gary and Mayo, Marjorie (eds) (1995) *Community Empowerment*, London: Zed.
Creed, Rupert (1992) 'Remould Theatre Company', in Pamela Dellar (ed.) *People Make Plays*, Beverley: Highgate Publications.
Cross, M., ed. (1992) *Ethnic Minorities and Industrial Change in Europe and North America*, Cambridge: Cambridge University Press.
Davis, Mike (1985) 'Urban Renaissance and the Spirit of Postmodernism', *New Left Review* 151: 106–113.
Ellis, Jean (1989) *Breaking New Ground: Community Development with Asian Communities*, London: Bedford Square Press.
Ford-Smith, Honor (1997) 'Ring Ding in a Tight Corner: Sistren, Collective Democracy, and the Organization of Cultural Production', in Jacquie Alexander and Chandra Mohnty (eds) *Feminist Genealogies, Colonial Legacies, Democratic Futures*, New York: Routledge.

Fortier, Mark (1997) *Theory/Theatre: An Introduction*, London: Routledge.

Friedman, C. (1995) *Cultural Identity and Global Process*, London: Sage.

Gaynor, J. Ellen (1995) *Theatre and Imperialism: Essays on World Theatre, Drama and Performance*, London: Routledge.

George, Vincent (1984) 'Community Theatre as a Strategy in Rural Development: The Case of New Market, Jamaica', *Community Development Journal* 19, 3: 142–150

Gilbert, Helen and Tompkins, Joanne (1996) *Post-Colonial Drama: Theory, Practice, Politics*, London: Routledge.

Gilroy, Paul (1987) *There Ain't No Black in the Union Jack*, London: Hutchinson.

Goldberg, D.T. *et al.* (eds) (1994) *Multiculturalism: A Critical Reader*, Oxford and Cambridge: Blackwell.

Gunew, Sneja (1983) 'Migrant Women Writers: Who's on Whose Margins?', *Meanjin* 42, 1 (March): 16–26.

—— and Rizvi, Fazal (eds) (1994) *Culture, Difference, and the Arts*, St Leonards, NSW: Allen & Unwin.

Hall, Stuart *et al.*(eds) (1992) *Modernity and its Futures*, London: Polity Press.

Hawkins, Gay (1993) *From Nimbin to Mardi Gras: Constructing Community Arts*, St Leonards, NSW: Allen & Unwin.

Hess, Karl (1979) *Community Technology*, New York: Harper and Row.

Hicks, Peter (1982) 'Community Arts, False Freedom and a Fight For Our Lives', *Art Network* 5 (Summer/Autum): 42–43.

Holderness, Graham (1992) *The Politics of Theatre and Drama*, London: Macmillan.

Honneth, Axel (1986) 'The Fragmented World of Symbolic Forms: Reflections on Pierre Bourdieu's Sociology of Culture', *Theory, Culture & Society* 3, 3: 55–66.

Jackson, Tony (ed.) (1993) *Learning Through Theatre: New Perspectives on Theatre in Education*, London: Routledge

Jellicoe, Ann (1987) *Community Plays: How to Put Them On*, London: Methuen.

Johnson, L. and O'Neill, C. (eds) (1994) *Collected Writings on Education and Drama*, London: Hutchinson.

Kelly, O. (1984) *Community, Art, and the State: Storming the Citadels*, London: Comedia.

Kenny, Susan (1994) *Developing Communities in the Future: Community Development in Australia*, Melbourne: Nelson.

Kershaw, Baz (1992) *The Politics of Performance: Radical Theatre as Cultural Intervention*, London: Routledge.

Lavrijsen, R. (ed.) (1993) *Cultural Diversity in the Arts: Art Policies and the Facelift of Europe*, Amsterdam: Royal Tropical Institute.

Lewis, J. *et al.* (1986) *Art – Who Needs It? The Audience for Community Arts*, London: Comedia.

Lippard, Lucy R. (1984) *Got the Message? A Decade of Art for Social Change*, New York: E.P. Dutton.

Marranca, Bonnie and Dasgupta, Gautam (eds) (1991) *Inter-culturalism and Performance*, New York: PAJ Publications.

Minh-ha, Trinh (1989) *Woman, Native, Other: Writing Post-Coloniality and Feminism*, Bloomington: Indiana University Press.

—— (1992) *The Moon Waxes Red: Representation, Gender and Cultural Politics*, New York and London: Routledge.

O'Toole, John (1992) *The Process of Drama*, New York and London: Routledge.

Pavis, Patrice (ed.) (1996) *The Intercultural Performance Reader*, New York and London: Routledge.

Phelan, Peggy (1993) *Unmarked: Politics of Performance*, New York and London: Routledge.

Poster, C. (ed.) (1992) *Community Education in the Third World*, New York and London: Routledge.

Rosenberg, H. (1987) *Creative Drama and Imagination: Transforming Ideas Into Action*, New York: Holt, Rinehart & Winston.

Said, Edward W. (1982) 'Opponents, Audiences, Constituencies and Community', *Critical Inquiry* 9 (September).

—— (1985) *Orientalism*, Harmondsworth: Penguin.

—— (1993) *Culture and Imperialism*, London: Vintage.

Salas, Jo (1993) *Improvising Real Life, Personal Story in Playback Theatre*, Dubuque: Kendall/Hunt Publishing Co.

Salverson, Julie (1996) 'Performing Emergency: Witnessing Popular Theatre and the Lie of the Literal', *Theatre Topics* 6, 2 (September): 181–191.

Shaw, R. (1987) *The Arts and the People*, London: Jonathan Cape.

Smith, Greg (1996) 'Ties, Nets and an Elastic Bund: Community in the Postmodern City', *Community Development Journal* 31, 3 (July): 250–259.

Soja, Edward W. (1996) *Thirdspace: Journeys to Los Angeles and Other Real-and-Imagined Places*, Cambridge, MA: Blackwell.

Spivak, Gayatri C. (1991) *The Post-Colonial Critic: Interviews, Strategies, Dialogues*, New York and London: Routledge.

Stourac, R. and McCreery, K. (1986) *Theatre as a Weapon*, New York and London: Routledge.

Turner, Bryan S. (1994) *Orientalism, Postmodernism, Globalism*, New York and London: Routledge.

Ugwu, Catherine (ed.) (1995) *Let's Get it On: The Politics of Black Performance*, Seattle: Bay Press.

Vickers, Jeanne (1993) *Women and the World Economic Crisis*, London: Zed Books.

Whybrow, N. (1995) 'The Art of Political Theatre-Making for Educational Contexts', *New Theatre Quarterly* 11, 43: 277–291.

Wilson, W.J. (1988) *The Truly Disadvantaged: The Inner City, the Underclass, and Public Policy*, Chicago: University of Chicago Press.

Woodruff, Graham (1989) 'Community, Class, and Control: A View of Community Plays', *New Theatre Quarterly* 5, 20 (Nov.): 370–373.

Zialcita, Fernando N. (1996) 'The Meanings of Community', *Philippine Studies* 44, 1: 3–39.

Zoon, Cees (1998) 'Een ontworteld Argentijns jongetje', *De Volkskrant* (Friday 20 November): 29.

Index